The Truth Within You

The Truth Within You

Faith, Gnostic Visions, and Christ Consciousness

by Wendell Charles Beane, Ph.D.

A.R.E. Press • Virginia Beach • Virginia

1st Printing, September 1998

Printed in the U.S.A.

A.R.E. Press
Sixty-Eighth & Atlantic Avenue
P.O. Box 656
Virginia Beach, VA 23451-0656

Library of Congress Cataloging-in-Publication Data
Beane, Wendell Charles, 1935-
The truth within you : faith, gnostic visions, and Christ consciousness / by Wendell Charles Beane.
p. cm.
Includes bibliographical references.
ISBN 0-87604-412-7 (trade paper)
1. Spiritual life—Christianity. 2. Gnosticism. 3. Cayce, Edgar, 1877-1945. I. Title.
BV4509.2.B43 1998
230'.998—dc21 98-26720

Cover design by Lightbourne Images

To
My parents: Olive and Sydney

———

Harmon and June,
Cliff, Ishwar, and Songhai,

———

and
Phyllis of Arlington

Contents

Preface

The *primary aim* of this book is to offer encouragement to persons who may be caught in a sort of spiritual "twilight zone" between traditional ideas and new insights germinating in heart, mind, and soul. I believe, sincerely, that there are literally millions of persons worldwide who are being lured not necessarily from without, but from the "Beyond Within," to broaden and deepen and lengthen their understanding of the possibilities of religion to offer new knowledge, especially self-knowledge. Although this is where it all begins, it is not all encompassed by this. There is also the prospect of discovering new opportunities to explore very powerful and engaging ideas, already in the Christian tradition, but long ignored by those whose hearts are too faint to enter into what Paul of Tarsus called "God's wisdom, secret and hidden." (I Cor. 2:7) This book also has the potential to enable one to feel free to venture into new territorial waters both in terms of one's belief system and interpersonal relationships in a very meaningful way. It thus aims to inform and to illustrate how such an exploration can be undertaken without abandoning long-cherished traditions and values. This is one of the reasons that throughout this book I have stressed that faith and spiritual knowledge are best understood in terms of one's spiritual progression along a line that begins in the one (faith) and ends in the other (spiritual knowledge—*gnosis*). *Spiritual knowledge, then, is not the opposite of faith but the fulfillment of faith.*

Another aim of this work is to draw out some of the very startling implications of a work by a spiritual colleague of mine, Dr. Richard Drummond, author of the pathmaking book, *Unto the Churches* (1978). Dr. Drummond did something extremely valuable for many souls when he gave us a sound, convincing, and inspiring testimony to the fact that the Christian faith, as manifested in the mystic seer, Edgar Cayce, was truly further fulfilling itself in terms of the soul's heavenly gift to explore what Jesus of Nazareth called "the mysteries of the Kingdom of Heaven." (Mark 4:11) A final aim of this book is to prepare the way for a companion volume in which I hope to present to readers a more conclusive perspective on how the idea of spiritual intuitive knowledge applies to some of the most difficult problems in the world today.

I wish fondly to acknowledge the role that my beloved wife, Peg A. Van Beane, played in support of my efforts to bring this book into reality. Her reading of the chapters included some bold and firm criticisms, but they have proved to be invaluable to me and the work. Harmon and June Bro receive my unending thanks for motivating me to do more writing in both the scholarly vein and in a vein that combines both scholarship *and* life experience such as in the present initial volume. Harmon (who still lives in the "Within Beyond") inspired me to rediscover the element of "community" in both my academic and devotional activities, while I was a Fellow at Pilgrim Institute in West Yarmouth, Massachusetts (1992-1993). And last, but not least, my thanks to John Van Auken, of A.R.E., for it was his idea that I write this book; although I hope, to his good pleasure, that I have fulfilled and gone well beyond what John initially envisioned.

May you, the reader, find here many biblical insights to make you wonder and much spiritual food to lead you to ponder. As you know, we are living amidst a generation of many modern adults who have turned away from the Bible as an ongoing repository of spiritual truth. Hence in this work I have continued a well-known tradition in the life of Edgar Cayce; that is, his deep devotional appreciation for the reading of the Christian Scriptures and their meaningful interpretation in relation to the mysteries of the Kingdom of Heaven. For that Realm still is among us, visits us, and invites us to enter in at every turn of our lives.

1

Faith as the Universal Human Adventure

Are you aware that no human being can live meaningfully on planet Earth without this thing called—faith? Or that, as a general principle in human life, faith is naturally rooted in the very structure of human consciousness? It has oftentimes been said, however, that as an individual, you have only three viable options regarding the matter of faith in a Supreme Being—and that is to doubt, deny, or believe. Yet when it concerns the reality of faith as a structure of human consciousness, it means that everyone needs faith, even if it is a faith *outside* of a religious framework. Hence physicist Max Planck (the father of quantum theory) could say that "faith is a quality which the scientist cannot dispense with."[1]

Thus you live by faith when you take for granted that

no monstrous asteroid or meteor will collide with Earth and cause all of our terrestrial hopes and dreams to vanish. You live by faith when you rely on the recurrent rising of the morning sun to give you light and warmth. You live by faith when you anticipate the coming and going of the seasons. You live by faith when you are told that earthquakes may now happen almost anywhere and yet you go on to function day after day. You live by faith when the tornadoes or floods come and you dare to return and rebuild. You live by faith when you trust that the airplane you are in will reach its destination and land safely. You live by faith, even unconsciously, when you trust there to be constant air to take your next breath. Were any of us to doubt these and countless other kinds of things, our lives would be characterized not only by the normal intensity of everyday existence but by the extraordinary anxiety of living in a universe without at least some certainty.

It is only when we consider the relation between faith and *religious* experience that faith, while remaining related to the previous concerns, becomes but something other, something more. And that *more* has to do with the fact that religious faith does not merely extend to the normal framework of life. Religious faith requires that faith have an *object;* and not just any object, but an object which is believed to be *the All-Encompassing Source of the total meaning of one's life.* Religious faith, then, has a frame of reference that pervades and a center of gravity that goes to the core of one's being and life-meaning. In the context of religious faith, therefore, the Book of Hebrews tells us two very important things about faith *and* the "Object" of faith (God).

First, it tells us (11:1) that faith "is the substance of things hoped for, the evidence of things not seen" (KJV); or it "is being sure of what we hope for and certain of what we do not see" (NIV); or, again, that it "is the assurance of things hoped for, the conviction of things not seen" (RSV). This biblical insight testifies to us both that we are capable of "hoping against hopelessness" and that we are capable of experiencing a link to other dimensions of Reality, at once, positive and precarious, but always glorious. Second, it tells us that "he that cometh to God must [first] believe that he is . . . " (11:6); or that "anyone who comes to him must believe that he exists . . . "; or, again, that "whoever would draw near to God must believe that he exists . . . "[2]

To me this means that the "substance" of faith refers to the metaphysical reality of God as the "Object" of faith that faith "hopes" to contact. The "evidence of things not seen" refers to life situations in which the convincing effect of the sprouting seeds of faith engender a meaningful assurance that one is in contact with God as the Invisible Presence.

With creative courage, therefore, a Harvard historian of religions has affirmed that faith is "a generic quality," and that its various forms in association with so many religious systems show that "God saves us in any way He can . . . "[3] He goes on to say what he means by saved in the most practical mundane terms:

> . . . saved from nihilism, from alienation, anomie, despair; from the bleak despondency of meaninglessness. Saved from unfreedom, from being the victim of one's own whims within, or of pressures without; saved from being merely an organism reacting to its environment.[4]

The nature of faith as a fundamental element in approaching the Divine is recognized among practically all major world religions, such as Judaism, Hinduism, Buddhism, Jainism, Christianity, Islam, Sikhism, Zoroastrianism, Shinto—and also among African, North American continental, and Asian-Pacific tribal religions.[5] Faith is, therefore, *fundamental,* but it is also a *submissive, grateful, optimistic, daring, firm, committed, cognitive, transformative,* and *totalistic* thing. The fundamental nature of faith is confirmed in a highly revered text called the *Awakening of Faith,* attributed to the Mahayana Buddhist monk, Ashvaghosha. Although there are four kinds of faith indispensable to attaining the highest salvation, "the first is the faith in the Ultimate Source."[6] Echoing Paul of Tarsus, a well-renowned modern Hindu mystic said that "God can be realized by true faith alone" (Ramakrishna).[7]

Moreover, faith is *submissive:* "What is faith? Unquestioning surrender to God's will" (Hinduism);[8] faith is *grateful:* "O my Father, Great Elder, I have no words to thank you, but with your deep wisdom I am sure that you can see how I value your glorious gifts" (African Kikuyu prayer); faith is *optimistic:* "My lord, boundless as the sun and moon light heaven and earth; how then can I have concerns about what is to be?" (Shinto);[9] faith is *daring:* " . . . if you say to this mountain, 'Be taken up and thrown into the sea,' and if you do not doubt in your heart, but believe that what you say will come to pass, it will be done for you" (Christianity);[10] faith is *firm:* "Unless you have believed, you will not understand" (Judaism);[11] faith is *committed:* "Faith *(iman)* is a confession with the tongue, a verification with the heart, and an act with the members";[12] faith is *cognitive:* "Consult thy heart, and thou wilt hear the secret ordinance of God proclaimed by the heart's inward knowledge, which is real faith and divinity" (Islam);[13] faith is *transformative:* "Let him do all manner of works, putting his trust in Me; for by my grace he will attain to an eternal and changeless state" (Hinduism).[14] But, in the end, faith is *totalistic:*

> There is nothing that so sanctifies the heart of

> man, that keeps us in such habitual love, prayer, and delight in God: nothing that so kills all the roots of evil in our nature, that so renews and perfects all our virtues, that fills us with so much love, goodness, and good wishes to every creature as this faith that God is always present in us with His light and Holy Spirit.[15]

Faith and the Use of Scripture as a Spiritual Catalyst

In our time there are many who continue to take the use of the Bible, or any other forms of Scripture, too lightly. For Scriptures represent the cumulative spiritual treasuries of countless souls who have entered the intellectual, experiential, and experimental quest for wholeness and holiness. Among those ancient writings, e.g., the Confucian (the *Analects*), Taoist (the *Tao Te Ching*), the Hindu (the *Vedas; Upanishads;* and *Puranas,*[16] especially the timelessly revered "Song of the Lord"; the *Bhagavadgita*), the Buddhist (*Lotus of the True Law* or the *Saddharmapundarika*), the Zoroastrian *(Avesta),* the Islamic *(Holy Qur'an),* and the *Adi Granth* of the Sikhs, all reflect that same quest-and-attainment regarding wholeness and holiness.

Though the typical Bible (which does not contain all the Hebrew Scriptures) is but one of a number of holy books on our planet, it has had an impact upon the world which is practically incalculable. One has only to ponder the wondrous effect that the teachings of Jesus of Nazareth, as revealed in the Bible, had upon Mahatma Gandhi;[17] or to reflect on the fact that America's most astounding mystic and seer, Edgar Cayce,[18] read the Bible in its entirety yearly, and his superconscious "readings" show a grounding in the essential, universal, and spiritual content of this sacred text. In his recent and startling book entitled, *Lost Christianity*, author Jacob Needleman, in conversation with "a certain bishop," candidly says that:

> I mentioned to him that in my own academic work as a professor of philosophy and religion *I had begun to perceive things in the Bible that I had never dreamed were there.* I was beginning to understand that everything I had seen in the Eastern teachings was also contained in Judaism and Christianity, although the language of the Bible was practically impossible to penetrate, because it had become encrusted with familiar associations.[19]

I *promise* you, the conscientious reader, that if you will take the time to read and reflect on all the biblical citations contained in this present work, in the light of the dynamic relation between the exoteric and the esoteric way of understanding,[20] that you, too, will see things that you "never dreamed were there." For what Needleman refers to as "practically impossible to penetrate" can become increasingly penetrable to your spiritual eyes, especially if undertaken with prayer and meditation.

The problem for many souls in our time remains a feeling of rebellion, either conscious or unconscious, against certain forms of institutional establishment or religious doctrines.[21] Though Martin Luther's German translation of the Bible was an original signal for many to grasp the opportunity to read the Scriptures for themselves, free of constraints, few rebels have ever come to realize, as the saying goes, that it is not wise to "throw out the baby with the bath water!"

First, there are those who need to ask themselves sincerely, "Are we afraid of the Bible?"[22] Suares says that we crave "static permanence" rather than face the reality of an upsetting, disturbing "flow of newness, of freshness," which the Bible shows us. Attributing this childish naiveté to a betrayal of the "biblical message of life-including-death" and to a misplaced promise of "existence after death" by "copyists, priests, rabbis, and theologians," Suares goes on to say this to all thereby daunted souls:

> We want the psychological security of a protecting deity, whereas we can become *as gods, knowing good and evil* . . . But the Bible is a Revelation only insofar as it includes death in life, thereby disrupting every psychological certainty . . . Death is actually here, as a vital aspect of our everyday life, at every moment. When we come to see that we are constantly waging a battle (psychologically) for the continuity of our existence against the life-death within us, and when we come to learn (from the Book of Genesis) that that combat must cease by our becoming that very life-death, a disruption occurs in our thought process and in our psychical armour, which *liberates us into life.* And this is precisely the thing, the life-stimulating thing, that we are afraid of.[23]

It is, of course, true that there are those who are not of the persuasion that on certain levels of spiritual consciousness the life-death mentality can become reorientated toward a purely Eternal Life psychological security ("Eternal Life Insurance"). But Suares's point is mentioned here because there still remains a lot of inexcusable naiveté within esoteric circles. There are souls, then, who have become so entranced by the rebellious joys of heterodox faith that they fail to recognize what a priest once said: that "the first mark of the gift of faith is the love of truth."[24] And the truth is that, though not an absolute ending of life, death for multimillions in their everyday life is still "the last enemy."[25]

Second, there are those who blame the church (or synagogue, or any other religious institution and its leaders) for their longtime disillusionment—even with God! In that act of rebellion and with no drive toward spiritual creativity, many have tragically overlooked the need to make a very critical distinction; and that is, for instance, between what is actually taught in the Bible about wholeness and holiness and what has often been taught by those of institutional religious authority who have taken to "holding to the outward form of godliness but denying its power" (II Tim. 3:5). Can either of the foregoing reasons justify the false assumption that it is somehow intellectually or religiously sophisticated to ignore the Bible, or the Bibles of the world's living spiritual traditions?

I have often said during my lectures on spirituality around the country that there are two kinds of people regarding this matter: those who insist absolutely on learning the lessons of life by themselves *alone*, and those who are willing to learn from their own experience *and* from the insights of the ages or the wisdom of the sages. Those in the former group tend to learn their spiritual lessons, but this process can only happen with greater suffering, not only for themselves but for others whom they will cause to suffer during the process. The latter group, too, will suffer (for, as Buddha knew, suffering is inevitable in history); but they will have avoided much unnecessary suffering, having gained an increase of faith, understanding, and encouragement from those who have gone before them and left their insights and wisdom behind to bless us.

All true seekers, then, whether in China, India, Palestine, or the West, need to endeavor to saturate their minds and hearts and souls with the spiritual gems, insights, or threads of wisdom found not only in the Bible but in all the various sacred books of the world. Such holy books are treasuries, they are spiritual diaries, they are sacred histories of the religious experiences of earlier seekers after truth. So they deserve our attention. Should the reader have any doubts about this fact, he or she is encouraged to browse, selectively, through the Bible, making sure to pause at Deuteronomy 30:11-20; Psalm 40, Isaiah 1:1-20; Jeremiah 31:31-34; Matthew, chapters 5-7 (the essential teachings of Jesus), I Corinthians 13:1-13; Galatians 5:22-23, Ephesians 3:14-19; I Peter 5:6-11; and John 4:7-21.[26] Moreover, there are priceless Scriptural anthologies and other spiritual writings, such as the incomparable fifteen-years-in-the-making collection by Whitall Perry entitled *A Treasury of Traditional Wisdom.*[27]

Through this and other treasuries, diaries, and sacred histories which reflect the encounter of souls with the ultimate origins of faith, the power of faith, and the consequences of faith, you and I and every other soul on earth can grow. Through such a rich spiritual heritage, we can see what other beings in ancient times and faraway lands have dared to believe and to know and to understand about the nature of reality, the nature of humanity, and the nature of human destiny. Let us read them! Let us meditate on them! Let us savor them so that they may inspire us to allow the "Lord of the Worlds" to "show us the straight path" (*Holy Qur'an,* Sura I:5).

The Glory of Religious Faith Beyond Mere Faith in Life

While you may be entitled by a democratic form of government to "life, liberty, and the pursuit of happiness," there is something that the long and cumulative search of our species for spirituality has discovered, confirmed, and reconfirmed. A mere faith in life itself, however—which usually includes faith in yourself alone, a community or institution, or even a material object—ever stands precariously on the shifting sands of time and change. Faith, then, in anything or anyone *finite* guarantees the probability, if not the certainty, that the object of such a faith is subject to perish. For millions, when that moment arrives, the individual is surely destined to suffer disappointment, disillusionment, depression, and, in many cases, either self-inflicted physical death or the death of hope itself, the thing for which religious faith is the substance, the surety, and the assurance.

The glory of religious faith beyond mere faith in life itself thus lies in the fact that religious faith does not exist in a mere time-bound framework but in a metaphysical macrocosm. To cite a revered Hindu philosopher, Radhakrishnan, on ethics (but which also applies to religious faith), "the question is inevitable whether the ethical ideal is a mere dream or *has the backing of the universe.*"[28] Choosing "patterns," therefore, according to the charisma of priests, prophets, seers, or messiahs has been a human need throughout time. But that choice has also included the need—especially in the beginning of one's participation in the universal human adventure of faith—to focus upon such symbolic human forms (e.g., Buddha, Christ, Laotze) as a means of both fulfilling that need and, ultimately, going on beyond the need for permanently focusing on and uniquely encountering what in the purest perception can only be known as—Spirit.

The Focus of Faith and the Faith Beyond Focus

Otherwise called many names, God, as the Eternal Mind and Spirit of all the "universes," has been conceived under the form of a Caring Presence, sometimes called "Father" and sometimes called "Mother" (if not,

"Father-Mother-God"); probably most often, "God," and at other times the "God-Force." An exciting medley of names, which we might call "focal options," is found in Shakti Gawain's insightful book, *Living in the Light.* (This work is intimately related to the helpful and healing art she gave us three years earlier under the title of *Creative Visualization.*) Gawain prefers "terms such as higher power, the universe, spirit, your higher self, or the light." Though in her book she uses such terms interchangeably, she suggests all of them by referring to "that highest creative intelligence and power within us."[29]

Likewise, the Christian mystic and seer, Edgar Cayce,[30] uses various names for the Ultimate Reality, including, among others, "the Mother-God," "Father-God," "Universal Consciousness," or "the Creative Force."[31] But he also tells us something vitally important about the use of nouns, pronouns—even *neuter* nouns—in relation to the issue of individual conceptions of God as personal or impersonal: "How personal is thy God? Just as personal as ye will let Him be! How close is the Christ as was manifested in the physical body, Jesus? Just as near, just as dear as ye will let Him be!" (1158-9)[32]

Focusing upon sacred names of divinities, charismatic personalities, or sacred Scriptures has undoubtedly been something very helpful to religious individuals. In fact, both in the Hindu religious tradition and in Roman Catholic Christianity, there are allowances for focusing upon personalities *and* icons as media with symbolic "transparency." This idea of the internationally renowned theologian, Paul Tillich, means that icons or any other such symbol, even human beings (e.g., Jesus of Nazareth; see John 14:9), have the potential to point beyond themselves to an Ultimate Reality (G o d).

One of the vital characteristics (among others) of what Tillich calls "symbols of faith" is that they "not only open . . . up dimensions and elements of reality which otherwise would remain unapproachable but also unlock . . . dimensions and elements of our souls which correspond to the dimensions and elements of reality."[33] It is only if symbols of faith become ends in themselves (thus becoming *opaque*) that idolatry ensues. Long, spiritual experience in both the foregoing world faiths or worlds of faith has confirmed that when the external and the internal are accompanied by repetitive prayer or the recitation of mantras (e.g., for Hinduism, the Gayatri, Om;[34] for Christianity, the "Hail Mary," "the Jesus Prayer"), the sacred power and presence of the Eternal Divine can be experienced.[35]

In this regard Hinduism knows three levels of worship of the Ultimate Reality: the gross (the use of external images), the subtle (the use of internalized images), and the paramount (the nonuse of images). The last is purely beyond any need to focus on anything less than experiencing the direct intuitive perception of the Divine. Roman Catholicism, avowing that icons in themselves are not worshiped, also knows, concerning holy beings, three levels of worship. They are the venerative (for saints), the supervenerative (for the Holy Virgin), and supreme worship (*latria,* for God only). The first two levels may include the use of images, external or internal. But the last (*latria,* hence the forbidden *idolatria,* idolatry) is a quality of focus and a form of adoration that is uniquely due to God alone. An important thing to remember is that whenever the focus of faith is upon sacred names of divinities, charismatic personalities, or sacred Scriptures, it must continue to be authentically experienced. This means that they must experientially correspond to the depth of your faith convictions. Thus "nonauthentic are religious symbols which have lost their *experiential* basis . . . "[36]

Whether in the spirit of hyperbole, as in the case of India's 33, or 33,000, or 330,000,000 gods, or Christianity's idea of the Ultimate Reality that is Three-Persons-in-One, the thing for us to remember is that, however helpful focusing on names, personalities, or Scriptures may be, "God" is not even the name of *God*. This is a truth which led theologian Tillich to dare to say that "God is [a] symbol for God."[37] The very application of the word *eternal*—without beginning, without end—to the Ultimate Reality is intended to send you that message.

This is why the most excellent sage of ancient Chinese mysticism, Laotze, says in the very first line of the immortal classic, the *Tao Te Ching*, that "the Tao [Way] that can be told of is not the Absolute Tao." Chinese philosophy thus has the concept of the named *(yu-ming)* and the Unnamed *(wu-ming)*. You can imagine that if, in fact, the Ultimate Reality cannot even be named and that there are so many superangelic, angelic, and soul powers in the universe, then all human pride of religion and life should immediately disappear! Richard Drummond would have us know that Cayce, too, knew that here we are dealing with "human concepts"; and that, for Cayce, even the Trinitarian symbolism is due to our experience of time and space and thus reflects "three-dimensional activity in a three-dimensional world." Further, Cayce points out that since you and I have the potential to "think in an eight-dimensional consciousness . . . the universal consciousness manifested or expressed in the three-dimensional as Father, Son, Holy Spirit . . . might be manifested or indicated in many more . . . dimensions in other realms than the earth."[38]

It is indeed our tendency to become addicted to *names* that has led many, religious and nonreligious, respectively, to think on the one hand that by naming the Ultimate Reality of the universe they can further assume to speak authoritatively and/or institutionally in that particular name; or, on the other hand, that they can to all intents and purposes control certain revealed modes of religious worship and even dictate proper human behavior. The damage to nature and other human beings caused by both priestly arrogance and spiritual ignorance regarding these matters has been nothing short of tragic in history. A warning from the Torah that "you shall not take the name of the Lord your God in vain" was indeed a safeguard both against the temptation to think that one could harness the power of God via magical means and to assert his Holy Name with arrogant autonomy—in the spirit of blasphemy. But today such a commandment must also refer to the human tendency to harness the energy of the Eternal under the form of atomic energy for the sake of political dominance and economic exploitation, as much as to curtail the spiritual freedom of souls for the sake of ecclesiastical and social domination.

The Hindus call the human addiction to names and forms *namarupa* (name-and-form). It is related to their concept of *maya* (illusion; although the term also refers to our capacity for self-delusion). For it is the self-deluding way of being in the world through attachment to names-and-forms,[39] which is both an expression of and the source of that spiritual ignorance. But it is not fundamentally academic or worldly ignorance. It is basically ignorance about the nature of *spiritual* Reality, which includes both your own true nature and your own true destiny. Shakespeare, who is considered in esoteric circles to have belonged to a medieval coterie of literary, mystical, and scientific visionaries, gave us a glimpse of this truth when he spoke of naming and the sweetness of the rose (see p. 133). Of course, there are those who still see in that saying only sweet words and not timeless wisdom.

The faith beyond focus is thus of the utmost importance for the future of religious experience and human unity. In the Hebrew Scriptures it was Solomon, in his quest to build Israel's most memorably beautiful temple to the glory of God (something that his father, David, had failed to accomplish), who at last declared: " . . . behold, heaven and the heaven of heavens cannot contain thee; how much less this house which I have built!"[40] In the New Testament, Jesus of Nazareth could, therefore, say to a woman who actually inquired of Him just where she should worship, down in Jerusalem or in the hills of Samaria, that "The time is coming *and now is* when the true worshipers shall worship God . . . God *is* spirit, and they who would worship him must worship him *in spirit* and in truth."[41] This is undoubtedly the most radical statement of Jesus regarding the most exquisite mode of worshiping God.

Later, Stephen, the first Christian martyr, managed to review in short the entire history of God's endeavors to save Israel[42] just before his final vision of the "glory of God" and of Jesus "standing at the right hand of God" and before his slayers could do their dastardly deed.[43] Stephen had reminded them of what Solomon had said before (see above) but more completely, which was that God had *through* Solomon asked, "What house will you build for me . . . or what is the place of my rest? Did not my hand make all these things?"[44]

But then Paul of Tarsus said it all when he uttered these stunning words: "The God who made the world and everything in it, he who is Lord of heaven and earth, does not live in shrines made by human hands, nor is he served by human hands, as though he needed anything . . . indeed he is not far from each one of us. For 'In him we live and move and have our being,' as even some of your own poets have said."[45] Does not all this throw revolutionary light on the matter of how we should then all look upon the temples, churches, and mosques, or any other sacred enclosures which humankind has in fact built "in God's name"?[46]

Endnotes

1. Margaret Pepper, compiler and ed., *The Pan Dictionary of Religious Quotations* (London: Pan Books, 1991), p. 178. For a brief assortment of opinions "on science and God's existence" by experts in science and other fields, see Mary Long's "Visions of a New Faith," *Science Digest* (November 1981), p. 42.

2. Several versions of the Bible are being used in this book: KJV, the King James Version; NIV, the New International Version; RSV, the Revised Standard Version. There is also the NRSV, the New Revised Standard Version, the translations of which follow the RSV very closely. Scholars worldwide generally respect the RSV. Contrary to popular opinion, variations in translation can often enhance creative reflection; where special issues are concerned, the author will comment on the same. Unless otherwise designated, the NRSV is being used throughout this work.

3. William Cantwell Smith, *Towards a World Theology: Faith and the Comparative History of Religion* (Maryknoll, New York: Orbis Books, 1989), pp. 172, 170.

4. *Ibid.*, p. 168; also see his remarks (p. 171) on what ought to be a form of "*Christian* delight" that God not only saves through other "forms of faith," but that He does "care about other men and women."

5. For brief summaries of these religions, see Andrew Wilson, ed., *World Scripture: A Comparative Anthology of Sacred Texts* (a project of the International Religious Foundation, New York: Paragon House, 1991), pp. 6-26.

6. *Ibid.*, p. 537.

7. Whitall N. Perry, *A Treasury of Traditional Wisdom* (New York: Simon and Schuster, 1971), p. 514.

8. *Ibid.*, p. 516.

9. Wilson, *op. cit.*, pp. 550, 553.

10. Mark 11:23.

11. Wilson, *op. cit.*, p. 536.

12. Perry, *op cit.*, p. 511.

13. Perry, *op cit.*, p. 514 (this and the preceding citation are attributed to the prophet Muhammad).

14. *Bhagavadgita* XVIII:56; cited in Kenneth Kramer, *World Scriptures: An Introduction to Comparative Religions* (New York: Paulist Press, 1986), p. 71.

15. William Law, cited in Perry, *op cit.*, p. 514.

16. For the interrelation between the Hindu mystical treatises (the *Upanishads*) and the metaphysics of Edgar Cayce, see I. C. Sharma, *Cayce, Karma, and Reincarnation* (New York: Harper & Row, Publishers, 1975); and a priceless gem by Geoffrey Parrinder, *Upanishads, Gita, and Bible: A Comparative Study of Hindu and Christian Scriptures* (New York: Harper Torchbooks, 1962).

17. A copy of Jesus' "Sermon on the Mount" was notably among Gandhi's sparse belongings.

18. On Edgar Cayce, see endnote #30 and chapter 6.

19. Jacob Needleman, *Lost Christianity: A Journey of Rediscovery to the Centre of the Christian Experience* (Brisbane: Element Books Limited, 1993), p. 2.

20. The *exoteric* refers to the overt, ordinary, everyday, commonplace dimension of religious learning and experience; and the *esoteric* refers to the covert, concealed, hidden, or secret dimension of religious learning and ex-

perience. See also chapters 2 (pp. 20-22) and 9 (pp. 233-235).

21. For an exemplary account of a disillusioned, former believer in the Christian "religion," particularly with "the indecent grovellings of . . . sin-obsessed Puritans," see Christopher Isherwood, "What Vedanta Means to Me," in Roger Eastman, ed., *The Ways of Religion* (Harper & Row, Publishers, 1975), pp. 69-74.

22. The title of chapter 14 of Carlo Suares's *The Cipher of Genesis: The Original Code of the Qabala as Applied to the Scriptures* (Berkeley, Cal.: Shambhala Publications, Inc, 1970), pp. 125-127.

23. *Ibid.*, pp. 125-126. Italics added. Of course, one needs to ponder that from the point of view of physical science, death is a reality; but that from the point of view of metaphysical religion, death is an illusion. Few persons, however, have effectively worked this out *in life:* "The reason that the tale of the talking serpent and the magic apple outlives every other fairy story is that we are afraid of it." Suares relates all this to "our wish to rationalize our sins of omission" (p. 127).

24. Pepper, *op. cit.*, p. 173.

25. I Corinthians 15:26.

26. See biblical readings recommended by Cayce "as an accompaniment of prayer and meditation" in Drummond, *A Life of Jesus the Christ*, p. 184.

27. New York: Simon and Schuster, 1971. Other remarkable sources of timeless wisdom are by Andrew Wilson, ed., *World Scripture: A Comparative Anthology of Sacred Texts* (a project of the International Religious Foundation, New York: Paragon House, 1991); Willis Barnstone, ed., *The Other Bible* (San Francisco: Harper & Row, Publishers, 1984), which includes the Dead Sea Scrolls, the Kabbalah, and the Gnostic Gospels; Lucinda Vardey, ed., *God in All Worlds: An Anthology of Contemporary Spiritual Writing* (New York: Vintage Books, 1995); Jonathan Star, ed., *Two Suns Rising: A Collection of Sacred Writings* (Edison, New Jersey: Castle Books, 1996); and Andrew Harvey, ed., *The Essential Mystics: The Soul's Journey into Truth* (HarperSanFrancisco, 1996).

28. S. Radhakrishnan, "An Idealist View of Life," in Frederick S. Streng *et al.*, *Ways of Being Religious* (Englewood Cliffs, New Jersey: Prentice-Hall, Inc., 1973), pp. 478-479. Italics added.

29. Shakti Gawain, *Living in the Light* (San Rafael, California: Whatever Publishing, Inc., 1986), pp. 6, 7. Gawain describes the moment at which she "received" the title for this work in terms tantamount to a genuine religious experience (p. xviii).

30. Edgar Cayce was more than a psychic in the superficial sense which the term has in many New Age and anti-New Age quarters (see also chapter 2). A dedicated Christian, he was really a mystic and seer whose prophecies, visions, and healings, though they included the unorthodox element of reincarnation, were generally based on a sound Judaeo-Christian biblical foundation. Though he is most deserving to be appreciated for his "readings" as guidance toward holistic spiritual healing, the splendor and the shortcomings of his ESP gifts are candidly discussed by his own sons Edgar Evans Cayce and Hugh Lynn Cayce, in *The Outer Limits of Edgar Cayce's Power* (Virginia Beach, Virginia: A.R.E. Press, 1971). Cayce is essential to this book for reasons those who have not taken the time to read his various biographies will never come to appreciate. For the best biography heretofore, see the late Harmon H. Bro's *A Seer Out of Season* (New York: New American Library, 1989). Dr. Bro is a University of Chicago graduate in the history of religions,

who started out as a healthy skeptic, but who also had firsthand knowledge of Cayce, the man. Almost no one who reads Bro's book with an open mind can come away the same. For further reading, see also Thomas Sugrue's *There Is a River* (rev. ed., Virginia Beach, Virginia: A.R.E. Press, 1992). For the argument against the charge of an A.R.E. cult, see Lynn Elwell Sparrow's *Edgar Cayce and the Born Again Christian* (Virginia Beach, Virginia: A.R.E. Press, 1985), chapters 9 and 10, especially pp. 98-103.

31. The need for a responsive flexibility is illustrated by Karen Armstrong (*A History of God: The 4000-Year Quest of Judaism, Christianity, and Islam*, New York: Alfred A Knopf, 1993), p. xxiii: "Thus in Arabic *al-Lah* (the surname for God) is grammatically masculine, but the word for the divine and inscrutable essence of God—*al-Dhat*—is feminine." In certain (gnostic) sectors of ancient Christianity, believers knew a "Trinity" of God the Father, God the *Mother*, and God the Son. See also chapters 3 and 7 of this book.

32. Richard H. Drummond, *Unto the Churches* (Virginia Beach, Virginia: A.R.E. Press, 1978), pp. 48, 147, note #73. Cayce *(loc. cit.)* did refer to the Supreme Being as "the Father-God *itself*" (italics added) in reading 1436-2. For anyone unfamiliar with the readings, the first number refers to a person's file name, the latter to the sequential number of a reading. Thus, 1436-2 was the second reading for the individual given the file number 1436.

33. Paul Tillich, *The Dynamics of Faith* (New York: Harper & Row, Publishers, 1957), p. 42.

34. That is, "the most important of Vedic mantras . . . [Rig Veda 3.62.10] repeated 108 times on a rosary in the morning facing east by the orthodox brāhmin"; for this and the mantra itself (which includes "Om," "the Queen of all mantras"), see Edward Rice, *Eastern Definitions* (Garden City, New York: Anchor Books, 1980), pp. 150, 279.

35. See Swami Prabhavananda, *The Sermon on the Mount According to Vedanta* (Hollywood, California: Vedanta Press, 1963), chapter 5: "The Lord's Prayer," especially pp. 77-80. Many Westerners still do not realize that the 150 Psalms in the Bible can also be seen as a vast collection of mantras, waiting to be meditatively utilized within the Judaeo-Christian tradition. Psalm 23 has traditionally served believers as such for centuries. Other memorably powerful ones are Psalms 27, 40, and 42 (which I call "the anti-depression mantra"); and especially a single verse revered worldwide: "Be still, and know that I am God!" (46:10) This Psalm-mantra is intimately related to the "Let go and let God" meditation in the traditions of Unity Church and the United Methodist Church.

36. Paul Tillich, "The Meaning and Justification of Religious Symbols," cited in Richard Grigg, *Symbol and Empowerment: Paul Tillich's Post-Theistic System* (Macon, Georgia: Mercer University Press, 1985), p. 44.

37. Tillich, *The Dynamics of Faith, op. cit.*, p. 46.

38. Drummond, *op. cit.*, p. 195.

39. For example, nationalism, racism, sexism, religious bigotry, class consciousness, etc.

40. II Chronicles 6:18.

41. John 4:23-24. Italics added. Note the RSV and NRSV versions: "God is spirit," compared to the earlier KJV translation, "God is a spirit." The former version lends itself far more strongly to an ecumenical religious perspective.

42. Acts. 7:1-56.

43. See Acts 7:57.

44. Acts 7:49-50.

45. Acts 17:24-25, 27-28.

46. For Edgar Cayce's views on this matter, see Drummond, *Unto the Churches, op. cit.*, pp. 205-206; and his *A Life of Jesus the Christ: From Cosmic Origins to the Second Coming* (San Francisco: Harper & Row, Publishers, 1989), pp. 188-189.

2

Faith and Its Primary Facets in Human Experience

F*aith as a* religious reality tends to be three-faceted: the first, as intellectual; the second, as experiential; and the third, as experimental. Faith is, then, the intellectual, experiential, and experimental link between the human soul and the Eternal Mind ("God"). While the intellectual facet of faith is intimately related to an individual's ever-growing confidence in the power of natural reason, the experiential facet of faith is intimately related to an individual's humble obedience to the Supernatural Being of divine forgiving love; and the experimental facet of faith is intimately related to an individual's courage to be creative in working out his or her salvation in any given human situation. But it is the experimental dimension of faith that eventually goes beyond faith toward spiritual knowledge *(gnosis).*

Hence what I call the experiential facet of faith tends to apply largely to the individual who, Paul of Tarsus says, is only capable of drinking "milk"; but the experimental facet can only apply to a soul decidedly advanced in spirituality at the level of *gnosis*, who is capable of eating "solid food."[1] Such an individual is one who has crossed the threshold of faith and has entered into Cosmic Consciousness and—if more—the Christ Consciousness (see chapter 9).

Faith is at once intellectual in that it includes your capacity to make sense out of the world at large or your personal and/or interpersonal worlds through the reliability of reason. Intellectual faith is thus born of human reason, as reason itself reflects God's Eternal Reason under the form of the laws of the universe, which includes the law of retribution, or karma (see "divine law" below). As I said before, reason as natural law has much to do, for example, with the idea of having confidence that there will always be enough air to breathe the next breath or that the world will not (necessarily) end momentarily.

So, as a religious reality, this form of intellectual faith can prove to be a source of spiritual comfort for an individual. Moreover, it is related to an idea associated with medieval and modern religious thinkers largely influenced by St. Thomas Aquinas. Such thinkers hold that there are four *harmonious* forms and levels of law in the universe that have much to do with our being. They are natural law (e.g., gravity),[2] human law (e.g., codes of justice), divine law (e.g., the Ten Commandments), and eternal law (i.e., the Absolutely Rational Foundation of the Universe, of which Universal Love *[agape]* is its essence). Of this last, you can well understand why Richard Lovelace, the English poet, could say that "Love is the life of the soul; it is the *harmony* of the universe." It has consequently been the quest of all theologians and religious philosophers to reason out the dynamics of that harmony, which is not always immediately seen but sensed between and among those four dimensions of law. That quest has in turn led to the affirmation of creeds, the proclamation of dogmas, and the preservation of ecclesiastical traditions.

In the final analysis, to say that faith can be intellectual means that even your confidence in the reliability of natural law is a form of faith; and it becomes something religious to the extent that the limitations of your human reason itself are humbly acknowledged in the face of things reason cannot fathom. Moreover, faith as intellectual conviction is a form of rational confidence in your human capacity to imitate the Creator's own powers of reason. But it also includes your willingness in the final analysis to acknowledge that in other life situations, as the French mathematician-philosopher Pascal said, "The heart has its reasons of which reason itself knows nothing at all."

Intellectual Faith and the Wonder of Our Place in Space

There are certain facts about the earth that naturally tended to inspire my intellectual faith at a very early age—around thirteen or fourteen. Reading science comic books for children and books of popular science for youth introduced me to the cosmic visions of George Pal, Werner von Braun, and others. Does this suggest how old I am? I was completely enthralled by the distances of planets and stars—and, even earlier, *shocked* by the realization that heavenly bodies seem to float! The entire visible universe made me feel that I was living inside an unbelievably large Christmas tree and that the planets and the stars were but decorations of light hanging out there—as if all by themselves.

But it should not surprise you to know that not even all contemporary "intellectuals" are fully aware of the scientific wonders that lie behind what they take for granted. What follows in facts and figures (that may vary) I knew rather early, except some of the latter portion of it. Consider, if you will, the fact that Earth is only one of nine planets in a solar system that is itself part of the Milky Way galaxy, which is 100,000 light years in diameter, has up to 400 billion stars, and is itself one of probably 2,000 million other galaxies. Our Earth is still forty times smaller than only a solar flare (fire bulging off the sun's surface to a height of 300,000 miles); with all the heat that the sun generates (27 million degrees Fahrenheit at the center), Earth at a distance of 93 million miles can still get pretty hot—and yet not too hot—for us to live on in general; as a body, Earth spins around on its own axis at over 17,000 miles per hour, and while itself spinning, moves around the sun at about 66,000 miles per hour—and yet you are capable of sitting down and comfortably drinking a cup of coffee without ever having to think about it. But how could all these things have become so systematized and harmonized to allow you to relax and not be thrown helter-skelter?

Although scientists can largely explain it (and it's not all gravity!), how can you live on it and take it so easily for granted without—at times—contemplating the wonder of it all? Suppose I add that if our Earth were tragically hurled out of its orbit, it would be subject to freezing within eight minutes! Does *that* grab you? Perhaps not. But then, just where is Earth, really, upon which you are having that cup of coffee? Fortunately, the saying, "billions and billions and billions"—whether Carl Sagan said it or not—has finally gotten to some who had not previously wondered enough.

Having already "wondered" throughout the years, I was indeed further awestruck when I later learned from

The Chronicle of Higher Education that it had been reported in a prominent international science magazine, *Nature*, that in 1989 "astronomers at the Harvard Smithsonian Center for Astrophysics . . . reported the discovery of *the largest known structure in the universe* . . . 'a great wall' of galaxies in the sky over the Northern Hemisphere, measuring 500 million light years long [one light year is approximately a distance of six trillion miles] and 200 million light years wide . . . and about 450 million light years from Earth."[3] I am glad you still feel comfortable about having that cup of coffee—but shouldn't you be less concerned about coffee and more astounded about just where *you* fit—meaningfully in spiritual terms—into this big picture? You can well understand how it is that a preacher who was once asked how he could possibly believe in the ridiculous idea of life existing in outer space promptly answered, "Where do you think *you* live? In outer space!"[4]

At a lecture at the Chicago Planetarium years ago, the guest speaker, an astronomer, informed the audience of what spectral analysis had confirmed: what he considered to be "the astronomical miracle" of how it was that so many of the very right atomic elements existed in this particular region of our universe to make the emergence of life at all possible. For anyone who remains skeptical of the statistical improbability of what has indeed happened on Earth regarding the birth of a single DNA molecule, a reading of the opinions of several scientists proves to be mind-blowing![5] In this regard, for example (allowing the bonus *preexistence* of other necessary right conditions), try to imagine—if you dare—there being only *one chance* in 10 to the 415th power (a number with 415 zeros after it). This is an unimaginably large number, which equals 10,000 (thousand), 000 (million), 000 (billion), 000 (trillion), 000 (quadrillion), etc., etc., etc.[6] Carl Sagan capstones all this with his opinion of what the statistical odds would look like regarding "the chance of life *itself* evolving on just one planet, i.e., the Earth." He "estimated this to be roughly one chance in ten followed by two *billion* zeros. A number this large would fill over 6,000 [paperback] books . . . just to write it out"![7] By now you may also well understand how it is that J.B.S. Haldane had a "hunch that 'the universe is not only queerer than we imagine; it is queerer than we *can* imagine'";[8] or that another thinker could say that "whether man is a product of nature, chance, or God, he is a miracle . . . "

In Sagan's novel, *Contact,* this miracle is presented in the form of the lifelong search and eventual transcendental experience of a radio astronomer who found the "miracle" hidden in what she already knew about physics. The fact that it lay hidden in something with which she was already familiar should become a spiritual object lesson for all of us. It suggests that God is both the source of metaphysics *and* the source of mathematics. For if we can perceive that the miracle of mathematics is intended to correspond to a *miracle of meaning,* then

> The universe was made on purpose . . . It doesn't matter what you look like, or what you're made of, or where you come from. As long as you live in this universe, and have a modest talent for mathematics, sooner or later you'll find it. It's already there. It's inside everything. *You don't have to leave your planet to find it.* In the fabric of space and in the nature of matter, as in a great work of art, there is, written small, the artist's signature. Standing over humans, gods, and demons, subsuming Caretakers and Tunnel Builders, there is an intelligence that antedates the universe.[9]

Experiential Faith and the Beyond in the Midst of Life[10]

Next there is *experiential* faith. Of course, this is not to deny that every thing you sense is in fact experiential. It does mean, however, that experiential faith is more than the mere contemplation of ideas of religion; it is more than the utterance of creeds; and it is more than the compulsory agreement with dogmas. It can include, for example, one's spiritual response to the event of actually having suffered because of some of those things mentioned of nature earlier (e.g., a tornado or even "El Niño"). Those acquainted with this kind of faith, for instance, are ready to affirm that there is a *real* and *direct* connection between the countless prayers offered in response to the vast flooding in North Dakota in 1997 and the magnanimous financial contribution made by one of America's most renowned philanthropists. That contribution, amounting to $35,000,000, provided $2,000 for individual persons and/or families suffering terrible losses. Another contributor soon followed the original example with less funds but no less spirit. But the caring presence and prayers of millions of other souls, no doubt, probably had an intangibly real (though non-monetary) effect on the lives of such victims.

Experiential faith directly implies trust in a Transhuman Agency (God) as the final focus for your heart, mind, and soul in the quest for spiritual liberation. Experiential faith combines both the reality of a soulful desire *for* and the reality of a heartfelt devotion *to* whatever you may conceive the Creator to be. But this is something that is finally beyond reason as such. Experiential faith is the supersensory awareness of the power of the presence of God in the commonplace. It is this kind of faith that is the point of convergence of all the other words associated with faith: "taking things for granted," "confidence," "anticipation," "trust," "belief," and others such as "knowledge," "vision," and "intention."[11]

Perhaps, by now, you have been wondering about the relation between faith and belief. It has been perceptively stated that while belief is "an intellectual, emotional, and cultural embodiment of . . . faith within the framework of a particular tradition," faith in the experiential sense used here "is the connection with the . . . beyond, however you choose to envision it."[12] Faith in this sense finally bears an experiential connection with the attainment of salvation. But there can be no experiential faith without (1) a firsthand, sacred encounter with the holiness of God; (2) an influx of the love of God into the heart by the power of the Holy Spirit; and (3) a deeply personal and practical internalization of the meaning of the words of Psalm 23: "Yea, though I walk through the valley of the shadow of death, I will fear no evil . . . " (KJV)

It is the combination of desire and devotion that makes experiential faith a cumulative reality. It builds upon its own reality through the establishment of what New Testament mystical theologian Leon E. Wright called a "continuity of faith." It "remembers" past moments of victorious trust, which prepares one for the next adventure in faith. In this sense, past victories in faith *no longer remain past or disconnected but somehow participate in present challenges of faith.* As no chain is stronger than its weakest link, so the strong and unbroken chain of faith in your life enables you to face the next, often unexpected, challenge in life with courage and—even more miraculously—with creativity.

Faith is fundamentally experiential because it is the one act with which you have been gifted by creation to open the portals of the heart to receive the saving grace of God. Over the centuries faith has been the source of much argument and confusion because of two enduring controversial opinions. One is that faith is never something that *you* do, really, as an act of spiritual will. Instead, God alone is the true giver of faith as an act of divine grace. The other opinion is that faith is something that you, *alone,* can and must do as a unique voluntary act both in order to verify your personal depth of desire for communion with God and to confirm your possession of authentic spiritual integrity. But it is really a paradox and not an enduring contradiction. A paradox, of course, is a moment or event in human life when one finds that two apparently contradictory ideas, forms, or experiences can somehow harmoniously coexist. For example, one of the greatest paradoxes in the history of Roman Catholic doctrine has been expressed in this way: "Mary is the mother of God; God is the Father of Mary"![13]

Faith as an Elusive Delicate Balance

The state of spirituality to which "childlikeness" points as a symbolic usage will be further commented on in chapter 9. For now, however, it is crucial to know that it is not only a highly elusive state of consciousness, but, like the Zen Buddhist "Samadhi," wherein there are swellings and dippings, dippings and swellings, of consciousness, one may at one moment manifest the fruits of it in its most pristine form and, at another moment, lose it like water slipping between one's fingers. Often I like to visualize it as trying to keep the bubble balanced exactly in the center window of a carpenter's level while standing quite still and holding it in one's hands. In the context of religious devotion, however, one is not merely trying to be precise about a horizontal line or plane but, rather, to balance both one's horizontal orientation toward one's neighbor *and* one's vertical orientation toward the God of Eternity. (This challenge I have elsewhere in this book referred to as *the quest to balance God-reliance and self-reliance* in one's life.)

One of the most illustrative moments of the swelling and dipping of spiritual consciousness occurs in the Gospel of Matthew. Jesus has decided to ask His disciples just who they thought He really was. The answers given included rumors that He was John the Baptist, the prophet Elijah, or the prophet Jeremiah. But, then, pressed further for their own opinions, it is Peter who declared quite boldly: "You are the Messiah, the Son of the living God!" Jesus was extremely impressed by this and complimented Peter, saying to him, "Blessed are you, Simon son of Jonah! For flesh and blood has not revealed this to you, but my Father in heaven."[14] But, later, Peter's spiritual consciousness "dips," and he becomes fearful.[15] He thus urges Jesus not to go up to Jerusalem lest He be arrested and killed. "God forbid it, Lord! This must never happen to You," he said. Being at that particular time in an entirely different (i.e., lower) state of spiritual consciousness, Peter is told in the sternest terms by Jesus, "Get behind me, Satan! You are a stumbling block to me; for you are setting your mind not on divine things but on human things."[16] Pristine faith must be rooted in a pristine state of childlike trust in God that empowers one to remain in a state of spiritual consciousness that, in turn, enables one to rise to the occasion amidst life's most daunting and tantalizing circumstances.

I know this to be true, for I have had my share of swelling and dipping, dipping and swelling. Yet I am still undauntedly optimistic! What about you?

Israel's Communal Biography and Your Spiritual Autobiography

Faith is, again, experiential because it is an adventure in your life that might be said to resemble either the collective life of Israel as the People of God in their adventurous journey toward understanding the will, knowledge, and action of God in history or else some personage or personages in symbolic terms.[17] This providential journey has been conveniently listed in the form of epic stages in the life of the Hebrews-Israelites-Jews: the religious visions of the patriarchs; emancipation from slavery in Egypt; the nomadic experience of wandering in the wilderness; the arrival at Mount Sinai for the reception of the Law (Torah); the emergence of kingship in the community of Israel; the return from exile and the hope of the Ingathering of Israel.

The journey of faith, to be sure, commences at once with the experiential faith of the first of the three main patriarchs: Abraham, followed by Isaac and Jacob. Abraham recalls having heard a voice telling him to leave his homeland and go into a strange land called Canaan. He moves, however, *both* in an act of faith, insofar as he knows that he has experienced something unique in his life, *and* in an act of faith in something so unusually convincing that he is willing to venture into a new world that he does not know. Herein lies the coinherent nature of the experiential and the experimental nature of faith. The experimental facet of Abraham's faith thus consists of his not knowing just how God intends to bring about the fulfillment of His divine promises.

When the Israelites were delivered from 400 years of slavery under the Egyptians, they were being challenged by the wanderings in the wilderness to develop the way of faith but in a God who had *not* told them where they were *really* going. Though they were shown miracles of sustenance and sternly disciplined during their journey, the way of faith in an invisible God was completely contrary even to what they had known of a visible though unacceptable pharaoh. The call to worship the Supreme (and Invisible) Spirit of the universe proved too scary as a call to God-reliance. The way of faith proved so difficult that some tried to assassinate Moses; others stirred up dissension over his failure to return early from his reported retreats to Mount Sinai; still others urged a return to the gods of Egypt for comfort; and there were those who frankly asked in utter despair whether there were not enough graves back in Egypt, since it appeared that God had merely brought them out in the wilderness to perish.

When the Law or Torah had finally been given, unfaith showed its head again. Eventually, the lack of conformity to the intended spirit of the Law made it necessary for the Israelite leaders to add increasing numbers of particular, often legalistic, additions to the original Law. That, in turn, made the Law something other than a guiding set of ethical-spiritual principles by which one could live in holy covenant with God (Yahweh). In fact, it remains a part of Judaeo-Christian esoteric tradition even today that the original Law itself delivered by Moses to his people was designed for a people who, if their hearts were right, would find no compulsion in that Law. The original Law has even been considered by some esoterics to have been a different set of (noncommanding) spiritual principles.

With the emergence of the Israelite Hebrew monarchy or the institution of kingship, the problem of a lack of faith in the benefits of following a consistent path of purity as against following a prideful path of vanity arose. The Hebrew monarchy became acutely torn between what the Jewish philosopher Martin Buber called the "Kingship of God" versus the "kingship of man." This tension, too, led to further self- and communal-enslavement, disfavor, suffering, and death. With the destruction of the glorious temple of Solomon and the eventual return from exile in the land of Babylon, the restoration of the land and even the building of another (but less glorious) temple were not enough. For they were not followed by a faith that could dare to envision in the very midst of an Israelite community lacking national independence under non-Israelite rule that what was happening in the *heart* was to be held more dearly than what was happening to the *land.*

Tradition has it that it was Alexander the Great, who knew much about territorial conquest, who uttered (on his death bed) the following words: “It is not lands that must be conquered, but the hearts of men.” The radical implications of this statement and that of Jesus of Nazareth about worshiping God in spirit and in truth for the modern Middle Eastern crises, the interrelations among religious denominations within particular world religions, and the dialogue occurring among world religions themselves, as such, are staggering.

Faith and a Rite of Passage

My experiential faith was well on the road when I discovered that my dearly beloved sister, Sylvia Patricia (“Paddie”), had contracted invasive bone cancer (multiple myeloma). Almost daily during her illness, I used to leave the Rutgers University campus where I was teaching, drive to the Bronx, pick up my mother, and then drive her downtown to Paddie who was in the hospital. Before this, Paddie had experienced a two-year remission period during which she practically traveled around the world. But later, she needed permanent hospitalization.

Paddie had led a very interesting life. She had graduated from Morgan State College (now University) and had gone on to teach for a while in Bermuda, where she was born. Later she returned to the U.S. and tried to earn a library degree part time. Mother, who had originally fallen in love with this country as a child (with subsequent visits to relatives), made a special trip from the

Bermuda Isles to this country in order to make it easier for Paddie to finish her degree. At one point both she and Paddie were working at the same library. Paddie went on successfully to become a principal librarian in the Bronx, New York.

Paddie's avocational life was full of unfulfilled romantic dreams. For example, one man deserted her just two weeks before their planned wedding. He ran off with a Swedish woman. By that time Paddie had, of course, even bought her bridal gown. Eventually, the very last man she loved abandoned her as soon as his wife passed away; she had been ill for a long time. Paddie thought that it was to be their moment of greatest fulfillment; that is, that they would get married. But after another desertion Paddie became a chain smoker. She soon knew what depression was. That man was later found to be in attendance at her funeral in the Bronx. He was discovered because he attracted so much attention by his deep sobbing near the back of the church.

Paddie became discarnate in October 1977. As you probably know, anthropologists and historians of religions recognize four universal Rites of Passage *(rites de passage):* birth, puberty, marriage, and death. Such passages are all potentially traumatic moments of truth, or momentous transitions in the soul's education to Spiritual Reality. But, as Elisabeth Kübler-Ross has shown us so well, the trauma can also affect others who are intimately related to the human being-in-transition. In my mother's case, her own traumatization was naturally the (universal) fear, as mentioned before, that she would probably outlive her own child.

Here is what else happened during the funerals, for there were indeed two of them for Paddie: one in the Bronx and one in Bermuda. They were to occur on two consecutive days. Mother had resolved to make thorough but secret prearrangements for the events, especially for the funeral in the Bronx. "Secret," to be sure, meant without Paddie's knowledge. Everything concerning mortuary business was in order. But a couple of days before the service a number of little things were not in order at all. Mother could not find her passport and other important papers; Paddie's burial gown suddenly did not appeal to Mother and having a different one became something quite emotional with her. Regarding the misplaced documents, I had earlier taught my mother how to pray for lost objects. Most of the time it was for her keys. But she had forgotten amidst the stress of events to use that God-given gift. She later recovered the prayerful-meditative finding mode and found her papers just in time.

The garment, however, presented another problem. It was a bad time to go out and look for one both in terms of prospects and the safety factor. The Bronx was hardly a place to begin shopping in the evening. DeAnna (my former wife) and I searched. All the stores we entered had nothing in size or color that seemed appropriate. Our faith was on the verge of trembling when we decided to go home empty-handed. But then, faith prevailed. We began to hope against hopelessness. So we drove and walked, walked and drove, and walked. At evening's end, when night seemed to signal the death of faith, we halted a moment and eyed a little dry-goods store across an unknown street. It could be entered only via a steep staircase. At the very bottom of it, right in front of us on a rack was *the* dress for Paddie, the right color and the right size! It was there waiting for us. She looked beautiful in it, and mother was happy.

For other matters, how can I explain in terms other than divine grace in the midst of experiential faith that the night an ambulance had to be called for Paddie to be permanently hospitalized I happened to arrive unexpectedly at my mother's door a few moments before? Or that I miraculously missed suffering a terrible collision with the car ahead of me in the funeral motorcade during a sudden stop for which I was not prepared because I was tired and not alert? How can I explain the fact that I did not swallow a spider trapped on my plate during dinner while on my plane trip to Bermuda?[18] How can I explain what happened when we all finally arrived at the church cemetery in Bermuda, which was different from where the funeral service took place? It so happened that the pallbearers who had been at the church earlier had somehow disappeared! Getting the casket from street level to the actual grave site would not be easy. But then, looking over my shoulder, I noticed certain beings coming at running speed toward us in and among the graves and tombstones. These were *not* the original pallbearers.[19] These were other beings. They were all my childhood buddies (with whom I had had no recent contact and whom I had not noticed at all at the church) coming to our rescue. To this very day, I look upon this rather complex experience as an unforgettable confirmation of the wonder and power of faith and what it is to be in a state of saving grace.

Experimental Faith and Mutual Spiritual Growth

Faith is finally experimental. It is so because it is the key to a door that leads not only to both hope and love *(agape)* but also to unpredictable spiritual adventure. In the final analysis it is the experimental facet of faith that reflects the Creator's willingness to allow you to test yourself, your own desires and motives, in the quest to have, sustain, and strengthen the vital link that you have to the Creator as Eternal Mind. The experimental facet allows you again to express not only your co-creativity with God[20] in the commonplace application of what we have received of spiritual laws and values but also the unexpected developments in our lives. Here is a list of insights taken by Drummond from the psychic readings of Edgar Cayce, the seer, which testify to that co-creativity. "The purpose of creation," according to Drummond, consists in "'God's desire for companionship and expression,'" that you and I might become "'companions with the Father-God . . . '" and "'co-creator[s] with Him . . . '"[21]

> "The universe He *called into being* for purposes that the individual soul, that might be one with Him, would have . . . those influences for bringing this to pass or to be in the *experience* of every soul. For hath it not been given that the Lord thy God hath not willed that any soul should perish? but He hath prepared with every temptation a means, a *way* of escape" (cf. II Pet. 3:9; I Cor. 10:13). "Giving of will to His creation, man, that man might be one with Him . . . "[22]

Here you will discern that all three facets of faith are present and underlined in that (1) there is an initial affirmation of the intellectual facet of faith that God is indeed the Supreme Being who is the Source of the universe as a Oneness-empowerment system; (2) there is the subsequent affirmation of the experiential facet of faith which is intended for every soul to come to know itself by experience in individuality and in oneness with the Source; and (3) there is also the affirmation of the experimental facet of faith, which is the way of creative triumph over all things and circumstances that can lead to the loss of one's soul.[23]

The experimental facet of faith can take various forms: the courage to entertain new ideas regarding the nature of Reality (e.g., is it the case, after all, that your God is too small?); human nature (e.g., have you ever wondered whether there is any chance that homosexuality is a transitionally incarnate state of consciousness?); or human destiny (e.g., are you inclined to believe it is possible that we are all ultimately intended to be saved?). Have you ever had to make a decision to end a marriage or to begin a new one after a divorce or death of a spouse (a new marriage that might even turn out to be international, or interreligious, or interracial)? Have you ever had to endure the risk factor in starting a completely new job not knowing for sure how the new workplace would be later on? How would you apply your faith to the discovery that you have been accused and will probably be convicted of a crime you did not commit? Could you make the decision to reenter higher education challenged by normal taunting doubts about whether you are intelligent enough to succeed? How would you faithfully handle the announcement with an unencouraging prognosis by your doctor that you have cancer? Or would you fare better if such a thing were to happen to your child with the fearful prospect that you might be going to outlive your own offspring? Would your faith tremble and buckle before the discovery that your sexual partner—or a husband or wife—has been unfaithful and in contact with the AIDS virus? Would your faith endure with the occurrence of a terrible accident that leaves you seriously handicapped and seemingly helpless?

The list can go on endlessly, but the need to experiment with one's faith during these precarious moments in one's life becomes imperative. Could you have faith that the Creator has gifted and allowed you to find a way of escaping disillusionment, depression, and despair during such moments? Are you assuming that it is inevitable that everyone go through the five stages defined by Kübler-Ross (i.e., denial, rage and anger, bargaining, depression, acceptance) when facing death?[24] Could not a faith that includes this experimental aspect be rewarded by an additional, advanced, and enhancing depth of meaning that surpasses ordinary belief systems?

From the list of precarious moments above, I shall now tell you about how I made the creative, experimental faith-decision to end a marriage and begin a new one. Although I had a clerical background, it was not so much that I had considered divorce or remarriage something absolutely taboo. It was that it never occurred to me in a million years that I would ever encounter such a prospect—or necessity. We had married young; she was nineteen, and I was twenty-three. DeAnna and I had met at our local United Methodist Church, where I was teaching Sunday school. It appears to be true for all of us originally in love that, at the time, romance is all we know; it is as if the past and the future cease to have any bearing upon the magic of the moment.

As far as some forms of Christian orthodoxy are concerned, there is only one criterion of marriage; and that is its rootage in a vow of "Sacramental Promise." Here the conception is that the marital form of love is not only inviolable but something not to be dissolved by any human being (the Roman Catholic "annulment" is the exception). "Till death do us part" is taken to be the segment of the vow that rules out any new relationship in romantic terms with any other person during your marital lifetime, whether due to events expected or unexpected. The Roman Catholic Church and a fundamentalistic reading of the Bible have decisively influenced all other Christian religious bodies holding such a conception. Of course, one must allow for variations of understanding among diverse denominations, for there are mainline denominations which now allow divorce-with-remarriage. But all of them agree that the original marital vows must be accompanied by the intention to remain with the same spouse throughout one's lifetime.

But there is another conception of marriage which I am convinced can be legitimately associated with what I regard as a criterion of "Mutual Spiritual Growth." This idea is rooted in a creative and integrative interpretation of the teachings of Jesus, and it allows one to act in the spirit of experimental faith for the benefit of the development of one's soul with a sense of divine guidance.[25] I intend to pursue this subject and other ethical-spiritual issues from a Christian gnostic perspective in a book to follow this one. For now, let me share with you how my new marital experience is a deeply vivid illustration of an adventure in experimental faith.

In keeping with the idea of mutual spirit growth, I had come to the point in my first marriage where I was convinced that we were no longer growing together spiritually. You are very fortunate, if in your case your mate should share your conviction, because it assures that parting, though not necessarily without some pain, can occur without bitterness or regret. And it can positively influence the disposition of children, property, or finances. By God's grace mine was a so-called "amicable divorce." I believe it is the only kind that has the possibility of being nonkarmic. It is the only kind wherein and whereafter neighbor love remains when romantic love has gone. We are after all not commanded to marry but to love our neighbors as ourselves. But marry we may, and not realize either what marriage means spiritually or that, though the Bible says of the marriage bond "Let no man put [it] asunder," (Matt. 19:6) it is not something that God Himself cannot put asunder—or lead one to put asunder.

My marital separation was not characterized by an initial mutual awareness and thus it was not a fully synchronized experience. In fact, the critical pre-separation phase would come gradually over a two-year period. Meanwhile, with the discovery that I had to leave my job for a new one in another part of the country, my spouse opted not to accompany me. She had good reason. She was tenured in her job, and the children were too positively settled in to be uprooted at the time. Thus we had a mutual understanding that my new job would need testing and vice versa. And we knew, after all, that she had a tenured job to protect. However, after the separation, almost ten years had gone by before my need for a new marital form of communion reached its peak. But the coincidence of an increasing need for separation and of my having to move away to another part of the country to work was an example of absolute "Providential synchronicity."[26] But then, it turned out to be that *that* need *coincided* with the need of another woman whom I was to encounter while she was also in the process of discovering that she and her husband were no longer growing spiritually together and that in their case, too, there was another possibility of a nonkarmic parting of the ways.

Her husband became disturbed at our friendship, for it was eventually to develop into what I would only later call a "spiritual romance."[27] But it is a process that can be short or long and drawn out, if the heart is faint or if foreordained purposes and/or karmic connections still linger.[28] He insisted on confronting me, but he was amazed at my initial attitude. He discovered within the first few minutes that I could actually put aside my sense of need for her and encourage him to try further to continue and renew their marital relationship. I knew Peg only as a friend for the next several years, lest it prove to be an unhelpful distraction. As it all worked out, on their part, however, no amount of counseling or search for renewal would work. Eventually, she separated from him, and we encountered each other again when she got a job at the University of Wisconsin Oshkosh (from which she had graduated in 1983), where I had assumed a teaching position in 1979. I have since considered it an example of "Providential asynchronicity" that Peg and I never cast our eyes upon one another during the years before we met, since we were both there within the same time frame. A subsequent view of a graduation program photograph under a magnifying glass, however, led us to believe that I was in fact in the audience among the faculty the day she received her degree.

Interestingly, the husband and I had earlier developed mutual respect and enjoyed the occasions when we challenged each other over the interpretation of the Bible and certain Christian dogmas. As things developed, both he and I remarried within one week of one another, in 1989. And it is significant that both of the women involved had spiritual orientations. The new relationships brought together individual temperaments that allowed for further mutual spiritual growth. I venture to say that, for each of us, then, it was not only an experiment in faith, but it was also, as Gandhi would say, an "experiment with Truth."

Several important insights emerge from this adventure in experimental faith. First, it was experimental because of its radical personal novelty for me. From a purely external (or exoteric) point of view I was, on the one hand, moving apart from my longtime mate; and, on the other, I was indirectly coming in between the longtime relationship of two other human beings. Thus only from an esoteric perspective (which transcends the forms of things: here the orthodox "unbreakable" vows) could I perceive without guilt, therefore, that something was happening to our souls that God Himself was intending. Gary Zukav, author of *The Seat of the Soul,* says with remarkable courage and spiritual insight that "All of the vows that a human being can take cannot prevent the spiritual path from exploding through and breaking those vows if the spirit must move on. It is appropriate for spiritual partners to remain together only as long as they grow together."[29]

Second, unrealized by many Christians and even some who have entered the esoteric perspective, the idea of "Providential synchronicity" appears in Paul of Tarsus's Epistle to the Romans (8:28). He mentions it in this way: "We know that all things work together for good for those who love God . . . " Authoritative translators say that that passage can also read: "God makes all things work together for good"; or "In all things God works for good" (all NRSV). The important thing is that we perceive the truth that God causes all of our saving and health-giving experiences to coincide (synchronize) in such a way that we are given the opportunity to find triangulative union (physical, mental, and spiritual) with another, but also to rise into higher levels of spiritual consciousness.

Third, this adventure in experimental faith testifies to the truth that all of us are still being guided by the Spirit into various situations, sometimes characterized by "not-still waters";[30] that is, sometimes and sometimes not, at the same rate of momentum, we are led into deeper and more precarious spiritual waters for the sake of advancing our soul development. But when we interphase with any other soul's relationships, we had better know what we are doing.[31] This is especially true in the case wherein the resolution of (negative) karmic things in a marriage or some other relationship may not yet have been completed. Interestingly, I recall, as an object lesson, that in a fragmentary gnostic-like text (the *Codex Bezae*) dated several hundred years after Jesus, a man whom Jesus came upon not fulfilling the Sabbath-day commandment was told the following: "Man, if you *know* what you are doing, you are among men most blessed; but if you do *not* know what you are doing, you are accursed!"[32] Experimental faith is, therefore, that focus of faith that is always on the edge of becoming a "gnostic faith"[33]—without a focus—and a love that fulfills the law in (what seems to some) often heterodox forms but which *trans*forms relationships.[34] Yet it is also something which ultimately requires a superconsciousness level of knowing that both prevents guilt resulting from one's action and which lures one into the deeper more radical dimensions of what John the Divine uniquely calls *doing* truth (John 3:21 KJV).

Endnotes

1. I Corinthians 3:2; Hebrews 5:12-14.

2. "Natural law" was a far more complex term for the early Church Fathers and for Thomas Aquinas; however, it is being used here in an intentionally limited way.

3. Jan. 3, 1991; pp. A5, A11.

4. See a marvelous statement of God as the Ultimate Source of the universe in terms of its immensity, complexity, the infinitely small, by Islamic thinker Fazlur Rahman, in Jacob Neusner, ed., *God* (Cleveland, Ohio: The Cleveland Press, 1997), p. 89.

5. See these views and other statistics in Appendix IV: "Life by Chance in Outer Space: Possible or Impossible?" in John Weldon (with Zola Levitt), *UFOs: What on Earth Is Happening?* (New York: Bantam Books, 1976), pp. 171-175.

6. *Ibid.*, p. 172.

7. *Ibid.*, p. 173.

8. Cited in Huston Smith, "The Reach and the Grasp: Transcendence Today," in Herbert W. Richardson and Donald R. Cutler, eds., *Transcendence* (Boston: Beacon Press, 1969), p. 12.

9. Sagan, *Contact* (New York, N.Y.: Pocket Books, 1986), pp. 430, 431. Reprinted with the permission of Simon & Schuster from *Contact* by Carl Sagan. Copyright © 1985, 1986, 1987 by Carl Sagan.

10. To the best of my knowledge, the phrase "the *beyond* in the midst of our life" was used by the European theologian, Dietrich Bonhoeffer.

11. Andrew Wilson, ed., *World Scripture: A Comparative Anthology of Sacred Texts* (a project of the International Religious Foundation, New York: Paragon House, 1991), p. 535.

12. Raimundo Panikkar, *The Intrareligious Dialogue* (New York: The Paulist Press, 1978), p. 12.

13. For more on this paradox, see my comments on Augustine in chapter 3.

14. Matthew 16:13-17.

15. See p. 27, point #3, on the elements included in experiential faith.

16. See Matthew 16:21-23.

17. See, e.g., Lynn Elwell Sparrow's *Edgar Cayce and the Born Again Chris-*

tian, pp. 210-215; cf. especially pp. 26-27.

18. See chapter 5, subsection: "The Totemic Spider."

19. I have since thought that the original pallbearers were of the A.M.E. Church only and thus did not thereafter follow us to Saint John's Episcopal Church for the burial. To the best of my recollection, no one had prearranged what did happen subsequently.

20. On co-creating, see Harmon Bro, *A Seer Out of Season*, chapter 9, especially pp. 183-190.

21. Consecutively, Edgar Cayce readings 5749-14; 1567-2; 2794-3.

22. Drummond, *Unto the Churches*, p. 82; Edgar Cayce readings 1347-1 and 900-20. Italics added.

23. Not quite clear to some, Cayce teaches that while the soul-force of God that is our metaphysical essence is never lost, the gift of our God-given individuality can after all be lost; the entity being referred to as having "submerged itself." Hence he says, "Can God lose itself, if God be God . . . The *soul* is not lost; the *individuality* of the soul that separates itself is lost" (826-8). The lost "soul" (as "individuality") would then be returned "to the One Force, but knows not itself to be itself any more"! (3357-1) This view presupposes, logically, an end of opportunities for reincarnation—even of sojourns in burning hells (5753-1) or states of consciousness. It is apparent that this loss is tragically worse a loss than even discarnate suffering as a prelude to reunion with its Maker (see also 3744-2 and 3744-4).

24. At a municipally sponsored divorce-counseling session I attended, I suggested to the group leaders that, with either divorce or death there could be a *sixth* state beyond "acceptance," which I called "renewal." They agreed. Kübler-Ross would probably agree in light of her belief in life *beyond* bodily death: that "we will be reborn again one day"; see "Death as Part of My Own Personal Life," in chapter 5 of her *Death: The Final Stage of Growth* (Englewood Cliffs, New Jersey: Prentice-Hall, 1975), especially p. 119.

25. See Marilyn Ferguson, *The Aquarian Conspiracy* (Los Angeles: J.P. Tarcher, Inc., 1980), chapter 12: "Human Connections: Relationships Changing." See also pp. 42-43 in this book and note #27 below.

26. *Synchronicity* is a term used (but not created) by psychologist Carl Jung. He defines it as "a meaningful coincidence of two or more events, where something other than the probability of chance is involved"; "On Synchronicity," in Joseph Campbell, ed., *The Portable Jung* (trans. R.F.C. Hull, New York: The Viking Press, 1973), p. 505. Jung realized that it was something that goes well beyond our human comprehension (as with his "archetypes" or "primal images"). I am using "Providential synchronicity" here to affirm that the Creator is the Supreme Source of the coincidence, sometimes of the convergence of events into meaningful spiritual adventures in intellectual, experiential, and experimental faith. This special type of ("Providential") synchronicity is inspired by Romans 8:28. It also means, however, that though every accident is a coincidence, not every coincidence is an accident!

27. A spiritual romance is one in which a romantic encounter is mutually perceived both as something destined to happen (either by "prevenient grace" or by preexistential karma), something whose spiritual purpose is intuited, and something that includes but ultimately transcends the typical original spell of romantic love, especially the form of a first marital love (or even a nonmarital relationship) that the soul has outgrown.

28. For a clarification of the use of the term *foreordained* by Edgar Cayce

in relation to the soul-mate concept, see Mark Thurston, *Visions and Prophecies for a New Age* (Virginia Beach, Virginia: A.R.E. Press, 1981), pp. 113-114.

29. Gary Zukav, *The Seat of the Soul* (New York: Simon and Schuster, Fireside paperback ed., 1990), p. 126.

30. Cf. Psalm 23:2.

31. See Proverbs 14:12; 16:25.

32. Italics added; see Luke 23:34.

33. "Gnostic faith": any experiment in faith that leads one into a spiritually enhancing direction wherein one has a deep sense within oneself of what is right for one's own life apart from external (orthodox) edicts or opinions, and wherein one has an unfaltering trust that, invariably, the Creator will compensate for the soul in any stressful situation, whether it be due to one's lack of adequate wisdom, or power, or love.

34. See "Mutual Spiritual Growth," p. 39 in this book.

3

Faith as Atonement and Gnosis as Attunement

In the light of all the previous remarks, it must be restated that all three facets of faith—the intellectual, the experiential, and the experimental—each tend to imply one another's coexistence. But it is the *experimental* facet or dimension of faith that is eventually bound to bring an individual to the threshold of a faith-beyond-faith and into the realm of "gnostic faith,"[1] and ultimately of pure gnosis. Hence, the importance of seeking to *know* what one is doing in spiritual terms.

But what was it about the previous adventure in experimental faith by way of a spiritual foundation that made it possible for the four of us involved? It was in large measure because of our collective and communal background in experiential faith. That collective and communal foundation of faith that made all this possible is the glorious teaching that we are capable of *both* atonement *and* attunement with the Creator-God. And the process whereby we may find either or both of these in some form often requires that the soul set itself free from the traditional belief and behavioral boundaries determined by persons who have been taken captive by the traditional past. I say taken *captive* by the traditional past because, though the past is always prologue in the lives of all spiritually reflective beings and, therefore, is never to be ignored or taken lightly, it should also never be allowed to take precedence over the developmental needs of the soul. This is the basis of the attitude of Jesus of Nazareth, when He used to say, "Ye have heard that it was said by them of old time . . . But I say unto you . . . "[2]

Faith, Atonement, and Self-Giving

Atonement, then, tends to be more typically linked to experiential faith; and attunement is more often linked to experimental faith. The relation between atonement and the experiential facet of faith in the Father-Mother-God is directly related to the foundation that the Judaeo-Christian tradition has laid for us in the form of its ancient Day of Atonement sacrifice.[3] Thus the idea of atonement preceded Christianity, but it was Christianity that converted the ancient Jewish atonement sacrifice into a sacrament-centered religion that has to this day remained linked to a substitutionary theory of atonement; that is to say, for the sake of salvation Jesus shed His blood in humanity's place, lest God punish the entire human race of uncleansed souls in hell which is demanded by His eternal justice.

Though this view intended us to believe that this uniquely ingenious Divine Plan of salvation was motivated by Divine Love, it has also tended to have ambiguous effects in the minds of millions. But a later parallel, if not adjoining, theory emphasized instead that Jesus saved humankind through the gift of His self-sacrificial spiritual love (John 4:10). Christ is really the very first "Christmas present" from the Creator! Thus Jesus died not in our place but rather *in our behalf!* Here the emphasis lies not on blood sacrifice but the morally motivating influence of human gratitude for this supremely unselfish act by one who was not worthy of suffering and death.

So it was Jesus of Nazareth who brought the Jewish understanding of atonement to its consummate individual level of meaning and understanding. He did this by teaching and demonstrating that all the previous ritual symbols of atonement pointed not to sacrifice per se, but to the glory of *self*-sacrifice in behalf of the spiritual wholeness of humankind.[4]

These two options are associated with two medieval thinkers, St. Anselm of Canterbury (1033-1109) and Pierre Abelard, French philosopher and theologian (1079-1142), respectively. The second option is much related to a theory well known to anthropologists, called the "Gift Theory of Sacrifice," whereby humans tender portions of their hunt or harvest as gifts in homage to the gods. In the Christian theory, however, it is God who renders a "gift" to humankind. Hence the immortal words of John the Divine (3:16): "God so loved the world that he *gave* his only Son, so that everyone who believes in him may not perish but may have eternal life." (Italics added.) In a word, the first option has a rather exoteric ring to it in terms of its conception of God (as Eternal Judge) and atonement (as a ritual transaction); the second option, though not purely esoteric, has the power to elevate the quality of one's frame of reference and the focus of one's faith in the moral sense. For love is the only power that can unite the exoteric *and* the esoteric in religion, and to unite persons who differ in how they conceive an individual can become at-one or have at-onement (atonement) with God.

Many intellectually oriented persons of faith might have remained in institutional Christianity had they been told of this latter option as a way of contemplating the meaning of Jesus' life for them. For the first option of bloody sacrifice has even to this day turned many persons, prone toward a largely intellectual faith, completely away from both the study of the Bible and the acceptance of establishment Christianity. Can you honestly say that, comparatively, the second option above does not appeal to your moral sensibilities in a more inspiring way? For this enables us to identify with others who at various levels of spiritual self-sacrifice have done the same, such as Socrates in Greece; Jason and the Maccabees in Judaism; the Islamic martyr, Husayn of Arabia; Gandhi in India; Martin Luther King, Jr., in the United States; and countless others elsewhere in the world who have lived-and-died in behalf of humankind. At any rate, a very important thing is to remain tolerant toward those persons for whom either one *or* both of these perspectives may continue to have profound meaning in terms of personal salvation. For in the end it remains irrefutably true that "you will know them by their fruits."[5]

As you might imagine, this view does not allow Christianity or any other religion a position of spiritual superiority as such. What it does mean is exemplified by two very important things regarding the relation between Judaism and Christianity. One is, as philosopher Hans Rosenzweig has put it (using one of several images to illustrate his point), that Judaism is the (historical) light or the fire of truth that burns most intensely at the core of divine revelation; and Christianity represents the rays that reach out in blazing dissemination of the light to humankind at large.[6] While citing Rosenzweig's *Star of*

Redemption, Lubarsky says, "To the Jew, God gave eternal life by 'kindling the fire of the Star of his truth in our hearts.' To the Christian was given the eternal way, guided by 'the rays of that Star of his truth for all time unto the eternal end.'"[7]

While Rosenzweig has some very seriously ambivalent reservations regarding tragic happenings during the Christian part of this process,[8] it nonetheless represents a potentially creative and meaningful way to link the two world religions in a common spiritual cause. Lubarsky notes that the question of superiority or inferiority is not finally resolved in order to make the two religions plainly symmetrical. I maintain, however, that the attitudinal problem is greatly improved if both Jews and Christians humbly realize that neither Judaism nor Christianity as a *religion* is the Absolute Source of the Light!

In spirit Rosenzweig's metaphor nonetheless implies quite strongly that Christianity, as a religion, still *needs* Judaism as its continuous spiritual foundation; and it means that Judaism, because of its historical tendency to conserve the presence of the Light of God in the world, especially in the face of recurrent persecution, *needs* Christianity to shine radiantly forth the glory of Torah to many lives in many lands. Neither Jews nor Christians should hesitate, therefore, to rejoice in the fact that Jesus of Nazareth could say, "Do not think that I have come to abolish the law [Torah] or the prophets; I have come not to abolish but to fulfill" (Matthew 5:17). An immensely important thing to remember is that Jesus Himself was a Jew. Does it then look anything but nonsensical for any individual whom God has enlightened[9] to declare that he or she hates Jews? Or vice versa?

But neither Jews nor Christians must ever forget that Jesus was more than a Jew *and* more than a "Christian," in any deeper spiritual perspective that goes beyond denominational and sectarian small-mindedness.[10] It was

Martin Luther King, Jr., who once said, "God is bigger than all our denominations." This is why in the case of Judaism Jesus was able to tear down or split the curtain that stood between large segments of humankind and the experience of the immediacy of God.[11] One may recall Paul of Tarsus's proclamation that Jesus of Nazareth also came to cast down the "wall of partition" (Ephesians 2:14 KJV) that separates Jew and Gentile;[12] and there is theologian Paul Tillich's extremely creative sermon on "Universal Salvation" in which he interprets the renting of the curtain or veil of the temple (the Holy of Holies) at the moment of Jesus' crucifixion (Matthew 27:50-54; Luke 23:43-45) as a permanent sign of what I previously referred to as experiencing the *immediacy* of God. In that sermon, Tillich bravely said:

> *This* curtain cannot be mended any more, although there are priests and ministers and pious people who try to mend it. They will not succeed because He, *for whom every place was a sacred place, a place where God is present,* has been brought on the cross in the name of the holy place . . . When the curtain of the temple was torn in two, God judged religion and rejected temples . . . The curtain which makes the temple a holy place, separated from other places, lost its separating power . . . [13]

This radically symbolic event thus pointed to the utter relativity of all religious sanctuaries (including churches) and rituals compared to the absolute accessibility of the Eternal Divine through atonement and attunement. Edgar Cayce could thus challenge and encourage a rabbi's limited spiritual perspective by urging him not to be "bound by creeds . . . modes . . . any law!" He also advised him to "*coordinate* the teachings, the philosophies of the East and the West . . . the new truths and the old . . . not the differences, but where all religions meet—*there is one God!* 'Know, O Israel, the Lord thy God is *one!'* . . . Hast thou not found that the *essence,* the truth, the *real* truth is *one?* Mercy and justice, peace and harmony."[14]

Thus Jesus was also more than a "Christian," insofar as, for Him, atonement meant that everyone can approach the Father-Mother-God directly (without intermediaries).[15] Furthermore, this now means that Jesus has confirmed the fact, as Teilhard de Chardin said, that God wishes to make us "present to one another." Each of us is thereby destined to be immediately present to the other as a loving neighbor, rather than separated by any present or new "veil" of institutional religion that could prevent the erection of an altar of love and devotion to God in the temple of the heart. For it is such veils that separate numerous beings everywhere who may be wearing the badge of some particular established religious institution or who are too uncritically prepared to profess the teachings of a particular religious doctrine. Indeed, Teilhard offered us a grander challenge when he said that the world had become a neighborhood, but it had not yet become a brotherhood.

Hence in the light of all the walls and partitions and veils that seek to separate one brother from another, one sister from another, one brother and sister from another, New Testament scholar Leon Wright has said, "The heavens are always 'opened.'" Likewise the Book of Proverbs says, "Keep my commandments and live . . . write them on the tablet of your *heart.*"[16] The day that we can witness the joyful and acceptable marriage of a Jehovah's Witness and a Catholic, a Mormon and a Seventh-Day Adventist, a Baptist and a Christian Scientist, we shall know that

> There is one body and one Spirit, just as you were

> called to the one hope that belongs to your call, one Lord, one faith, one baptism, one God and Father of us all, who is above all and through all and in all.[17]

Jesus of Nazareth was undoubtedly the most convincing personification, the greatest living fulfillment, and the boldest manifestation of the character and destiny of the prophet Isaiah's vision of the Israelite community as the suffering servant of God *(Eved Yahweh).* Isaiah 53 is in essence a redemptive Judaic "Hymn of Nonviolent Self-Sacrifice." It was uttered not only in the face of the Jewish experience of Babylonian exile, but ultimately in the face of every human oppression and every demonic foe. But even today, the hymn remains one of restorative and saving promise. For it contains, in a word, a reaffirmation (if we forgive gender usage) of a saying which was once uttered in behalf of the human species itself: "Man will not only endure; he will prevail!"

But, in a historical context, the vision of Isaiah was a promise to Israel that she would prevail over all her foes not only in the ancient world, but throughout time—if she would dare to trust, to have faith in the living God's power; that is, His power to make His Eternal Light shine through her by way of her loving obedience to Torah under the form of a communally—but also *ecumenically*—lived Word (recall Cayce and the rabbi above). This, too, would unfortunately mean the inevitable physical death of more Jews, as the European Holocaust has uniquely demonstrated.

However, in the context of the hope of immortality, as the prophet Isaiah also declared of Israel, " . . . he shall see his offspring, he shall prolong his days" (Isaiah 53:10). It, therefore, represents a new vision—nay, indeed, the recapturing of an old vision that God had earlier given to Israel but which had been forgotten and unfulfilled due to the ups and downs of what seemed to so many a sacred history and a sacred promise gone awry. For what with traumatic community exile *(Galut)* and disheartening dispersion *(Diaspora),* Isaiah's vision lay probably dormant until the Essenes emerged. Not that all Essenes were the same. For there were, and are, varieties of religious temperamental responses and understandings concerning what the "War of the Sons of Light and the Sons of Darkness" in the Qumran scriptures really meant. Was it really an external, gargantuan group conflict of Jews and/or all righteous souls against the demonic nationalistic powers of this world and/or the influence on earth from subastral demonic powers? Or, for example, was it not as some have perceived, symbolic of what Sufi Muslims especially call "the Greater Jihad" ("struggle"), a striving within oneself to submit to the way of nonviolent forgiving love—the way of peace?

Yet the apparent vision of an Israel newly committed to an unswerving loyalty to Torah, but now without war, can be linked to God's earlier call to Israel not only to remain apart from profanely oriented peoples for the sake of being nurtured in the art of holiness, but also to accept her destiny to become "a light to the nations."[18] It is now apparent in the light of recent history, however, that the nations cannot perceive that Light without Judaism's and Christianity's common communal commitment to witnessing to that Light!

Three extremely important facts remain, therefore, about Israel, despite the occurrence of the Holocaust and its demonstration of how far evil can go. One is, according to sympathetic persons of various religious backgrounds, the wonder that the Jews were not all centrally located and were thus prevented from being completely and tragically wiped out. The Creator, therefore, turned their "Diaspora" (dispersion) into a form of salvific or saving separation for many. Another is that their persecutors did not in fact prevail even though Jews endured what must seem too much, too long; and again Judaism continues to be a living faith today, despite the presence of some Jews who in post-World War II times became and have remained atheists. Yet despite the continuation of forms of oppression not unlike but in some sense more depressing than she experienced from her ancient enemies (i.e., facing modern terrorism), the faith of Israel has prevailed over all her enemies throughout time.

Unfortunately, when it comes to war, Israel has not historically had the necessary, exceptional quality of faith—and, one must say, neither have the Christians—to accept the Creator's ultimate spiritual challenge uttered through the mouth of the prophet Isaiah:

> *He* was wounded for *our* transgressions,
> crushed for *our* iniquities;
> upon *him* was the punishment
> that made *us* whole,
> and by *his* bruises *we* are healed.[19]

This vision of Isaiah of collective Israel but fully realized in the life of Jesus of Nazareth challenges, again, the idea of the "Holy War," which has been a part of all three of the exclusively monotheistic religions: Judaism, Christianity, and Islam. It still baffles the enlightened mind how for socio-politico-economic reasons, under the guise of divinely ordained (bloody) "Crusades," souls professing religious devotion can seek to conquer land rather than the hearts of humankind (recall Alexander the Great's dying words). Believe it or not, there is something more questionable about this than the war fought against Hitler! No wonder that the internationally renowned scholar of philosophy and interreligious dialogue, John Hick, who has been writing and contemplating the warring relations among the various world religions (including the problem of evil) has said that, perhaps, it is the Buddhist world community that has come the closest to achieving some collective consistency in this regard.

Gnosis, Attunement, and Self-Transcendence

The relation between attunement and the experimental aspect of faith in the Eternal Mind is more directly related to something that has throughout time lain deep in the heart of Judaism and Christianity (via Kabbalism and Gnosis), but which both have largely shied away from because of its esoteric implications. Yet it is something that reflects the search of many for a deeper and more intimate experience of the Eternal One. Daniel the Prophet uttered the following words that should give many persons reason to pause who think that the extension of faith into the realm of Gnosis was never intended:

> Blessed be the name of God from age to age, for wisdom and power are his . . . he gives wisdom to the wise and knowledge to those who have understanding. He reveals deep and hidden things . . . To you, O God of my ancestors, I give thanks and praise for you have given me wisdom and power and have now revealed to me what we asked of you.[20]

Traditionally, the deeper dimensions of historical Christianity have been variously understood to include such things as the mystery of the cross, the mystery of baptism, the mystery of the atonement, the mystery of the church, the mystery of the resurrection, and the like.[21] It is tremendously significant, however, that these mysteries have been passed on by teachers, interpreted by theologians, and celebrated by priests entirely and only within doctrinal frameworks. Ordinary believers have not been informed that these "revelations" are themselves based on Cosmic Truths reflecting ever-deeper dimensions of Reality and thus the cumulative understanding of our ancestors about the nature of God, human nature, and the universe.

The time has indeed come to move on toward exploring, experiencing, if not accepting, the metaphysical mysteries that now lie behind the "mysteries" of the sacramentarian, bureaucratic church itself! Understanding the mystery of the cross *(mysterium crucis),* in the theologian's words, as "the epitome of the structural law of the universe,"[22] does not mean, as Christian orthodoxies would have it, that it can be understood apart from all the other mysteries revealed in the ancient world before the coming of Jesus of Nazareth. Ultimately, Jesus of Nazareth did not come to pontificate but to demonstrate the practicability of the mysteries in terms of our ethical-spiritual lives.

Attunement to the structural law of the universe—whether conceived as Muntu (African), Ma'at (Egyptian), Dharma (East Indian), Torah (Hebrew), Logos (Christian), Tao (Chinese), Asha (Persian), or Wakan Tanka (Sioux), etc.—is ultimately intended to bypass both the religious frameworks and individual limitations imposed even by the traditions that have discerned them. Only one who perceived this truth at the deepest level could thus say, "Man was not made for the sabbath; the sabbath was made for man." Here, Jesus, because of His radical attunement to the Spirit behind and beyond the Law, was fulfilling the spiritual purpose of the Law, not contradicting the Law. But what is behind and beyond is a Cosmic Law which the Torah itself merely reflects. Cosmic Law, itself, does not belong to anyone. In truth it has kinship with, but it is also as uncontrollable as the natural laws of the Cosmos which, again, no one owns. This Law, then, which I am not the first to call Eternal Law, is something which one can never harness but only with which one must seek to be in harmony. The Christian mystery, then, is fundamentally distinguished from every other mystery we know only by its unparalleled emphasis on the inseparable relation between Love (which is the form of Eternal Law) and Grace.[23] Hence both atonement *and* attunement come to nought without Divine Grace. And the person through whom that truth has been permanently and ineradicably revealed is Jesus of Nazareth. And He did not reveal this by speaking in the form of doctrines or in tongues but, rather, in spirit and in truth. "The kingdom of God depends not on talk but on power"![24]

Attunement is thus spiritually inseparable from the intentions of Greek Christian mysticism or Oriental systems of meditation. It can even be looked upon as a way of penetrating the purposes of doctrine which the perpetrators of doctrine themselves have not often penetrated. Atonement and attunement are thus two sides of the same coin, as Cayce implied about prayer and meditation; or atonement and attunement are as yin and yang as they function in the lives of men and women scattered across the face of the earth.[25] But both atonement and attunement are capable of levels of intellectual, experiential, and experimental interpretation. Yet in the final analysis, should one consider oneself to "understand all mysteries and all knowledge," (I Cor. 13:2) whether in terms of at-One-ment or attunement-to-the-One, without love (agape), it all means nothing.

These previous remarks have more credibility when one considers that Jesus of Nazareth linked His own cross to the crosses which He challenged His followers to bear. They, too, were to bear both in His day and long after Him their own crosses![26] This flies in the face of those who would use Jesus as a "scapegoat"; for that attitude is certainly in keeping with what a gem of Chinese mysticism *(The Secret of the Golden Flower)* calls the two main obstacles to salvation: laziness and distraction.

In other words, there is a vital link between what Jesus already understood of the Eternal Mysteries and what He wanted His followers and even others not of His immediate fold to understand as well.[27] And this, in order that they might correlate their ordinary and their extraordinary experiences with the same Eternal Mysteries. Among those mysteries is the truth that, in part, we, as rational beings, have been given to live in a universe whose first startling mystery is ecological-religious in nature: that life is relentlessly driven to feed upon life—a mystery exoterically given most dramatically in the animal and human sacrificial (including cannibalistic) rites of the ancient world. But it is also a mystery esoterically (symbolically) given in the previous words of Isaiah the prophet (p. 55), as well as in the words of Jesus:

> Those who eat my flesh and drink my blood have eternal life . . . for my flesh is true food and my blood is true drink. Those who eat my flesh and drink my blood abide in me, and I in them. Just as the living Father sent me, and I live because of the Father, so whoever eats me will live because of me. This is the bread that came down from heaven, not like that which your ancestors ate, and they died. But the one who eats this bread will live forever.[28]

Yet this particular mystery encompasses, again, the wonder that we ourselves have been given the spiritual task to prove that there is something in this universe that is even greater than life itself—and, of course, that is *love*. Only when life feeds on love, then, can life cease to prey on life and, ultimately, to merge with love, whereby it can be said that "No one has greater love than this, to lay down one's life for one's friends."[29] Recall the saying by poet Richard Lovelace: "Love is the life of soul; it is the harmony of the universe."

Thus that which is greater than life itself is love—Eternal Love, or as a well-known hymn says it, "Love divine, all loves excelling." This in turn is part of another wonder: that we as human beings have been infused by God's grace within our historical and spiritual evolution, in order to make the vital transition from animal sacrifice to human sacrifice, and finally to human self-sacrifice as a sacramental way of being in this world. In the very words, "Father, forgive them, for they do not *know* what they are doing," (Luke 23:34, italics added) lies a cosmic secret. Those who crucified Jesus, then, did not have *gnosis;* therefore, they did not *know* what they were doing—in cosmic terms—to obstruct the advancement of the Kingdom of God! Yet they lacked not only gnosis per se but gnosis possessed by the Christ Consciousness. For this reason even Gnosticism itself as an elitist esoteric movement failed in the early centuries (see I Cor. 8:1-3). Too many of its adherents did not perceive, indeed, that in all cosmic times and places where souls have really known what they were doing, spiritual love (agape) has been understood to be the very essence of gnosis.[30]

Hence it is the element of attunement as an esoteric means of at-one-ment-as-union (or a unitive experience of the Holy) that allows for the radical transformation of the egoistic tendencies of the ego. It is the Oriental traditions that have contributed a treasury of attunement experiences to the Near Eastern-Far Western worlds, since it seems to have been given to the Orient by the Eternal Divine One to become the masters of the art of meditation (e.g., Yoga, Dhyana, Zen). The idea of meditation (which goes to the heart of attunement) was, of course, not unknown to early and later Judaism (e.g., kavanah); or Christianity (e.g., hesychasm).[31] Meditative attunement as a mode of salvation, nonetheless, was probably an infusion of the Palestinian and the Graeco-European worlds by highly specialized meditative techniques of the East (especially via Buddhism). It was most likely this that enabled the Essenes, for example, to become, among others, the forerunners of the art of harmonizing both prayer and meditation for individuals and communities all across the Near Eastern and the Western worlds.

The Buddhist vision of the contemplative way of being in the world is believed by some scholars to have penetrated the ancient Near East during the missionary zeal of the Indian emperor Ashoka (fourth century B.C.) and to have reached as far as northern Syria.[32] This event has been understood to account for the apparently unique nature of the Essene community in Palestinian Judaism—a monastic Jewish community where none should have existed. The Essenes, therefore, are a treasurable communal example of experimental faith, insofar as they dared to heed the call of the prophet Isaiah to go out into the Judean desert and prepare the way for the coming of One who would become the paragon of the Christ Consciousness, Jesus of Nazareth.

Thus far in describing faith as the universal human adventure, it should by now have occurred to you that faith, in the truest sense of a religious reality, is multifaceted. It is multifocal. It is multipractical. Faith is multifaceted because we are after all multidimensional beings; that is, body, mind, and soul. And the art of prayer and meditation, one petitioning, one listening, is the primary means for helping to integrate body and mind, to bring them into final harmony with the soul in which lodges the Pattern of the Eternal (i.e., the Christ Consciousness). So that as we go about our daily round of life in and through the intellectual, experiential, and experimental facets of faith, we must continue the quest to find wholeness in the quest for holiness. The substance of our faith is thus inseparably linked to our hope to be able to (intellectually) contemplate, to (experientially) integrate, and to (experimentally) create saving moments for the Eternal Spirit and Its eternal things in our lives.[33] The final and most convincing evidence of the Unseen Reality that makes all this possible consists in how our faith is translated into spiritual values, into living, loving, and learning how to become the most wonderful of human beings—the servants of God. Faith is multifaceted because the three facets of faith, being indeed facets, are not necessarily stages but variously interphasing dimensions of the operation of the soul through our minds and our bodies. There is a sense, then, in which the "evidence of things not seen" (Heb. 11:1 KJV) requires the increasing integration of all three facets of faith. This means, therefore, that they represent interpermeating phases of spiritual consciousness.

Faith is multifocal because the object of faith is the Eternal Being who is willing to be conceived in ways and degrees personal or impersonal without offense. You might recall (when it comes to this fact about God) not only Edgar Cayce's insights given earlier on, but also the title of Joseph Campbell's monumental four-volume masterpiece, *The Masks of God.* The word *masks* says an awful lot about the ways of God (as Divine Providence) in trying to meet the needs and temperaments of all His children in the world.[34]

Faith is multipractical because the "substance" of faith as "things hoped for" (Heb. 11:1 KJV) also includes the anticipation that there *are* practical solutions to the most perplexing problems that can confront us as developing souls; that we can be guided into the practical truth of any given personal or social situation which may negatively affect our progress toward final salvation.[35]

Is it any wonder that when Paul of Tarsus wanted to let us know what we could absolutely count on in the midst of an ever-changing world—a world in which many even now are paying more attention to the emphasis on change than the changeless example of Jesus of

Nazareth (Heb. 13:8)—he includes along with hope and love as the only three things that endure forever—the wonder of faith (I Cor. 13:13).

Endnotes

1. See chapter 2, note #33.
2. E.g., Matthew 5:21, 22, 27, 28, and elsewhere. The reader should note that much of that "old-time" religion was held to have come from God—hence Jesus (and we today) looked quite bold and arrogant to the religious leaders of His time.
3. See Leviticus 16.
4. See Leviticus 16; John 1:29; Isaiah 53.
5. Matthew 7:16, 20.
6. See Sandra B. Lubarsky, *Tolerance and Transformation: Jewish Approaches to Religious Pluralism* (Cincinnati, Ohio: Hebrew Union College Press, 1990), pp. 49-72.
7. *Ibid.*, pp. 66-67; cf. Rabbi Yonassan Gershom, *Beyond the Ashes* (Virginia Beach, Virginia: A.R.E. Press, 1992), pp. 224, 289.
8. Of the Jew and the Christian, then, Rosenzweig in *The Star of Redemption* (New York, N.Y.: Holt, Rinehart and Winston, 1971), p. 415, also says that God "cannot dispense with either. He has set enmity between the two for all time, and withal has most intimately bound each to each." Cf. p. 413ff.
9. John 1:9.
10. See chapter 7 and the Gnostic cross.
11. Luke 11:2; Rom. 8:15-16; Gal. 4:6.
12. Exoterically, Paul of Tarsus believed in "churches," but, esoterically, he knew that for us the human body was intended to be conceived as God's temple: see I Corinthians 3:16, 17; 6:19.
13. Paul Tillich, *The New Being* (New York, N.Y.: Charles Scribner's Sons, 1955), pp. 177-178. Italics added. Cf. the disciple Steven's speech before his martyrdom: chapter 1, p. 15.
14. Edgar Cayce reading 991-1.
15. This is an insight truly given in the body of teaching known as *A Course in Miracles*, which I will comment on in my next volume; however, we must remember that the notion of divine or human intermediaries and of blood atonement properly belongs to an essentially exoteric framework of understanding. Like the question of images, therefore, it is to be regarded as a mode of understanding to be surpassed before being outright rejected as such; for there are those who of old were—and even today who have been—introduced to the process of redemption (i.e., being drawn to the Christ Consciousness) by such an exoteric means. See the milk/solid food reference in chapter 2, p. 21.
16. Proverbs 7:2, 3; cf. Deut. 6:4-5; Lev. 19:18; Mark 12:29-31.
17. Ephesians 4:4-6.
18. Isaiah 42:6 RSV; see also John 12:46; Matt. 5:14.
19. Isaiah 53:5; italics added.

20. Daniel 2:20-23; see also I Cor. 2; James 1:5-8.

21. Hugo Rahner, "The Christian Mystery and the Pagan Mysteries" in *The Mysteries* (Papers from the Eranos Yearbooks, Bollingen Series XXX.2; ed. by Joseph Campbell, New York, N.Y.: Pantheon Books, Inc., 1955, p. 358) reduces the Christian mystery to three distinguishing points: it is (1) a mystery of revelation, (2) a mystery of ethical law, and (3) a mystery of salvation by grace.

22. *Ibid.*, p. 375.

23. I say "emphasis" because the idea of grace is known in the Orient, though there, too, it has been variously understood.

24. I Corinthians 4:20.

25. See chapter 6 and the relation of faith and gnosis as paradox. This author prefers the continuum analogy.

26. Mark 8:34.

27. See John 10:16. There are those who perceive this as an esoteric saying that refers to persons of other world religions, especially in light of psychics and seers who say that Jesus did travel to lands outside Palestine.

28. John 6:54-58.

29. John 15:13.

30. I Corinthians 13:2 contains the words, "And if I . . . understand all mysteries and all knowledge *[gnosis]* . . . but do not have love, I am nothing."

31. See Aryeh Kaplan, *Jewish Meditation: A Practical Guide* (New York: Schocken Books, 1985), pp. 49-50; James Aerthayil, "The Hesychast Method of Prayer," *Journal of Dharma* (Vol. 2, No. 2, April 1977), pp. 204-216.

32. The wonder of the Essenes as monastics may have been due to the arrival of Buddhist monks in northern Syria in the third century B.C. which contributed to the development in the Qumran community of a reclusive mode of being (though all were not so) and an austere way of life including, alongside Jewish baptisms and communal meals, the art of meditation and healing. For the Buddhist-Jewish connection, see the article, "2,200-Year-Old Inscription Suggests Jewish Monastics Drew Inspiration from the Ideas of Buddhism," *New York Times* (Sunday, April 26, 1970), p. 12; see especially Glenn D. Kittler, *Edgar Cayce on the Dead Sea Scrolls* (New York, N.Y.: Paperback Library, 1970); on the Buddhist-Near Eastern gnostic connection, see Elaine Pagels, *The Gnostic Gospels* (New York: Random House, 1979), p. xxi.

33. Galatians 5:22-23.

34. Cf. Acts 17:22-23, 28. Was God present but wearing a "mask" among the Athenians? Cf. W.C. Smith, chapter 1, pp. 2-3: "God saves us in any way He can . . . " This view is, of course, contrary to the Carthaginian theologian, Tertullian, who asked, in terms of salvation in Christ, just what Athens had to do with Jerusalem.

35. John 16:13; *Holy Qur'an,* Sura 1:5.

4

Faith, Freedom, and Fulfillment

Probing the Riddle of Faith, Freedom, and Divine Power

The question is whether faith is an entirely free and voluntary act or whether it is a matter of divine determination. It was St. Augustine (fifth century A.D.) who tried to resolve the question of faith in relation to God's grace in a most creative way. He tells us, first, that on the plane of eternity God is the ultimate Source of a form of grace *(gratia)* universally operating[1] in behalf of the entire Creation. This means that nothing can really exist or function without His Divine Power (e.g., the sun shines on all, Matt. 5:45); and, by implication, even Satanic powers derive their power from God's Power (Job 1: 6-7; John 19:11).

Second, since you, as a human being, are created uniquely (i.e., in God's image, Gen. 1:26-27), you have been miraculously constituted to have the inborn power to decide upon an original course of action or to choose a saving mode of being in cooperation with God, i.e., through God's cooperative grace.[2] Third, there is a sense in which God reserves the divine prerogative to predestine the fate of your soul (Rom. 8:29-30). Moreover, that includes His intention to intervene in the life of any individual He chooses or elects by His prevenient grace[3] for the sake of accomplishing an ultimate good which would otherwise not come to pass. Being the most controversial point of the three modes of grace, this last has again been restated in this way:

> God's sovereignty over the human will, according to Augustine, is absolute. *Grace*, unmerited, precedes all good actions, including faith. Here Augustine's theories of illumination and grace are at one. Nevertheless, man's *will is free*. God's foreknowledge reconciles both elements in the problem.[4]

Opponents of Augustine hold that there is never an excuse for lack of faith. After all, look at all the things we have faith in every day that we can see (and often that we do not even understand—our cars for instance!)—to say nothing at all about all the things to which we give our faith that we cannot see! Have you seen an electron lately, or your own thoughts mentally? Opponents of Augustine continue by saying that faith is an act so fundamental to human nature and human freedom that it makes the idea of cooperative grace (even more so prevenient grace) unnecessary.

Thus faith to those who see no excuse for lack of faith in God say that this is mainly why Jesus was so impatient with some unbelievers,[5] because He was trying to tell them that it is an inborn capacity of human nature, and also that faith involves a dimension of common sense.[6] Faith is a matter of uncompelled decision. Here, again, the thought is that faith in Him is the one original religious decision that even God cannot empower us to make, except to give us the potential to make choices as such, but not the actual particular choice of believing and trusting in God. The preeminent rabbi, Soloveitchik, in his powerful and perceptive little book entitled *The Lonely Man of Faith*, says that according to the Halakhah "the initiative . . . belongs to man; the successful realization, to God." For Soloveitchik, then, "The Lord wants man to undertake the task which He, in His *infinite grace,* completes."[7]

Nonetheless, there were those who came centuries after Jesus—even many today—who say much like Augustine that we cannot on our own muster religious faith of the kind that Jesus wanted us to have. Such persons continue to echo the words of a demon-possessed son's father to whom Jesus said, "If you are *able!*—All things can be done for the one who believes." But the father "cried out, 'I believe; *help* my unbelief.'"[8] You can see why Augustine would state that it is not enough to say that we are gifted by God's operative grace with the capacity to have faith in general terms. Like the father answering Jesus, we also need the help of God's cooperative grace to *en*-able us to believe, so that "all things can be done." In this view, then, that extra or additional gift to accept, believe, and trust in the religious sense is something of supernatural origin.

Augustine's view of grace has not ceased both to impress and distress audiences with differing religious temperaments. The feeling is that he did not really work out the details of grace and freedom as a living paradox, so that it would not still appear that *God* is doing everything, and that you and I are doing nothing at all—a rigid predestination. Augustine, himself, would seem to have shown his real hand, however, in these words: "Now I would ask, if there is no grace of God, how does He save the world? And if there is no free will, how does He judge the world?"[9]

Nonetheless, reflecting on Augustine's conception of prevenient grace, there are still those who wonder, for example, about the extremely controversial events of how (considering Sarah's negative attitude toward Hagar) Isaac got to be preferred over Ishmael in the mind of Abraham as the right thing to do; Jacob's "devious" way of having been chosen over Esau to inherit the blessing of their father Isaac; David's appropriation of Bathsheba through his machination of her husband Uriah's death;[10] Bathsheba, the mother of Solomon, (in political intrigue with the prophet Nathaniel) having "deviously" arranged for Solomon to have been chosen over his brother Adonijah to inherit the throne of David—and a host of other biblical incidences.

The other problem that Augustine could never answer satisfactorily for many, and especially for any Holocaust victim, is how God's power, indeed His Eternal Love, could have anything to do with evil whatsoever. Nonetheless, there is one thing to say for Augustine in the matter. He directs our attention toward the fact that there are serious consequences to affirming that God is indeed all-powerful and all-knowing. For this means that, contrary to those who say that "God helps those who help themselves"[11] or, as the Persian Islamic proverb bids, "Trust in Allah, but tie your camel," Augustine would say that "God helps us to help ourselves!"[12]

Before I leave Augustine, however, I wish to point out partially in Augustine's behalf that in the history of religious experience it seems that, in a religious sense, the paradoxical nature of grace and freedom has indeed been borne out recurrently. A paradox, of course, is an experience in thought, feeling, or action, in which two seemingly contradictory things can somehow harmoniously coexist.[13] There is a real sense in which if God is, as the Lord's Prayer says, "the Kingdom *and the Power,*" then even our particular choices must go back to God as their ultimate Source of Cosmic Energy, even if the transmutation of that Energy into qualitative choices is attributed to us as free moral and spiritual agents.

In this sense it would pay in all practical purposes for us to come down on the side of human free will and to affirm with the friends of the seer, Edgar Cayce, that *"Faith is developed by the use of it.* It cannot be taught or forced, neither can true faith be destroyed."[14] So there are two camps: those who think in Augustine's way (saving faith is a special, supernatural gift) or those who think lack of faith is inexcusable (it is naturally given to us to decide to have or not have faith). To both I say that there is an intimate and ultimate sense in which we as divine-human creations are the result of supernatural grace; but that what may be difficult to comprehend at the level of intellectual thought may be easier to grasp at the level of experiential encounter with God in the act of faith; and that what may be experientially encountered yet needs further to become a matter of continued experimental faith that leads to spiritual knowledge; so that one is no longer living with a question or seeking an answer—but only *knowing* the Reality that is God.

Yet most of us are not ready for this level of living and moving and being in a state of constant grace. So there may even be those who would opt not for Augustine's but Richard Bach's view of freedom-and-grace implied in his memorable book, *Illusions: The Adventures of a Reluctant Messiah.* There, Bach, for instance, does an extremely creative but no less controversial thing in portraying the relation between God ("Infinite Radiant Is") and the "Messiah," Don Shimoda. Bach turns topsy turvy the New Testament version of Jesus of Nazareth's suffering, soulful petition to God for release from the obligation to be crucified. In the Gospel of Luke (22:42) Jesus says, "Father, if you are willing, remove this cup from me; yet, not my will but yours be done." Thereafter, God's gesture is to send an angel to minister to Jesus in order to strengthen Him (22:43).

In Bach's *Illusions*, however, the "Messiah" utters the same words, "not my will but yours be done," except he adds instead, "let me lay aside this impossible task." And, contrary to Luke's version, Infinite Radiant Is answers his "Messiah," rather startlingly, in this way: "Not my will, but *thine* be done. For what is *thy* will is mine for thee . . . "! This insight from Richard Bach, though it has greatly upset many fundamentalist and liberal Christians, contains a vital esoteric truth. It is the fact that in harmony with the Cayce vision of the intended co-creatorship of human souls with God, it should not then be considered strange that in a state of radical spiritual communion with God a soul can say, as did Jesus, "My Father is still working, *and* I also am working" (John 5:17 NRSV); or, as Paul of Tarsus, " . . . work out your *own* salvation with fear and trembling; for it is God who is at work in you, enabling you *both* to will *and* to work for his good pleasure" (Phil. 2:12-13).[15] Perhaps the most intriguing yet paradoxical statement on this entire mystery was written by Thomas Sugrue, who again, echoing Cayce, said that "free will and predestination coexist in a person."[16]

Inherited Faith and Inherent Reason

I have elsewhere defined religion as "humankind's quest to discover a universe-of-meaning in relation to an Ultimate Being, Consciousness, and Bliss, for the sake of self-security, world-transformation, and life-continuum."[17] But in that same essay I added that whether we examine, for example, the myths of Africa, Babylonia, India, or the Western-Near Eastern monotheisms (to include Islam), all of them seem to sense that "something is *amiss* or *incomplete* about humankind . . . [that] *there is a human predicament.*"[18] What is that predicament? I believe that it is essentially a recurrent, if not perpetual, conflict within the soul about accepting its destiny to transform into a living paradox the precarious balance between self-reliance and God-reliance.

The human predicament has been defined in terms of its cause or causes in many ways. Some say that the tendency toward evil in human nature was the result of an original mistaken divine message and/or misdemeanor, as among many African peoples; others say that there is something mixed in the constitution of human nature, something part god, something part demon, as among the Babylonians.[19] You can imagine what that means for psychologists of the Freudian persuasion! Others, still, say that it all started out as a form of cosmic ignorance (a lack of knowledge of the nature of Spiritual Reality, especially the soul), as in India; and then there are those who insist that there used to be a Paradise, but that a "primeval fall," an "original sin" or act of disobedience took place; and, thereby, both human nature—and nature-at-large—became corrupted. This view is most well known to be held by adherents of the Christian religion.[20]

It is important to recognize that Christianity is the world's largest religion. It is forecasted that around the year 2000 it will have well over two billion followers. This is so important because of the impact that this religion continues to have on so many persons (though not all agree with it) through the notion that we are inevitably sinners and at the same time capable of becoming sanctified (holy) in this world. Unfortunately, on the whole, it does not seem to have worked as a religious outlook. It has backfired, many say, and has instead caused more damage to human self-esteem than the preached promise of conversion can begin to heal. A significant recent development has occurred, therefore, that makes it even more important that increasing numbers of persons try to develop a more profound view of human nature.[21] In an encounter between theologians and psychologists, it was discovered that though they both recognized that there is a human predicament, these disciplines generally held completely opposing views about the crux of that predicament. While the theologians were inclined to say that the human predicament stems from persons thinking too much of themselves, the psychologists were more inclined to say that it was due to the fact that persons tend to think too little of themselves![22]

This in itself should urge us to question whether you and I should confine ourselves solely to the orthodox view of the human predicament. For it does not seem likely that we will ever be able to explain the varieties and subtleties of evil in the world on the basis of any Sunday school version of a "primeval fall." Indeed, the effects of such a doctrine on human personality, according to psychoanalysts and psychotherapists, have been well nigh spiritually tragic, if not catastrophic. Perhaps one can hardly do better amidst so many definitions of sin (e.g., missing the mark, prideful rebellion, seed-transmission, etc.) than to consider these simple words attributed to Saint Bernadette: "A sinner is one who loves evil." This would seem to go to the heart of the matter, for here, sin is more perceptively understood to be rooted in a negative ethical-spiritual disposition than in the breaking of commandments.

I must point out that the tragedy or catastrophe is not that the Genesis story is out-and-out untrue in the esoteric sense. For in this regard, Adam and Eve mirror the predicament as underlined above not in the sense that they merely wished to become wise, but that they wished to become wise without faith in the wisdom of God. The problem is that the exoteric version which our previous

Church Father, Augustine, and others left us has been taken and made into an official doctrine of universal sin based on a highly doubtful psycho-physiogenetic assumption. Sin, according to Augustine (though it was preeminently rooted in pride and not sex) was passed on from Adam and Eve in the Garden of Eden to humankind basically via sexual intercourse—through the medium of human semen! Taking Adam to be what the New Testament scholar Elaine Pagels calls "a corporate personality," Augustine thus said, "For we all were in that one man [Adam], since all of us were that one man who fell into sin through the woman who was made from him."[23] There is no absolutely unanimous agreement about this among Christians, Catholic or Protestant. Nonetheless, Augustine's outlook has, unfortunately, been forced upon all subsequent generations as a thing they are to believe unquestionably.

There have been many critics of this idea from among the faithful, but, in modern times, it is especially through Elaine Pagels that Augustine's view has been shown to be biblically unsound. It is in her book *Adam, Eve, and the Serpent* that Pagels does our own and subsequent generations a priceless favor. She points out that Augustine's theological ideas of what Paul of Tarsus said about sin (in Romans 5:12) represent a gross misinterpretation. She tells us that Augustine, having read the foregoing passage in Latin and not Greek, "either ignored or was unaware of the connotations of the Greek original." He thus read the crucial phrase in Romans 5:12 as "in whom" all sinned (Adam, as if we were all potentially [actually?] in his loins), and not as "in that" or "because" we all sinned, which would *not* allow for a psycho-physiogenetic basis for a doctrine of "original sin."[24]

This point is supported by the prophet Ezekiel. See the entire chapter 18 (which goes against both Exodus 20:5 and any such doctrine), especially verse 20: "A child shall not suffer for the iniquity of a parent . . . the wickedness of the wicked shall be his own."[25] However, among those who are not afraid to oppose faith and freedom when faith becomes oppressive without reason, Pagels asks a question that strikes a reasonable chord: "How can one imagine that millions of individuals not yet born were 'in Adam' or, in any sense, 'were' Adam?"[26]

This clarification by Pagels is important, indeed, for certain readers, upon whom I wish to impress the point that it is not enough to ignore or be against learning from the Bible, if in fact much of what one may be thinking or may have heard that the Bible is saying is not even true to the Bible!

We can thank God that we now know that other Christians called Gnostics existed even prior to Augustine's time who sensed that it all had to do with a much vaster and longer history of the soul in the universe.[27] Pagels, for instance, tells us that the Gnostics were very much concerned with the "pneumato-psychodynamics" or "the interaction between the *pneuma,* the spiritual element of our nature, and the *psyche,* that is, the emotional and mental impulses."[28] They were not, therefore, confined to what was later to become the Doctrine of the Fall of humankind through an "original sin," committed in the Garden of Eden. Thus they used the Adam and Eve story in Genesis in different ways to express even more profound spiritual truths about human nature.

For example, sometimes, she says, one or the other of these two beings, the male or the female, was used to symbolize the power with which the other had to become joined in a sacred marriage to become a whole being. In another instance both beings were essentially coequal but needed to realize their destiny in that regard:

> . . . death began when . . . the woman separated

> . . . from the man—that is, when Eve (the spirit) became separated from Adam (the psyche). Only when one's psyche, or ordinary consciousness, becomes integrated with one's spiritual nature—when Adam, reunited with Eve, "becomes complete again"—can one achieve internal harmony and wholeness . . . only the person who had "remarried" the psyche with the spirit becomes capable of withstanding physical and emotional impulses that, unchecked, could drive him or her toward self-destruction and evil.[29]

Above I emphasized the need for reluctant Bible readers to realize, in the face of unacceptable things they may have thought or heard from others that the Bible is saying, that such things may not even be true to the content of the Bible itself. Here I call your attention to the fact that it is not even necessary for you to accept merely a single interpretation of things found in the Bible. For the esoteric dimension of any such teaching allows for levels of truth according to whether the Spirit gives us a decisive increase of understanding. Such an esoteric level of understanding requires (1) that your mind be ardently desirous of finding a new and deeper perspective; (2) that your mind be receptive to being raised to a higher level of spiritual consciousness; and (3) that your mind anticipate being empowered by the Holy Spirit of Truth with what one theologian calls "unconquerable good will" (agape) to relate to others who may yet be confined to exoteric frameworks of understanding. If you are a person who feels that you have spiritual knowledge transcending an exoteric perspective, it is imperative to remember that it is not the esoteric per se that "saves" in the end, but the presence of agape in your innermost being.

Faith and Your Personal Identity

Within this profound spiritual perspective, let me say that should you be addressed by an angel who asks, "Who are you?" and you happen to answer, "My name is John Smith" or " . . . Mary Hamilton," you can be certain that you do not know who you are! As the saying goes, we usually identify ourselves in terms that reflect one of three perspectives: (1) we are who others say we are, (2) we are who we think we are, or (3) we are who we *really* are.

No more dubious source of your identity can be imagined than to believe that you are to be essentially associated with a family, an ethnic group, a national loyalty, or even a religious body. As I said earlier about name and form, there are illusions everywhere, especially when it concerns the matter of personal identity. This factor has been of absolutely crucial importance in the history of human experience when it concerns the matter of human relationships and human health. To be sure, there is hardly any authority in the modern psychological, sociological, or theological disciplines who would hesitate to say that this is humankind's "Achilles' heel."

In a healthier perspective, then, you are divine spirit. And you are divine spirit because you come from Divine Spirit;[30] or as theologian Paul Tillich said, "Man comes from the eternal and goes to the eternal." You are an emanation and an incarnation of the One and intended to be guided by the God Who Is One, or the source of the Law of One.[31] You are a son or a daughter of the living God and intended to love and be loved by God's other spirit-souls. You are infinitely valuable, because, though from one ultimate Source, you are unique in the Eternal "Eye" of that Source.

You are needed. And that is because, though God is infinitely independent, the Creator through his own eternal creativity has chosen to have you share in his

Eternal Glory. You have chosen to share in an Eternal Experiment in being, consciousness, and bliss, which includes the winning of agnostic (un*know*ing) souls to the Eternal Glory of the Creator.

You are also the potential incarnation of a "universalizing faith."[32] That faith requires that you relinquish all the time-bound illusions of identifying yourself with becoming or having become outstanding in the worldly sense. For a universalizing faith demands that you not even allow false religious identities to define who you really are. Fowler says of a "universalizing faith" (his "last" developmental stage):

> Heedless of the threats to self, to primary groups, and to the institutional arrangements of the present order that are involved, Stage 6 becomes a disciplined, activist *incarnation*—a making real and tangible—of the imperatives of absolute love and justice . . . the self . . . engages in spending and being spent for the transformation of present reality in the direction of a transcendent reality.[33]

Faith, therefore, requires that differing religious dogmas or worldviews should not become powerful enough to prevent the expression of your love and compassion across all cultural boundaries. But in our present state of affairs, for example, the Protestant-Catholic conflict in Northern Ireland, one must ask just how many times does Jesus have to die on the cross for persons to reach the stage described above? In addition, religious faith even requires that economic status or occupation, per se, should not be the sole determinant for choosing a marital partner; that thin or fat should not prevent the giving of oneself in love or in friendship; that handicapped body or mind should not rule out the birth and manifestation of love in noble and precious form; that ethnic-linguistic accent should not deter the willingness to understand another divine spirit; that political party should not allow uncommon concerns to override common causes.

So, in sum, you are a cosmic incarnation, you are spirit, you are a divine son or daughter of God. You are valuable, and you are needed.

Thus in a world of false identities—social, political, economic, and religious—you can afford to acknowledge and appreciate all the subidentities that have been a part of your spiritual evolution. But, in the final analysis, you are something more than these. Your true identity really surpasses all these subidentities, for, as the poem *Desiderata* declares, "You are a child of the universe." Therefore, be who you *really* are, and the world itself will stand a better chance of becoming what it was *really* meant to be—the Blessed and Loving Community of God.

The Creatures of God and the Children of God

Though in a general sense all of us are children of the Creator, it has been because so many of us have not been willing to spend or be "spent for the transformation of the present reality" or to give ourselves over to "the imperative of absolute love and justice" that the phrases "Children of God" and/or "Sons of God" have been used by Jesus and others.[34] However, before we pursue that distinction, a matter of perspective should be clarified. This means that from an exoteric perspective God created the heavens and the earth and everything in them. Human beings are therefore naturally creations of God, but, in this perspective, too many tragically hold that they are basically mere creatures of God, despite the fact that they are said to have been made in the image of God (*imago dei,* Genesis 1:26-27).

In an esoteric perspective, however, two decisively important truths about us must be perceived in order to deal with the question of why the initial distinctions above were ever made in the first place. One is that the mere reference to you as being a "creature" does not mean that you are not essentially a spiritual being; after all, Jesus Himself is referred to by Paul of Tarsus as being "the firstborn of all creation";[35] yet, indeed, is there any believer today who would be willing to declare that Jesus was merely a creature of God because He was very early referred to as one of God's creations? The other truth is that both the Gnostics and mystic seers (of various countries and religions), including the Christian example of Edgar Cayce, tell us that, originally, we were in fact emanated and not merely created as if human beings were originally only "God's mannequins."

Thus the division "Sons and Daughters" vs. "Creatures" oftentimes arose because of the lack of metaphysical knowledge and understanding on the part of the guardians of various religious traditions, who, themselves, have either forgotten or do not wish to remember their own esoteric heritage. Recall Jesus' impatience with Nicodemus, a member of the Jewish inner circle (the Sanhedrin), who in his time did not seem to understand earthly things, such as physical rebirth! So it is fundamentally not only a matter of "lost Christianity" but of "lost Gnosis"—uninfused love (Agape) and unpracticed wisdom (Sophia).[36]

A few examples of such a vital distinction, including and going beyond the Scriptures themselves, take us back into the distant past—and into eternity. According to Revelation there was a "War in Heaven" (Rev. 12:7-9), after which it is implied that the universe was thereafter divided into exalted and fallen angels. This occurrence is echoed in the Book of Jude, verse 6, "the angels who did not keep their own position, but left their proper dwelling" and in Jesus' testimony (Luke 10:18) that He "watched Satan fall from heaven like a flash of lightning."

In Genesis 6:2 another division is implied by the act of the sons of God (angels), seeing that the daughters of men were fair and, prematurely, taking them as wives.[37] In the Essene "War Scroll" there is "The War of the Sons of Light with the Sons of Darkness."[38] And in the New Testament, Jesus likens those who know who they really are and who act accordingly to "the children of God" (Matt. 5:9: "the peacemakers") or "sons of the Father," "sons of God," or "sons of the Kingdom."[39] And in typically radical fashion, Jesus said in response to the cry that His mother and brothers were outside waiting to speak to Him, "Who is my mother, and who are my brothers?" Then, pointing to His disciples, He said, "Here are my mother and my brothers! For whoever does the will of my Father in heaven is my brother and sister and mother"![40] Paul of Tarsus makes the same distinction when he says, "For not all Israelites truly belong to Israel, and not all of Abraham's children are his true descendants" (Rom. 9:6-7). Moreover, John the Divine speaks of those who have received Jesus as God's gift as persons to whom God gave the power to become "the sons of God" (John 1:12).

This signifies that all of God's soul-emanations, though originally His very beloved offspring, are yet to be distinguished by their possession or nonpossession of a crucial state of spiritual consciousness, sometimes called the "Kingdom of Heaven," or that which has been called "The Christ Consciousness." The Kingdom of heaven is, therefore, within you (Luke 17:21-22); and this essentially is why the gnostic Gospel of Philip dares to say that "Those who say they will die first and then rise are in error. If they do not first receive the resurrection while they live, when they die they will receive nothing."[41]

Resurrection is, then, a state of spiritual awareness of the truth of the reality of immortality (John 11:26); and the "Kingdom of God" has no proper geographic address—it is *also* a state of pristine spirituality, a dimension of transcendental consciousness rooted in the most concentrated, formless Essence, from which all things have been emanated. So it has had to be that in the light of the tragic reluctance of so many men and women to be willing to spend or be "spent for the transformation of the present reality" or to give themselves over to "the imperative of absolute love and justice" (Fowler) that there continues to be the vital distinction between the creatures of God and the children of God.

Read the story of a "child of God" who, because she was so certain of who she was, could invite others to share in her anticipated blessing of deliverance from terror. Though in hindsight you will certainly ask just how many persons can stand under a single umbrella, is it not possible that even standing near the sacred space of faith one might be saved? In a gem of a book with no less than thirty-five hardcover printings, *The Healing Light*, author and healer Agnes Sanford writes:

> A missionary once taught an ignorant Chinese woman that she was God's child. This newborn child of God stood at the railway station when a bombing raid began. She raised her oil-paper umbrella. "I am God's child, so I can't be hurt!" she screamed to the crowd. "Whoever gets under my umbrella with me will be safe." Four helpless ones crowded under the umbrella with God's child. When the raid was over, only those five stood alive and unharmed amid the shambles. Under the umbrella of the Almighty they had found their refuge until this tyranny was overpast.[42]

If ever there was an instance of human adventure in faith that confirmed the words of Jesus that God has "hidden these things from the wise and prudent and revealed them to babes," (Matt. 11:25) this is it! It is not so much that the incident is characterized by unbelievable naiveté, as much as how it illustrates with pristine power that single attitudinal quality without which Jesus insisted no one could enter into the Realm of God.[43]

In the matter of developing one's true, divine identity, there can be no avoidance of the role that education in family, school, and community can play in that process. As has already been mentioned, Freud and Jesus had a common—but subtly different—concern with childhood consciousness.[44] But, whether you are Freudian or Christian, the translation of either psychological or religious ideals into educational reality requires that maturer souls live by example for the sake of rearing physically, psychologically, and spiritually healthy children. For just as a baby inappropriately shaken by a parent or a nanny can suffer irreversible brain damage, a "budding" incarnate soul's evolvement can be irreversibly "shaken" by the trauma of discovering that adults do not really know who they are.

Moreover, parents who do not know who they really are, but expect children to act in ideal ways to which the parents themselves will not be committed, can engender sickness and evil—with all their typical consequences. Psychotherapist M. Scott Peck calls our attention to the fact that the worldviews of patients are too often ignored in the process of therapy. As we apply this insight to parents without self-knowledge, there are doubtless numerous cases of developing children who are growing up in "a universe of rigid law in which they will be struck down and cast away if they step even slightly out of line."[45] And, of course, such children, themselves, grow up in turn to become parents without a positive foundation of identity; and they, in turn, proceed to "shake the foundations" of their children, in a vicious and tragic cycle.

Such is a part of the thesis of the author of a startling book published almost forty years ago entitled *Summerhill*.[46] As with all idealistic visions of what life could be like in the schools for growing children, there were those who claimed, of course, that there is no such thing as children needing "approval and freedom to be *naturally* good"; that human nature, though pliable, did not outweigh, as A.S. Neill claimed, children's need for "discipline," "direction," "suggestion," "moral training," and "religious instruction";[47] or that, though noble in vision, it simply could not be done on a large enough scale to affect significant sectors of the world. Nonetheless, Neill saw something in the natural attitudes of children that Jesus of Nazareth would admire, despite Neill's radical rejection of the dangers of dogmatic "antagonism to natural life" and doctrines of "the antithesis of body and spirit." A selective glimpse of this work whose basic insights were to be reincarnated in other visionary frameworks on education is as follows:

> Children do not need teaching as much as they need love and understanding. They need approval and freedom *to be naturally good*. It is the genuinely strong and loving parent who has the most power to give children freedom to be good . . . the world . . . is suffering from too much hate . . . A *new* religion . . . will praise God by making men [and women] happy . . . [it will] find God on the meadows and not in the skies . . . [48]
>
> Salvation lies in love . . . [49]

Faith, freedom, and fulfillment are, therefore, interrelated with life, light, spirit, and love. It was *never* true, as an old hymn was sung to say, that "God has no hands but our hands." Nonetheless, though it is yet true that God has got the whole world in His hands, He has also called us to be co-creators with Him so that we can save the children.

Endnotes

1. Lat. (Latin), *gratia operans.*
2. Lat., *gratia cooperans.*
3. Lat., *gratia praeveniens.*
4. John J. O'Meara, ed., *An Augustine Reader* (Garden City, New York: Image Books, 1973), p. 21. Italics added. Augustine emphasized two biblical passages in this regard: I Cor. 4:7 and John 15:5.
5. Mark 9:19: "You faithless generation, how much longer must I be among you? How much longer must I put up with you?"
6. See Matthew 16:2-3.
7. Joseph B. Soloveitchik, *The Lonely Man of Faith* (New York, N.Y.: Doubleday, 1992), p. 90. Italics added.
8. Mark 9:23-24. Italics added.
9. "Two Letters from Augustine to Valentinus and the Monks of Adrumentum" in *The Works of Aurelius Augustine,* Vol. 15, ed. by Marcus Dods (Edinburgh, Scotland: T&T Clark, 1926), p. 4; cf. p. 14.
10. A controversy over the extremely esoteric (supportive) interpretation of David's actions concerning Bathsheba, for instance, by the modern Muslim gnostic, Frithjof Schuon, existed between scholars Richard C. Bush and Huston Smith. See their respective "con" and "pro" responses to Schuon's book, *The Transcendent Unity of Religions,* in the *Journal of the American Academy of Religion* [JAAR], Vol. 44, No. 4 (December 1976), pp. 715-719, 721-724; especially Bush, p. 717f.
11. Incidentally, contrary to a widespread assumption, the Bible says no such thing.
12. This highly illuminating paradox in divine-human relations is still best stated by Paul of Tarsus in Phil. 2:12-13; see p. 70 in this book.
13. One of the greatest paradoxes of Roman Catholicism is the belief that God is the Father of Mary, but that Mary is also the mother of God!
14. Reflecting the views of the seer, Edgar Cayce, in *A Search for God, Book I,* compiled by Study Group No. 1 (Virginia Beach, Virginia: Association for Research and Enlightenment, Inc., 1988), p. 51. Italics added.
15. Italics added.
16. Thomas Sugrue, *There Is a River: The Story of Edgar Cayce* Virginia Beach, Virginia: A.R.E. Press, 1942), p. 317.
17. W.C. Beane, "Karma and the Law of Love," *World Faiths Insight,* 1984, p. 37. The last three terms refer to identity, community, and the afterlife. Subsequently, via restatement, "world-transcendence" was changed to "world-transformation," lest the impression of sheer otherworldliness be given. The most authentic and spiritually developed beings via diverse means are certainly working for a better world.
18. *Ibid.* Italics added. Various "Paradise Lost" accounts worldwide and

exemplary human events are contained in psychoanalyst Theodore Reik's book, *Myth and Guilt: The Crime and Punishment of Mankind* (New York, N.Y.: G. Braziller, 1957).

19. In their Creation story (*Enuma elish,* Tablet VI:5-9), the original human being is called "savage-man."

20. The Jewish faith contains the Genesis story on which this is based (chapter 3), and it did allow that there are two basic inclinations in human nature (toward good or bad); but it did *not* allow the sin of Adam to become a doctrine of "original sin" (whereby everyone is born in, and has the predominant tendency to, sin) as in Catholic and Protestant Christianity. Islam inherited the Genesis story, but Allah warns Adam and Eve's offspring against, rather than punishes them with, the tendency toward evil. See Pagels's comments, pp. 73-75 in this book.

21. See a more profound view by the early Gnostics, p. 74 in this book.

22. Peg A. Van Beane, "Transitions: Psychological and Theological Concerns in the Process of Counseling University Nontraditional Undergraduates" (an unpublished graduate seminar paper, Andover New Theological Seminary, Boston, Massachusetts, 1993), p. 20.

23. Elaine Pagels, *Adam, Eve, and the Serpent* (New York, N.Y.: Random House, 1988), p. 109. Augustine also argued, of course, that Christ was born without sin, since He was born of a virgin and thus without the means of semen *(loc. cit.).*

24. *Ibid., loc. cit.*

25. One needs to remember that by divine revelation the prophets of Israel bring us closer to the redemptive will of God beyond the permissive will of God that sometimes allowed narrow tribalistic traditions (Ezekiel 20:25), but could not overshadow (Ezekiel 20:22) God's "steadfast love" (*chesed*; e.g., Exodus 34:6; Psalm 136; cf. Hosea 11:8-9).

26. Pagels, *op cit.*, p. 109.

27. See Elaine Pagels, *The Gnostic Gospels* (New York, N.Y.: Random House, 1979).

28. Pagels, *Adam, Eve, and the Serpent, op. cit.,* p. 68, of the chapter entitled "Gnostic Improvisations on Genesis."

29. *Ibid.*, pp. 68-69.

30. See Psalm 82:6, which is often understood in this manner by esoterics.

31. See Deuteronomy 6:4-5; and Jon Robertson, *The Golden Thread of Oneness* (Virginia Beach, Virginia: A.R.E. Press, 1997), pp. 56-58.

32. A term borrowed from James W. Fowler, *Stages of Faith: The Psychology of Human Development and the Quest for Meaning* (New York, N.Y.: HarperSanFrancisco, 1981), especially chapter 6.

33. *Ibid.*, p. 200.

34. Historically, in the Jewish tradition, the kings and princes of the earth, who could display both Godlike qualities *and* yet fail to do so because of their vanity, were at one time complimented by God (as in note #30): "I have said, 'Ye are gods, children of the Most High'"; but yet, at another time, be told, "nevertheless, ye shall die like mortals, and fall like any prince" (Psalm 82:7). Thus this text has its exoteric *and* esoteric meanings.

35. See Colossians 1:15.

36. Paul of Tarsus could thus say, "God's love has been *poured* into our hearts through the Holy Spirit" (Romans 5:5); and Jesus, "Wisdom is vindicated by her *deeds*" (Matthew 11:19 KJV: "Wisdom is justified by her *children*"). Italics added.

37. Esoterically, we know that, beyond patriarchal language, this means "the sons and *daughters* of God . . . the daughters and *sons* of men . . . " In II Corinthians 6:18, Paul recalls a text saying, " . . . I will be your father, and you will be my sons and daughters."

38. See Willis Barnstone, ed., *The Other Bible* (San Francisco, California: Harper & Row, Publishers, 1984), pp. 235-242. Barnstone grants that "Myth is myth—that is, fantasy as opposed to history—only to skeptical outsiders. To the faithful, the intended myth is revealed truth." I hold, nonetheless, that the text also requires esoteric interpretation.

39. Matthew 5:9, 45; 8:12; Paul of Tarsus: Romans 8:14, Galatians 3:26, I Thessalonians 5:5; as opposed to the "sons of this world" (Luke 16:8).

40. See Matthew 12:46-50.

41. The Gospel of Philip, Codex II, in James Robinson, *The Nag Hammadi Library*, p. 153.

42. Agnes Sanford, *The Healing Light* (Plainfield, New Jersey: Logos International, 1976), pp. 173-174.

43. See Mark 10:15.

44. Freud was concerned with infantilism ("childishness"); Jesus was concerned with "childlikeness" (humility—before God).

45. M. Scott Peck, *The Road Less Travelled* (New York, N.Y.: Simon and Schuster, Inc., 1978), p. 186.

46. A.S Neill, *Summerhill: A Radical Approach to Child Rearing* (New York, N.Y.: Hart Publishing Company, 1960).

47. *Ibid.*, p. 4; see especially pp. 239-266.

48. *Ibid.*, pp. 118, 241, 242.

49. *Ibid.*, p. 119.

5

Faith, Prayer, and Spiritual Encouragement

Faith and the Mystery of Prayer

While *faith is* said to be "the substance of things hoped for, the evidence of things not seen" (Heb. 11:1 KJV), prayer has been said to be "the soul's sincere desire" to commune with the Source of one's being.[1] Faith relates to prayer by projecting and focusing the desire of the soul upon the Supreme Being as a responsive Personal Reality. In his classic work on prayer, Friedrich Heiler said that "Prayer is . . . a living communion of the religious [person] . . . with God, conceived as personal and present in experience, a communion which reflects the forms of the social relations of humanity."[2]

There are basically three forms in which prayer has been traditionally passed on in human experience: the vocal, the written, and the contemplative.[3] Yet, like the question of the use of icons—and mantras—prayer also has its subtle, symbolic links to levels of efficacy. For instance, James, the brother of Jesus, says that "The effectual fervent prayer of a righteous man availeth much" (James 5:16 KJV). The vocal aspect of prayer as an aspect of faith is older than any other form. This is true in terms of physical or earthly evolution. The written form of prayer, as an aspect of faith (which presupposes the invention of writing of some kind and includes liturgical traditions), is a later manifestation of the faith experience.[4] But it can also be synchronized with oral recitation with no less effect, according to the individual's level of consciousness and if the soul's desire remains sincere.

The contemplative form of prayer as an aspect of faith, though largely unspoken, has the potential to resonate so much deeper in the soul that it eventually links itself to the "faith beyond faith" (Gnostic faith)—a deepening form of mystic knowledge. Thus contemplative prayer can become a state of recurrent or, if more, of perpetual reaching out to God from the deepest depths of the soul. Contemplative prayer is both as the Psalmist said, "Deep calleth unto deep," (Ps. 42:7) and as Paul of Tarsus bids, "Pray without ceasing" (I Thes. 5:17 KJV). All these three forms of prayer are nonetheless interrelated, insofar as the soul that prays may express its sincere desire more emphatically in one form or in combination in any given encounter with God.

But there are two absolutely amazing things about prayer, whether uttered, written, or contemplatively experienced. One is that prayer "as the mysterious linking of [the soul] . . . with the Eternal . . . is an incomprehensible wonder, a miracle of miracles which is daily brought to pass in the devout soul."[5] Prayer is like the seed that Jesus of Nazareth said is placed in the ground but which, when it sprouts and grows, the "pray-er" "does not know how"![6] The second thing is that prayer always receives an answer, though that answer itself requires the maintaining of a prayerful attitude (akin to meditation) to receive it.[7]

The reason that there remain those who would protest this saying is that they do not understand what the word a*nswer* can mean in purely spiritual terms. An answer in material terms (e.g., money, physical health) is always, of course, preferred by millions. For that is the form in which so many of our everyday problems and difficulties need to be resolved. Yet, more often than not, an answer in emotional terms is a far greater need (e.g., forgiveness) and would tend to influence our physical well-being; but it tends to be less sincerely desired or unambiguously desired. An answer in purely spiritual terms presupposes that one knows not only *how* to ask[8]—ask what one may—but, finally, that one only asks for what one may in relation to what God sees would move the soul closer and closer to the fulfillment of the soul's even more ultimate desire—to become fully attuned to the Universal Soul which is the Creator. Moreover, there is a real sense in which no genuine prayer goes unanswered, because the act of prayer itself, like the way Socrates thought of knowledge as its own true reward, always involves the spiritual reward of drawing the soul closer to the God to Whom one is making one's petition.[9] This prereflective response of the Creator to the soul's need to pray (and which reminds us of the paradox of Divine Grace) is illustrated by a line from an old Afro-American spiritual:

> Every time I feel the spirit moving in my heart
> I will pray.

This overall foregoing viewpoint, however, is not unrelated to the often described answers of God: "yes," "no," and "wait."[10] Yet it does not all begin to make sense until our prayers begin to make sense! They must, therefore, be understood within the framework of a process of soul-salvation beyond the goal of ego-satisfaction. Paul of Tarsus says, "I will pray with spirit, and I will pray with the understanding also . . . "[11] Praying, then, *can* be acceptable prayer, but it cannot become contemplative prayer until we purify our prayers of ulterior motives, hidden agendas, and earthbound fantasies—even other-worldly desires. Perhaps the most radically sincere nature of pristine prayer is symbolized by the memorable attitude of the Islamic Sufi mystic, Rabiah, who approached God in this way:

> O God! If I worship Thee in fear of Hell, burn me in Hell; and if I worship Thee in hope of Paradise, exclude me from Paradise; but if I worship Thee for Thine own sake, withhold not Thine Everlasting Beauty![12]

The faith-motivated prayer is also daring.[13] It resembles the way in which Penny stepped into a cosmic mirror on an episode of the TV series *Lost in Space.* It was, indeed, a mirror that led into another world, like the world into which Dorothy entered in *The Wizard of Oz;* or in which Natalie Wood's character lived in *The Miracle on 34th Street.* Prayer presupposes the willingness of the mind to suspend the reason and logic it has known, in order to become enshrouded by but not granted the Eternal Reason and the Superlogic of the Realm of the Creator. Yet prayer, though it may appear to be the magnification of, is really the surpassing of the land of make-believe; for it *is* the entrance into a whole new universe of fantastic possibilities. Prayer, therefore, always has the potential to surprise the "pray-er" even when he or she should know only too well what God can do. For though prayer means that you have to anticipate a response from the Creator, it tends to surprise even the believer, because the Creator's answers are always new to the heart. It is as if one had never prayed before.

Prayers answered tend to usher in a genuinely pious smile, do you notice? This is often followed by a loud or whispered, "Thank You, Lord."[14] Prayer is faith's secret key to penetrate the very heart of God and to opening the doors of gnostic perception. It is the ultimate way of coping with any of life's uncertainties. Yet the soul's most sincere desire can be no less than to hear God "speak" and not to prove that He can or will answer or "speak." To hear God "speak" should mean more to the soul than to be concerned that God might say no.

What, then, is the speech of God? It is, to the surprise of many—though it should hardly be so—pure silence! Silence is God's most exquisite language.[15] It is a "tongue," of course, that, when it speaks, does not speak. As we, too, therefore, are willing to become mute both to the urge to tempt God with words of honey and to show others how well we can pray, then we may be ideally ready to hear God speak the unspoken language. Rabiah warns us, for example, that "seeking forgiveness (merely) with the tongue is the sin of lying."[16]

The reason that silence is the most exquisite language of God is mainly because the Creator is Pure Spirit. But it is also because of the din of the forms of expressed desires, lust, and restlessness that lie at the core of humanity's hearts. Getting quiet, then, should also mean that we are willing to *not* hear the Creator's yes, even to the things that we have asked of the Creator in the humblest spirit of prayer. For it is only when we are willing to forsake the concrete things typically asked for in prayer that we can begin to discern that for which we really need to pray. You have certainly heard the truism before, that you may not get what you want, but you may get what you *need* instead. This is no clever rationalization. It is a crucial realization.

Every experience, therefore, wherein we receive concretely what we pray for—with later regret—is intended to make us aware of the need not to pray without the willingness to say, finally—before asking anything of God!—"Not my will, but thy will be done" (Luke 22:42 KJV).

But when prayer is without pretense, the mere asking (according to age-old traditions of piety) can sometimes bring a miraculous response before the utterance of it is complete. Prayer accompanied by daring faith,[17] then, is as it was with the centurion whom Jesus encountered. When Jesus was asked to go and heal the centurion's servant, and Jesus said that He would go there and do it, the centurion answered that it need not be so; for Jesus, he believed, could do it merely by saying the word. Jesus Himself was completely amazed! He said, " . . . I have not found so great faith, no, not in Israel!" (KJV)[18]

A recent adventure in faith and prayer is the story of what has been called "the magnificent seven." However, this does not refer to the movie by that name, but to the miraculous birth of Kenneth Robert, Alexis May, Natalie Sue, Kelsey Ann, Brandon James, Nathan Roy, and Joel Steven McCaughey! For all the hoopla that surrounded the decision of twenty-nine-year-old Bobbie and twenty-seven-year-old Kenny to surge forth in childlike faith regarding the birth of these children, there were others who saw only a terrible gambling with the consequences of taking fertility drugs. But the event turned out to surpass anything seen, at least in known medical history—the newborns became "the first *living* septuplets."[19]

What is extremely important for any discussion of faith are the following factors: (1) the McCaugheys were sincerely rooted in an authentic religious tradition in which simple childlike faith is placed in a living God and the wonders the Creator can perform; (2) the task of the multiple births was undertaken despite the warnings of negative odds and the threat to Bobbie's health and safety;[20] (3) the wondrous event was not an isolated family affair but a full community-wide commitment, to the extent that we are reminded, as Hillary Clinton echoed from the African tradition, that it takes a village to raise a child—"and then some," as one writer added[21]; and this meant there had to be awesome financial assistance by many;[22] (3) the communal aspect of the "miracle" also included all the hospital workers: doctors, nurses, specialists, assistants, even "the elevator operator";[23] (4) it was an event in which both medicine and faith worked hand in hand, and thus it was a testimony to a gloriously holistic adventure; (5) the larger national community showed empathy (despite some naysayers who rightly feared the encouragement of unwise imitators) with corporate business pledges of untold amounts of baby needs: diapers, infant wipes, baby formula, loads of laundry, etc.;[24] (6) Bobbie's doctor, Paula Mahone, was already of the conviction that "God is in the center of this"; and (7) Bobbie, herself, said that "God could have given us one, but God's entitled to give us seven"; and Kenny said that "We were trusting in the Lord for the outcome."[25] If all this does not strike one as a miracle of divine response to a daring faith, then there must be more doubt and cynicism in the world than has been heretofore imagined.

Prayer, again, can be concerned not only with the advent of new life, but also the event of death and the gift of the soul which enables one to enter into other dimensions of reality. Do recall that the rich man Dives[26] was told that "a great chasm has been fixed," separating "those saved and others who are lost"; so that "those who might want to pass from here to you cannot do so, and no one can cross from there to us."[27] Yet it still remains an esoteric reality that prayer is the one medium through which the love of God permeates both the soul of the “pray-er” and affects the one to be redeemed across the gulf that separates one soul in subastral planes from another who dwells on a higher plane (e.g., “the bosom of Abraham”). Even the fire of hellish confinements, though hard to pass beyond, cannot ultimately confine “the hidden fire” of the heart that sincerely wants to reconcile with or become attuned to the Creator. James Montgomery’s (1771-1854) hymn still echoes down the ages with the ring of saving truth:

Prayer is the soul’s sincere desire,
Unuttered or expressed;
The motion of a hidden fire
That trembles in the breast.

Prayer is thus the only power that can pierce the veil of ignorance, penetrate the force-field of estrangement, or permeate forbidden dimensions to “Rescue the Perishing,” as another old hymn has it. It is indeed this glorious fact that has led the visionaries of exoteric and esoteric Christianity, including other Eastern faiths (e.g., Chinese Buddhism) to say that we *can* pray for those souls who are undergoing further purification (“purgation” or “catharsis”) in postmortem states of existence. In Christianity, this is a Roman Catholic insight into the depths of the love of God too often overlooked by Protestant believers. For prayer echoes even in the halls of hell![28] Prayer, to be sure, has often caused God to “wink” at the weaknesses of humankind.[29] Prayer is, indeed, the only thing in the entire history of religious experience that has cross-culturally emboldened some incarnate souls to affirm that it is not only intended that all souls be saved, but that the Creator has even made arrangements for the same.[30]

Prayer is humankind’s ecumenical spiritual S.O.S. (Save Our Souls). Prayer is an integral universal religious rite that requires no understanding of the mysteries of religion, or the dogmas of religious faith, or the sacraments of religious tradition. Prayer is inner prostration. Prayer is humble petition. Prayer is sincere penance. Prayer is pervasive purification. Prayer is hopeful prognostication. Prayer is blissful pacification. Prayer is spiritual plenitude. To paraphrase the Psalmist, it is "deep (soul) calling unto deep (God-Soul)."[31] Prayer is the spirit of the Creator, moving our hearts to speak to the heart of the Creator, so that the Creator can answer—sometimes with "a still small voice" (I Kings 19:12)—sometimes in utter Silence.

Faith Experiences and Spiritual Encouragement

Faith and the Totemic Spider

Totemism is an intimate and sacred bond that exists between a "species of animal, plant, or inanimate object in nature"[32] and a tribal community and its ecosystem which includes its food economy. It is also sometimes understood as having to do with an individual who senses being guided by the spirit of a thing or an ancestral spirit, an angelic guardian, or spiritual presence. When I first gazed upon a huge spider (adult hand-sized) just about a foot away from my bed on the wall of my small bedroom in Somerset in the Bermuda Islands, I felt extremely uneasy about this entity. Such sightings would continue to happen recurrently at home and abroad rather unexpectedly, yet without my having any conscious feeling of their potential religious significance.

For some time after having left my home at fifteen and a half to enter into a boarding school in Sedalia, North Carolina, I had no memorable encounter with such creatures. Not until I had finished graduate school did I reencounter a form of this mysterious creature but in a totally unexpected way. It was in the middle of my dinner plate! I was on a flight to Bermuda on the occasion of conveying my sister's body back home for burial. There it was, a relatively small, very delicate-looking, silver-glistening but beautiful thing that I was just about to pick up with my food and put into my mouth! I was stunned when I considered that such could have happened had I been distracted enough. I could not resist taking it as a sign. It marked the first transition in my mind toward thinking that perhaps it bore some religious significance in my life. I recalled later that during the funeral services in the Bronx a number of circumstantial miracles had taken place which involved solutions both to arrangement problems and deliverance from personal danger.[33]

Without running out to read about this fascinating creature, it later occurred to me on the basis of my studies in comparative religion that in many countries the spider has been recognized as a symbol of divinity, the presence of a god. I later contemplated an age-old tradition that the web of the spider is a symbol of the wondrous integrity of the universe. And that the design and destiny for entrapment were a rather paradoxical expression of both the reality of purpose and the existence of pressure in the journey of the soul toward the remembrance or the rediscovery of its relation to its Eternal Source. Moreover, the spider has been symbolically associated not only with both fearsomeness *and* creativity, but also with the idea of self-sacrifice. To be sure, attention has often been called to the fact that female spiders, along with mantises and beetles, share "the rather unpleasant habit of eating their consorts during or soon after their fertilization."[34] I am more positively moved, however, by the possible symbolic meaning this can have for you and me on our plane of existence for the spiritual value of human self-sacrifice and interdependence.[35]

It would eventually become my intuitive conviction that whenever a spider appeared it was either a sign in the sense of a warning or a blessing, or both. Here are a few instances of its appearance to me at different moments of my life:

- it appeared well enough ahead of a potential argument between me and my wife;
- it appeared when I had become very sad and needed a lift;
- it appeared one day, creating a very dramatic experience, during the very moment when I was actually relating its existence in my life to my secretary—to her utter amazement;
- it appeared to me from beneath the shade of the lamp by which I was reading;
- it appeared one night while my son and I were waiting in a restaurant to ride back to pick up my daughter. We had decided to do this because she would be leaving late from work in an area of town where gang slayings had recently occurred. The spider appeared and crawled right across the table while my son was ordering some food;
- it appeared once near my shoulder while I was driving my car down the highway on a trip;
- it appeared one day after my wife, Peg, and I had had difficult moments, and I had decided rather spontaneously to call and remind her that she had forgotten something she had wanted very much to take to work with her. It dropped right in front of me, startling me and causing me to drop the phone receiver. I stayed a little after the call and talked to it . . . as if to the Creator. It has continued to appear to this day.

The Most Delicate Moment of Its Appearance

It was 1981 and I was in the process of changing apartments. I had been staying on the second floor of the home of an elderly woman and her daughter in Oshkosh. In one of the bedrooms there, I had earlier observed that a daddy longlegs was up in a far corner of the room. It looked different somehow. But eventually the time came to clean the room thoroughly before leaving; so I had the broom in my hand, ready to do the usual thing—swish right over all those cobwebs in all those corners and be done with it!

But that particular day, I found myself hesitating to do that "swish." I decided to walk over and took a closer look at this creature whom many find far less intimidating than the big and bulkier ones that I saw in my home in Bermuda. While standing beneath and looking up intently, it happened. As if a flower were budding in a field of daisies, as if in slow motion, I saw these very small creatures fan out into the surrounding web. They were spider-children being born before my very eyes! I had the broom in my hand and thought what a tragedy it would have been had I not hesitated and chosen to eradicate rather than contemplate. I had been given the privilege to be present at a procreation, an event fraught with religious symbolism. I had seen not only the web of the universe but also the maternity of God. I had seen not only the maternity of God but the wonder of new life emerging in a microcosm. And I had seen it all because of the presence of Something in my heart that gave me pause for reverence. For while a certain phase of my life was closing—I was again learning to be as the song says, "on my own," I was also sacredly touched by seeing that the cycle of life itself was opening for the newborn little ones—the children short-legs of "Mommie" (not Daddy) longlegs![36]

Faith and the Night Train

It had been a long, lonely afternoon and evening for me and my former wife, DeAnna, as we waited for an expected train. It was to take us from what seemed an Indian village that belonged to "the lost world." We had ended up in the outlying areas in an attempt to see more of the life of the common people rather than spending time with intellectuals in the institutes and the universities. During our wait, time had passed so slowly that we had the opportunity to take baths in huge cylindrical tubs that helped to ease the heat of weather and a bit of the anxiety that could so easily threaten two foreigners who had decided to explore places beyond the usual guided tour routes. But it was far into the night before a train came at last. The station master had already promised us that, as foreigners—especially Americans—we would surely be given special treatment by the train conductor. It was not to be. The train did come, and amidst its own misty steam, it seemed to coast toward us as if it had come from out of a kind of twilight zone.

The conductor got off the train, as usual, but, all at once, it was an army sergeant who quickly took charge. He abruptly told us that the train was full and off limits, mainly because it held many soldiers being transferred to—we were not told where. The station master was embarrassed. We were completely taken by surprise, and all seemed lost. But then, swelling up inside of me was the thought that, though we were far way and beyond our familiar terrain, the God who has indeed brought us thus far could not be that far off. I thought of how I had learned in seminary that the Israelites, too, as they found themselves far from home, in Babylon, had to cope with being away from Sinai, God's popularly held dwelling place. Moreover, I remembered that the Bible said that God went before them in a "pillar of cloud" to guide them. Like them, my heart had to decide whether the God who could perform the unforgettable nature-miracle would in this case perform what I now refer to as "the circumstantial miracle."

As it was often my way when I need serious divine guidance and support, I cast my eyes toward the firmament and past the misty singing of the train engine. I found myself asking God to get us on that train. The exact words are not recalled, but my prayer went something like this (I learned this way from Jesus): "Father, I know You hear me always; please open a way for us to get on this train." All at once, I heard the voice of the sergeant beckoning us to climb aboard. I gave a silent smile as I have done so often when overwhelmed by the saving grace of God. Once on the train we saw quite plainly that there was in fact no room just as the sergeant had said. One could barely stand. We moved further in among what seemed countless soldiers sharing cots barely wide enough for two. He once again spoke abruptly. But this time he was speaking to one of his men lying on a cot in a makeshift space. "Get up!" he said. And then to us he said that if we did not mind lying down together on that cot in the presence of his soldiers, we could go along. We gladly lay down but had to sleep on our sides, with my arm falling over her waist from behind. The night could not pass without our recurrent whispering to one another about the wonder of how the Almighty "works in mysterious ways His wonders to perform" and thanking the Creator for doing what seemed the impossible—getting us on the night train.

Faith and the Light in the Darkness

For myself, I recall that I had been afraid of the dark since a child, far into my young adulthood in college. In my original home, the Bermuda Islands, an expensive tourist mecca, many an individual may have to work at two jobs of some kind just to make ends meet, like building their own homes, for example. My parents were longtime musicians. Dad was a calypso singer—in fact, the granddaddy of calypso there. Mom was a pianist for many years. They, too, had to work more than one job, and it took them out at night. My sister and I used to cuddle together. And God help us if we had seen a horror film recently! It was on one of those nights, after we had moved to Somerset and Paddie and I had our own rooms, that I saw that large spider just inches away from my bed. I was thirteen.

Years later, I met my "Christian-Buddhist" guru, the Reverend Dr. Leon E. Wright, a Harvard *summa cum laude* graduate in the New Testament. Though fundamentally a Christian, he had learned meditation from Burmese Buddhists while a cultural attaché there. My life was to change decisively. This highly spiritually developed being—to say the unusual—had had a vision of *Jesus* in a *Buddhist* temple, in Burma, in 1957. Dr. Wright simply pointed something out to me that, dramatically, struck more than an intellectual chord. He uttered a saying of Jesus of Nazareth: "Ye are the light of the world." (Matt. 5:14) That utterance is all too often thought to refer only to the ethical commandment to Christians to strive to be examples amidst the darkness of the sin, immorality, and degradation of the world. What I suddenly "realized"[37] was that those words of Jesus, for me and my problem, did not merely refer to the call to be a spiritual example to the world. They applied even metaphysically to how our auras shine amidst the very natural darkness in this physical dimension. Dr. Wright thus followed up that saying of Jesus with the statement, "Wendell, the solution to your problem is to realize that *you* are the light in the darkness."

Suddenly, my entire mind-set was transformed! I

came to realize further that, should demons themselves dare to come near, one must in one's inner self be aware that any such malevolent discarnate entity will, instead, tend to be afraid of you. There are also those who say that such fear is generally unfounded. Such entities, it is claimed, are not able to tune in to your "auric space" so easily across the great gulf that separates you and them. But, granting the possibility that our fears may be the very thing that so quickly bridges that gulf, one needs to know that "we are more than conquerors through Him that loved us."[38] So that, should one be lying alone in a dark room or caught off guard in a darkened public building, or even cast adrift in darkness at sea, one need not abandon one's cumulative spiritual experience to fear, for it is we who are the light in the darkness.

On the basis of the existence of the Kirlian aura, your physical, mental, and spiritual health will make certain that you will shine in the darkness brighter than any candle—for ultimately the darkness itself is an illusion. To rephrase what Augustine said about good and evil, the darkness has no palpable existence: it is merely the absence of light. Here, in this case, the light itself is only absent if one has failed to realize that wherever one is is where the Light of God is!

This truth has been demonstrated to millions in a story found in the memorable work, *The Healing Light*, by the venerable healer, Agnes Sanford. She tells us that the Norfolk reporter who wrote the story most likely made no connection between it and God, Whom she calls here "the Father of Lights."

> Pilots flying over the ocean at night . . . saw a circle of light upon the water. It was too dim and flat to be the light of a boat. They decided that it must be a man upon a raft, signaling for help with a flashlight, and they flew down to save him. They

found a man clinging to a spar. But he had no light of any sort! Only the Lord was his light and his salvation.[39]

Faith and the Christ Encounter

This is an account with added commentary of a unique happening in my life, while at Cook Dormitory, Howard University, during my college years (1954-'58). It was 1957 when I had the following religious experience. I continue to regard it as the most significant religious experience of my life.[40]

I had been secretly communing with God under the form of Christ; that is, using an abandoned "Bleeding Heart" portrait of Him (and candlelight, before which I kneeled) in the basement of the dormitory for how many months, weeks, days, I do not remember. But eventually the dormitory director discovered me in my secret place and, to my surprise, asked me whether he could join me in prayer. For a while we used to commune there together. In those days I was deeply into a form of Christ-mysticism. Christ became my daily object of adoration, and the wind became the Spirit of God against my face.

One day it so happened that I came to commune with God seven times. Although I do not recall the context of every event of communion, it all began with the suggestion of a rather verbose but brilliant young idealist. His idea was that several of us should gather at 6 a.m. in front of the university library to pray for the state of the world. It was barely light when I got there. No one else came. Sad I was, but I prayed anyhow; and just when I was about to leave, a strange wind came upon the leaves on the ground and gathered them around my feet. Perhaps this is not an unusual thing, but, at the time, it seemed that God was saying "Hello"! I returned to the dorm.

Later that day my girlfriend and I went to the chapel

to pray together, for we had resolved that there would be no sexual relations before marriage; and we shared the challenge to resist together through prayer and mutual confession. Late in the evening, while I was alone in my room, three students, all alcohol drinkers, dropped by and asked to enter. I obliged them, but soon they were making fun of what they perceived to be my consistent religiosity. They took my Bible and began tossing it around among themselves. I instinctively reached for it, but to no avail, as they taunted me about my religious faith and my overheard verbal witness to the wonder of Christ.

Finally, when left alone, I prayed before I went to sleep.

Sometime around 3 to 4 a.m., I was lying on my right side, and just as familiar as the next thing might seem to be to millions (for it has happened to me before but without a mystical experience), I simply and calmly opened my eyes. But at this particular time, there was standing there a bare-footed being in a long garment, the upper part of whom I could not really see. I intuitively sensed that this was neither an ordinary figure nor an ordinary occurrence. For the figure—which I sensed was male—took his hand, which seemed unusually larger than any normal adult hand, and placed it on my shoulder. Then he gently squeezed my shoulder in his hand exactly three times. But the distinct feeling was that the strength in that hand was so great that even an uncalculated squeeze would have crushed my shoulder completely. Yet the unforgettable awareness I had was that I was being told not to despair or discontinue searching for Truth. It was a literally comforting spiritual experience somehow related to the seven encounters with God during the previous day, although I did not think of this until later reflection upon the event.

I have meditated on why I was not led (or allowed?) to

see the face of the figure, and my thoughts have usually settled upon the idea that I was not spiritually ready, if not worthy, to do so. Later, I found that I could speak of anything *other* than the vision; then perhaps my not seeing my Visitor's countenance corresponds to Zachariah's not being able to speak at all. The wonder is that from beginning to end I *knew* that it was Christ whom I had encountered.

The next day, when I met my special friend, DeAnna, I discovered I could greet her and talk of anything *but* the experience I had had. For when the moment came for me to share the experience with her, I could absolutely not speak a word of it, even to the point of crying and facially giving the impression that I was choking on a bone in the throat. Every attempt to even begin to tell her of the experience ended in vain, as we sat upon the steps in one of the out-of-the-way stairwells of the library.[41]

She reached out to help me as if I were being strangled at my every renewed effort to testify to her of it. Yet there was an almost immediate release from that constriction once I relented from making such an effort.

Eventually—I cannot say exactly when—I was able to testify of the event. I later realized that it was not merely a gesture of comfort but a form of anointing of my soul for a special work in behalf of the advancement of the Creator's kingdom on earth. I was eventually to enter the pastoral ministry and departed the little church where I had served for four years in Arlington, Virginia, only after a memorably successful ministry. I had been called, ultimately, to enter academia (what I call the "teaching ministry," though not directly in the evangelistic sense).[42] To this day, notwithstanding that I have seen many "little miracles" along the Christian way, that experience stands uniquely among all my experiences with God as the most significant, long-lasting, and confirming one that I have come to treasure. I know intuitively that Jesus

Christ made His Presence known to me at that time.

I have been asked, of course, just why I think that this experience happened to me. Well, I had been seeking a more intimate communion with the Creator with all my heart and mind and soul and strength with the spirit of a little child. I was His, and I felt that He knew that. The Presence came, I am certain, to answer the ridicule experienced during (and even prior to) that "seven-prayer day" mentioned previously, as well as to fully comfort and encourage me to know that I was walking on the right path and that His hand (spirit) would be upon me in life and in my lifework.

During that period in my life, there was perfect coincidence and no conflict. I was fast growing into a state of spiritual consciousness wherein the incredible wonder of His working in my everyday life was becoming increasingly natural.

Did I do anything that would lead me to believe that I somehow deserved this visionary experience? Absolutely nothing. In my life I had seen other wonders of God, but this was a gift of Grace—neither producible by the human will, nor to be sought as if such experiences would automatically follow upon certain forms of thought or behavior.

As to the kinds of spiritual exercises I carried on that may have led to the experience, I can only testify to prayer and meditation morning and night. Special mantras in the morning; prayer as spontaneous experience during the day; the night schedule always set at bedtime just before sleep; the prayer mode comes alone at times; meditation mode comes alone at times; yoga, with approximate lotus posture, comes infrequently, unless the "prayer as spontaneous experience" is considered to be a form of bhakti-yoga (ardent devotion to a chosen personal divinity), which I believe to be the mode in which Jesus found me. Yoga, in the Oriental sense, came into my life several years later through Dr. Leon Wright; although I seem to have known some of its techniques via preexistential experience. It was during my encounter with Dr. Wright as my teacher in seminary that the unity of Cosmic Consciousness and the Christ Consciousness took place (see chapter 9).

Now for a few words concerning the sharing of this experience. At first, no one heard of it beyond my wife-to-be; later one or two small groups; later still, my mother and at least two larger audiences. And, of course, I have shared this with audiences gathered at the Association for Research and Enlightenment at Virginia Beach and especially at a meeting of the A.R.E. at the University of Wisconsin Whitewater. It was there that I had the pleasure of working with Glenn Sanderfur, author of *Lives of the Master: The Rest of the Jesus Story.*

My present spouse, Peg, has also been told. The responses have generally been characterized by attitudes of acceptance of a kind that have led me to believe that I was meant to speak of the experience at those times. It always takes a humble boldness to speak of it, and those who hear it seem to be spiritually inspired.

Sometimes I am asked whether this experience precipitated any significant changes in my life or lifestyle. No immediate changes took place in my outlook or behavior, except that when later I saw my first wife-to-be, I experienced the choked-up attempt to speak of the vision. No doubt the experience took me into a deeper dimension of the experience of the Holy. Later, therefore, in my ministry at Arlington, Virginia, there were signs that I was developing the capacity to be used as a channel of His healing power, to preach with unusual charismatic influence, and to love with a love (agape) that others continue to testify is a manifestation of His Divine Grace.

I am humbly convinced that it was a divine anointment empowering me to become a channel through which His Light can shine before humankind, that they may see it and glorify its Source. Those around me have not generally known me to have been otherwise—perhaps just more so now—although I have discerned that some individuals have to be with me for a time to notice that *their* lives are changing. But, like many others, I have not been able to maintain the same level of spiritual consciousness in all situations.

I must emphasize, nonetheless, that this visionary experience has reconfirmed its authenticity during the years through other events, personal and interpersonal. I have discovered time and time again, for instance, that in the midst of temptation I can be strengthened to overcome. But, like others who have had genuine visionary experiences, I have felt no temptation to think that I have reached perfection or that I am the source of the power I have received in my life. There are, indeed, persons in the world who continue to believe in so-called "self-salvation" (without a theory of Divine Grace). Yet I am persuaded that once one has had an authentic encounter with the Holy, one knows only too well who God is as a matter of divine sovereignty and that without the Creator we can do nothing. No amount of power or praise, fame or fortune, privilege or promotion can easily turn away the heart of a man or woman who has had a genuine encounter with the Living Christ.[43]

All these foregoing experiences are manifestations of what I have entitled this part of the chapter: "Faith Experiences and Spiritual Encouragement." Needless to say, no one has a monopoly on these kinds of experiences. A perusal of G. Scott Sparrow's book, *I Am with You Always,* will testify to the occurrence of other visionary encounters with Christ that will certainly seem far more glorious than what I have testified to here.

The important thing for any individual who really

wants to have such an encounter is to realize that all things are possible to them that believe. It is still amazing what we are capable of experiencing when we relinquish our preoccupation with things and begin to focus our minds on spiritual realities and spiritual values. But sheer, undaunting persistence in striving for more humility before God, purity of heart, and universal love is one of the keys to experiencing the mystery of the Presence. As the Creator said through the prophet Jeremiah, "When you search for me, you will find me; if you seek me with all your heart, I will let you find me . . . "[44] And as Jesus said to us, "Listen! I am standing at the door, knocking; if you hear my voice and open the door, I will come to you and eat with you, and you with me."[45]

Faith, Expectancy, and Disappointment

There can be no true faith in the deepest sense of the term—even beyond the working of miracles—if there is not the will and the power to remain steadfast in the face of sheer disappointment. Of course, one might ask, what can disappointment mean to a soul who has a history of encouraging faith experiences? Yet not everyone is so far along a spiritual path that there does not remain some remnant of vulnerability to disappointment, even depression, upon being turned down—even by the God who is Eternal Mind. To many, therefore, it appears at once that there may be a discrepancy between expectation and disappointment, if one needs to be in a state of anticipation of faith's fulfillment during and after the act of prayer.

For what can you think and what can you do when that academic degree you worked so hard for cannot be completed for one sad reason or another; that job opportunity or promotion so long awaited fails to come through; that much anticipated date or marital proposal does not materialize; that Olympic trophy strived for with heart and mind and sinew finally goes to someone else; that yearning to have a child of one's own flesh—or through adoption—goes unfulfilled year after year; when prayer does not seem to work—at least for you—concerning a special wish in your life?

On the basis of cumulative personal experience, I am convinced that there is a creative way to begin to deal with this problem. I begin by taking seriously the idea that because God is the God of Eternal Mind, there is a need to distinguish among the following three things, not unknown to pastors and theologians: (1) God's purposive will, (2) God's permissive will, and (3) God's redemptive will.

This multidimensional perspective of the divine loving consciousness allows for me to consider some important implications in relation to my prayer requests. First, God's purposive will refers to what the Creator sees as the direction He wishes the entire universe, which includes you, as an individual, to take in the broadest and most ultimate terms. Second, God's permissive will refers to what the Creator will directly permit to happen in nature, allow us to be, have, and do, as well as what can be temporarily tolerated especially regarding the unfolding of current human events. Third, God's redemptive will refers to what the Creator wills for us individually and communally, but for which the Creator will intervene with powerful Grace, in order to guarantee that all things will ultimately work together for the good of the Whole, the universe of souls. This accounts for the arrival of the Christ Spirit on earth.

The crux of the entire adventure in faith regarding disappointment resides in our understanding that true faith presupposes that before you approach the Creator with your particular desires, it should be your most fervent wish that your desires be in attunement with the

Creator's purposive will. Should this element be missing in the heart of our consciousness concerning even the most cherished of your dreams, then God becomes a means to an end and not the End in Itself. Recall that in perfect attunement with God, Jesus could say, "I am the Beginning and the End." (Rev. 22:13)

When an anthropologist was asked to distinguish magic and religion in the briefest terms, he said that "Magic says, 'Not thy will but my will be done,' but religion says, 'Not my will but thy will be done.'" This means that in the most pristine state of faith, one never asks anything of the Creator that one does not hope will be in attunement with what the Creator foresees; so that if He permits it, it will work toward one's own final spiritual redemption (salvation). Thus, in the immortal definition of the Epistle to the Hebrews, "Faith is [also] the substance of things hoped for"; but that hope should mean not only the fulfillment of an ardent desire but also the hope that one's prayer will not only be "lawful" but also "beneficial."[46] The *bene* in "beneficial" literally refers to what will turn out to be *good* for you.

Yet what the Creator will permit takes us back to my previous reference to an insight found in Richard Bach's novel, *Illusions*. For long, cumulative experience in prayer has taught millions of devout believers in all religions that the saying is literally true that "You must be careful what you pray for, since you may just get it!" For the permissive will of the Creator is intimately sensitive to your heart's desire, even (to reverse Pascal's remark) when your heart does *not* have reasons that reason does not know.

Yet it is also true that often there are prayers answered so fast that (as part of ancient prophetic tradition) God may answer them sooner than the words can fully leave one's mouth. The thing that amazes me perpetually, however, is not only the fact that (as a folk spiritual goes)

"God Specializes," but that the Creator compensates! God is the Great Compensator in the universe of worlds and in the universe-of-meaning in the lives of earth's billions. As another perennial insight has it, God never closes one door without opening another. In the face of utter disappointment following the glow of your original expectancy, God will always do something else in response to the unfulfillment of your particular prayers and dreams. For His purposive-permissive-redemptive will is One Will. And it is a Will that, though multidynamic in nature, will always provide a way out, a way in, a way through, a way around, under, or above and beyond any human predicament or any obstacle to the prevalence of your peace of soul in your life circumstance.

God Even Answers the Foolish Heart to Save It

But since faith and prayer by far tend to transcend reason as such, the Creator will sometimes give you what you ask for. Foreknowing, even in your unknowing, the Creator has the will to bring the Kingdom, the Power, and the Glory to bear on the fulfilled events of your often foolish heart, so that you will not be ultimately deterred from your greatest intended spiritual fulfillment. Hence God will then literally respond to you in Bach's words saying, astonishingly, "Not my will, but *thine* be done. For what is *thy* will is mine for thee . . . " The divine-human paradox here is that God knows better than this! Yet God loves you so much that the Creator is less concerned about the foolishness of your request (your "foolish heart"). The Creator does your will because the Creator knows that through the consequences, joyful and/or sorrowful, S/he can ultimately guarantee an increase in your wisdom *(Sophia)* if even in your recurrently misguided petitions you manage to retain a genuine, sincere desire to know the truth about yourself—and a sincere inclination to accept the Divine Sovereignty. Thus it should come as no surprise to you that Paul of Tarsus could write these timelessly poetic but ironically wise words:

> For God's foolishness is wiser than human wisdom, and God's weakness is stronger than human strength.[47]

The truth is, nonetheless, that there are some things that one should *not* ask God at all—thus there are some things that one has already been empowered to do; there are some things that one should not want to be, have, or do—thus asking God could constitute not merely a foolish act but an act of vanity; there are some things that God would not want to do for you; thus in some cases no number of prayers can bring forth a desired response; yet there are many things that God probably wants to do for you, for which you have not asked. Often, then, the problem may not simply be to get what we desire but, basically, as Buddha said, the problem is desire itself! Or the matter may be that your attitude may need to change from being primarily concerned with getting-what-you-want from God, and only secondarily concerned with accepting- or wanting-what-you-get from God. "For," said Edgar Cayce, "all prayer is answered. Don't tell God how to answer it."[48] Jesus' saying, therefore, "Ask and you will receive" (Matt. 7:7) still presupposes the priority of love of God beyond self-love or neighbor-love.[49] Moreover, in the Lord's Prayer, the words "Thy will be done" precede the words "Give us this day our daily bread." In a deeply perceptive sermon years ago, a preacher managed to capture this insight while speaking of the many spiritual implications of the "Parable of the Prodigal Son." He said that while the son as "lost" said initially to his father, "Give me . . . " the son as later "found" said, "Make me . . . "[50]

Faith and the Amazing "But If Not" Experience

Almost no greater and more exquisite incident in the sacred Scriptures of Judaism and Christianity has ever been recorded than that of the story of Shadrach, Meshach, and Abednego (Daniel 3). These are the "Three Musketeers" of the Bible who faced the challenge of idolatry and the threat of "the fiery furnace" (KJV) during the reign of the wicked Babylonian king, Nebuchadnezzar. Set against the background of the enslavement of the Jewish people following defeat at the hands of the Babylonians and the traumatic destruction of the Temple of Solomon, it teaches us something of the nature of pristine faith that is hard to surpass. And it serves as an *esoteric* prototypical model of the sufferings of the Jewish people in the modern Holocaust, regardless of the fact that, unlike Shadrach, Meshach, and Abednego, Holocaust Jews were literally tested by fire! For in that single event, the entire multidimensional reality of the will of God is dramatically illustrated and consummated.

Having been accused of not obeying the royal command to bow down before the king's colossal statue, the three men were threatened with being thrown into "a furnace of blazing fire" (3:6, 11, 15). Moreover, they were asked by the king, "Who is the god that will deliver you out of my hands?" Their answer was:

> O Nebuchadnezzar, we have no need to present a defense to you in this matter. If God whom we serve is able to deliver us from the furnace of blazing fire and out of your hand, O king, let him deliver us. *But if not,* be it known to you, O king, that we will not serve your gods, and we will not worship

> the golden statue that you have set up.[51]

Having indeed been thrown into the furnace, the subsequent miracle of their survival is captured in the words of Nebuchadnezzar himself who said:

> But I see four men unbound, walking in the middle of the fire, and they are not hurt; and the fourth has the appearance of a god.[52]

The KJV, of course, says of the fourth being that he was "like the Son of God," a saying that has greatly appealed to Christians who regard this as another preview of their Messiah, Jesus, in the Hebrew Scriptures. Others, of course, are satisfied to say that it was probably some kind of angelic being. To be sure, this reminds us of the fact that the appearance of a being of light in near-death experiences has some saying it is Christ Jesus; others, that it is an angel of God; and others still that it is the god Krishna, etc.

But the important thing here for laypersons, ministers, and theologians of all persuasions is not even that in the story these three individuals were miraculously delivered from a horrible death. It is rather their mind-blowing affirmation that even if it should happen that God did not deliver them, they would not abandon their faith in God! This biblical event is not, then, merely a story of God's power to perform wondrous deeds, or even that we are not finally alone facing death. It is a faith experience that should encourage every religious person to ask within, "Does my faith in God depend directly upon whether the Creator does exactly what I ask and—for some—'tell' Him to do for me?"

The story of this faith experience was obviously, in its own time and later, passed down through the generations as a source of spiritual encouragement for a people whose entire history had been characterized by the recurrent threat of persecution—and death. Again, the mysterious figure who appeared with the three may well have been an angel, if not, as many Christians say, the Christ. But regardless of who it was, the important thing is that in every truthful asking of anything of God in faith, there must be a greater consciousness and desire, even in the midst of the very act of asking, to know and to do what God may be asking of us than what we are asking of God. True faith is, then, a persistent, powerful, and pervasive desire always to give God the edge in everything. God, therefore, purposed that His "chosen people"[53] become a communal witness to the Creator's Kingdom, Power, and Glory; God permitted their enemies to persecute them in order to confirm that nonviolent love is humankind's only "final solution" to evil in history (see Isaiah 53); and God is ultimately redeeming His chosen people, through whom Jesus of Nazareth came into the world, which (in the spirit of Rosenzweig) has something to do with both the Star of David and the Star of Bethlehem.[54]

In one dramatic instance in my life, I witnessed a grieving sister who would have literally pulled the casket of her dead brother off its rest to the floor had she not been restrained by other participants at the funeral. During subsequent funerals I have had the occasion to ask mourners, "Shall we bury our faith in God with our dead?" Thus it is only with a faithful, childlike attitude that we can safely approach life's crises, an attitude reminiscent of the earlier and more daringly confident Job, who said, "Though he slay me, yet will I trust him."[55] Thus one must be able to say, "I have asked God to take away this cancer, this bipolar disorder, this multiple sclerosis, this Alzheimer's, this AIDS—having faith that to the Creator nothing shall be impossible—*but if not,* I still shall not bow down to the idol of depression, despair, and defeat. And I shall not bow down because, through Jesus of Nazareth and others, I have been taught to "hope beyond hopelessness." Paul of Tarsus would have us not be ashamed of suffering in any form, "*knowing* that suffering produces endurance, endurance produces character, and character produces hope, and *hope does not disappoint us,* because *God's love* has been poured *into our hearts* through the Holy Spirit that has been given to us." (Rom. 5:3-5; italics added)

The wonder of the post-Holocaust period for Jews who suffered in the Holocaust is not merely that there were survivors, but that there were survivors who did not abandon their faith in God. It is significant that Holocaust survivor Elie Wiesel's statement that "One can be a Jew with God, one can be a Jew against God, but one cannot be a Jew without God" also can apply to any of God's children, especially those who have ever had to face the terror of radical evil. Let no one competitively seek to impress you with comparative statistics about whose people have suffered most. The Talmud offers us, instead, a universal challenge by telling us that he who saves the life of one child, saves the life of humankind. For both Jews and Christians, then, there are moments in history when the children of God have been tested by real fire! Recall that the Christians, too, had their turn in the Roman arenas and in other missionary ordeals throughout history. But, for the individual, there are moments in history when (as one wise elderly woman told my mother during my sister Paddie's battle with cancer), the cross we are given to bear can be a steel cross. During such moments we cannot help but ask for deliverance from such a gruesome ordeal, *but if not . . .* may the Creator grant you and me the grace to say with Paul of Tarsus:

> Who will separate us from the love of Christ? Will

hardship, or distress, or persecution, or famine, or nakedness, or peril, or sword? As it is written,

"For your sake, we are being killed all day long;
we are counted as sheep to be slaughtered."

No, in all these things *we are more than conquerors through him that loved us.* For I am convinced that neither death, nor life, nor angels, nor rulers, nor things present, nor things to come, nor powers, nor height, nor depth, nor anything else in all creation, will be able to separate us from the love of God in Christ Jesus our Lord.[56]

Endnotes

1. No less than thirty definitions of prayer by various religious—and nonreligious—thinkers are listed in the Introduction to Friedrich Heiler's *Prayer: A Study in the History and Psychology of Religion* (New York, N.Y.: Oxford University Press, 1958). Indeed, Ludwig Feuerbach, to whom "all religion" was "an illusion," could venture to say that "the innermost essence of religion is revealed by the simplest act of religion—prayer."

2. *Ibid.*, p. 358. Heiler was fully aware both that persons vary in how they conceive of their relation to God; e.g., child with Father, bride with Bridegroom (see chapter 1, pp. 10-11 in this book); and that "prayer appears in history in an astonishing multiplicity of forms" (see his p. 353).

3. Cf. Larry Dossey, *Healing Words: The Power of Prayer and the Practice of Medicine* (New York, N.Y.: HarperSanFrancisco, 1993), p. 6.

4. All the Psalms, for example, can be used as prayers, though they can also be used as mantras—a fact that has eluded the imagination of many who only look to the East for such a medium of sacred power.

5. Friedrich Heiler, *op. cit.*, p. 363. According to Kenneth L. Woodward, "Is God Listening?" (*Newsweek*, March 31, 1997, p. 58), "in a new *Newsweek* poll, a majority of American adults—54 percent—report praying on a daily basis, and 29 percent say they pray more than once a day. For them, it is not an unrequited relationship: 87 percent say they believe that God answers their prayers at least some of the time."

6. Mark 4:26-27.

7. The idea of prayerfulness is perceptively presented by physician, Larry Dossey, in his masterpiece, *Healing Words, op. cit.*, especially pp. 24-28.

8. Dossey, *op. cit.*, see chapter 5, "How to Pray and What to Pray For."

9. For an excellent chapter on "Unanswered Prayer," see chapter 7 of that name in Harry Emerson Fosdick, *The Meaning of Prayer* (New York, N.Y.: Association Press, 1946). Devotional daily (Bible) readings are included.

10. In his *Conversations with God: An Uncommon Dialogue*, Book I (New York, N.Y.: G.P. Putman's Sons, 1996, p. 13), Neale Donald Walsch mentions "yes," "no," and "maybe, but not now" as typically but mistakenly associated

with the way God really is.

11. I Corinthians 14:15.

12. Cited in Karen Armstrong, *A History of God*, p. 226.

13. See Chapter 1, p. 4 in this book.

14. See Walsch, *Conversations with God, op. cit.*, p. 11. I regard "supplication" and "gratitude" as the yin and yang of prayer (see them together at I Thessalonians 5:17-18), and Walsch's "appreciation" as the *tao*—hence prayer, too, has its esoteric dimensions. Persons on different levels of understanding are, therefore, at various stages in mastering the paradox at the heart of prayer. We glimpse the esoteric when Jesus says that "your Father knows what you need before you ask him" (Matthew 6:8).

15. I am echoing "Trappist monk Father Thomas Keating [who says], 'Silence is the language God speaks . . . and everything else is a bad translation'"; cited in Larry Dossey, *op cit.*, p. 87.

16. Margaret Smith, *The Way of the Mystics: The Early Christian Mystics and the Rise of the Sufis* (New York, N.Y.: Oxford University Press, 1978), p. 187.

17. See chapter 1, p. 4 in this book.

18. Luke 7:9; the NRSV says that Jesus was "amazed."

19. The story is momentously and excitingly presented as "The Magnificent Seven," by John McCormick and Barbara Kantrowitz, in *Newsweek* (December 1, 1997), pp. 58-62; cf. pp. 62-66.

20. See "selective reduction" (*ibid.*, p. 61) involving the decision where, in the case of more than three births anticipated, there is the option to "kill some in the womb" in order to save at least a set of twins.

21. *Ibid.*, p. 62.

22. The estimated cost for one year's care for the septuplets was expected to total $39,000. For examples of corporate assistance, see *ibid.*, p. 61.

23. *Ibid.*, p. 59.

24. See *ibid.*, p. 61, for estimated numbers and note the need for thirty-five to forty-nine "volunteer helpers."

25. *Ibid.*, pp. 60, 62.

26. See chapter 6, p. 157 in this book.

27. Luke 16:26.

28. See Psalm 139:8: " . . . if I make my bed in hell, behold, thou art there" (KJV). "Hell" here is literally *sheol* in Hebrew (death, the gravesite, or even a shadowy postmortem state of existence), and not eternal hellfire as many Christians think. But the point is that, esoterically, God's love can reach into the depth of any realm (including the fiery hell itself, say others!) whenever the Creator hears "the contrite sinner's voice" (from verse 4 of Montgomery's hymn, "Prayer is the soul's sincere desire").

29. See Acts 17:30 (KJV).

30. That is, "universal salvation"; otherwise known as "universal restitution." This and other related matters will be pursued in a separate volume.

31. Psalm 42:7.

32. David S. and John N. Boss, *A History of the World's Religions*. 9th ed. (New York, N.Y.: Macmillan College Publishing Company, 1994), p. 19.

33. See chapter 2, subsection: "Faith and a Rite of Passage."

34. Doris F. Jonas, "Life, Death, Awareness, and Concern: A Progression," in Arnold Toynbee and Arthur Koestler, *et al.*, *Life After Death* (New York, N.Y.: McGraw-Hill Book Company, 1976), p. 171.

35. Jonas adds, for instance *(loc. cit.)* that by her act the female is "thus

keeping the bodily matter of the male in the service of his species," for there is also danger in "giving birth for many of the females."

36. In this case I had the God-given power to show compassion at a moment symbolic of Creation. For a thought-provoking treatment of the spider as religious symbol, see the subsection "Spider, Keynote: Creativity and the Weaving of Fate," in Ted Andrews's *Animal-Speak: The Spiritual and Magical Powers of Creatures Great and Small* (St. Paul, Minnesota: Llewellyn Publications, 1996), pp. 344-347.

37. "Realized," meaning experienced as a state of superconscious awareness.

38. Romans 8:37.

39. Agnes Sanford, *The Healing Light* (Plainfield, New Jersey: Logos International, 1976), p. 175. Sanford's usage of "Father of lights" and her last sentence are from James 1:17 and Psalm 27:1, respectively.

40. This experience first appeared in G. Scott Sparrow's *Witness to His Return: Personal Encounters with Christ*, ed., Mark A. Thurston (Virginia Beach, Virginia: A.R.E. Press, 1991), pp. 130-133 (now out of print). See also its expanded and revised version, *I Am with You Always: True Stories of Encounters with Jesus* (New York, N.Y.: Bantam Books, 1995).

41. See Zachariah unable to speak in Luke 1:21-22: "He kept motioning to them and remained unable to speak." Though linked here to his not believing Gabriel's words (1:20), the "struck dumb" experience has occurred to many under various visionary circumstances.

42. In a state university, more than in a seminary, by contrast, the aim is never to evangelize but to expose students to a number of options through teaching them about the awesome varieties of religious experience that characterize the history of humankind.

43. In early and later Christian circles, it was controversial whether such a man or woman could ever fall back into a state of spiritual perdition; and, if so, whether a return was possible. See Hebrews 5:4-6.

44. Jeremiah 29:13-14.

45. Revelation 3:20.

46. I Corinthians 10:23.

47. I Corinthians 1:25.

48. Edgar Cayce reading 4028-1.

49. See Mark 12:29-31.

50. See Luke 15:11-32, especially v. 12 and 19.

51. Daniel 3:16-18.

52. Daniel 3:25.

53. The difficulty of the Jews being God's "chosen people" should pose no problem for the Christian (or any other religious being, for that matter), as long as one perceives that they were originally chosen in behalf of humankind and not because they are God's favorites; see Amos 9:7.

54. See chapter 3, pp. 49-50 in this book.

55. Job 13:15.

56. Romans 8:35-39. Italics added.

6

Faith Beyond Faith: Gnostic Visions

Hast Thou the right to reveal to us one of the mysteries of that world from which Thou has come . . . Whatsoever Thou revealest anew will encroach on men's freedom of faith . . .
—Fedor Dostoevski, *The Brothers Karamazov*

Introduction

T*he major concern* of this chapter is to speak to the question of how one can approach the problem and the prospect of how to *rethink* fundamental spiritual ideas beyond traditional religious frameworks. The idea is to make sure that one feels comfortable about what one holds to be true. The aim is to make sure that what one holds true is also true to one's inner being and to bypass any onslaught of anxiety about no longer being accepted by others or being dubbed as a heretic. Earlier, religious faith was described as the intellectual, experiential, and experimental link between the human heart and the Eternal Mind. It just so happens, however, that we are also mind and soul. The word *heart* is often preferably used in many religions as a symbol that really points to the core of a person's very being; therefore, "as he thinketh in his heart, so is he" (Prov. 23:7 KJV).[1] But as long as we continue to exist in the human body and to possess a thinking brain, we are going to remain composite beings—hence body, mind, soul.

Faith, then, at the deepest level usually has to do with things of the heart. But in the deeper dimensions of its lived expression, the need eventually develops to integrate all three facets of faith to a depth that involves the heart, mind, and soul within the realm of Gnosis. One way to conceive of Gnosis is that Gnosis is Agape plus Sophia. Agape (Divine Love or Universal Love) is that aspect of Gnosis that marks our development of the power of caring for others for their own sake and because the Creator loves us all. But that Divine Love is also for the sake of encouraging others now confused or lost in their search to find salvation in the Kingdom (or Realm) of God. Sophia (Divine Wisdom) is that aspect of Gnosis that marks our development of an understanding of the mysteries of the Kingdom of God. And that Divine Wisdom also aims at its own practical application in the round of daily affairs for the solution to life's endless problems. Gnosis does not, however, mean that we can claim to have understanding of "all mysteries and all knowledge" (I Cor. 13:2). Gnosis can mean, nonetheless, that one has firsthand (experiential) practical knowledge of metaphysical realities in the universe. Primarily, in this sense, Gnosis means that we have come to possess an understanding of the mysteries of redemption; that is, the workings of God in the process of winning the souls of men and women back to their Eternal Source.

Gnosticism as a Religious Movement

But, then, what is Gnosticism per se?[2] It is a very broad mystical intellectual movement running like an underground stream penetrating and erupting in and among many varieties of religions in the ancient world,[3] but centered in the concept of revealed knowledge and not faith as the way to achieve final liberation from the world of duality, darkness, and damnation. Gnosticism is, again, a belief system rooted in a divine saving truth; it can also be a mystical mode of religious experience. However, it need not, as stated before, be conceived as anti-faith but, rather, the deepening of faith that leads to spiritual knowledge. It were better seen as an immediate, intuitive perception of the cosmic truths that lie beneath the surface of ordinary reality. My briefest definition is that Gnosticism is the quest and attainment of radical spiritual freedom through mystical intuitive knowledge. But, in terms of Christian Gnosis, it is always *Agape* (Divine Love) plus *Sophia* (Divine Wisdom), the freedom by Divine Grace to be loving and wise, in spirit and in truth, as a way of life.[4]

The living link between Christian Gnosis and the ancient movement known as Gnosticism, however, remains the desire to become radically free from the apparently unsolvable mystery of evil (in a universe originally valued as good),[5] the terrors of time (disease, decay, death),[6] and the limitations imposed by ignorance of the nature of Spiritual Reality (hence, the substitution of immortality for every resurrection doctrine).[7] It is, therefore, time for the traditional and modern religious prejudice characteristic of ministers and theologians against the idea of gnosis to be overcome. For it has heretofore resembled the conditioned response that the word *Communism* did and, perhaps, still does, stimulate in the European-American consciousness. Likewise, the use of the word *gnosis* has perennially conjured up the worldview of radical dualists in the ancient era who thought that the world was inherently evil, that it was created by another divinity (called the Demiurge) who is not *God,* and that gnosis is an idea necessarily associated with arrogant and conceited elitists who considered themselves immune to sin and knowledgeable of things ordinary Christians cannot imagine. The highly respected philosopher of religion, Huston Smith, hit the nail right on the head when he wrote that

> Esoterics do not constitute a moral or even a religious elite. As a group they are not more righteous or holy in the sense of maximizing the spiritual potential that is theirs. Only with respect to truth can it be claimed—by them; exoterics will naturally resist the claim—that they see more.[8]

No doubt the oft-painted picture of proud, pretentious, and problematic gnostic elitists was true of some; but it does not describe every type or form of gnostic thinking that existed amidst the earliest Christian communities. And Smith's statement, "that they see more," will certainly continue to be problematic for those who cannot stand the word "gnostic"! It is, nevertheless, important to be informed that there was no one, all-encompassing school of Gnosticism in the ancient world. There were only varieties of gnostic groups, attitudes, and experiences.

In his book, *Unto the Churches,* Richard Drummond thus tells us that gnosis had a diversity of meanings during the early Christian centuries, that gnostics as foregoingly described were not all alike, and that the word *gnosis* was used by New Testament Christians themselves in a manner that did not exclude the idea that original Christianity could speak of its own mysteries *(mysteria).*

> The time has surely come, therefore, to correct the older, facile dismissal of *Christian Gnostic* mythopoetic depiction of the heavenly spheres as

> "fantastic speculation" and *recognize it for what it is.* It represents, first, a concern which was in fact *faithful* to the ancient Hebraic affirmation of Yahweh as Lord of the heavenly hosts—realities to be not denied but "known"—and, second, imagery symbolic of the moral and spiritual growth of the soul in this and other dimensions of life. This *growth process* . . . was seen by most Christian Gnostics not as some kind of titanic effort to penetrate by man's own power the unseen realms, but as a journey homeward made possible *by grace* from on high, most specifically by *the cosmic significance and power of the Christ event.*[9]

What so many pastors, theologians, and laypersons do not realize and/or find hard to accept is that the idea of gnosis (though not ultimately derived from) goes back to original Christianity itself (Jesus of Nazareth, Paul of Tarsus, John the Divine, and others);[10] and it is intrinsically linked to the idea of Jesus as the incarnation of the fulfillment of the hopes and dreams of all gnostics and non-gnostics, Jewish or Christian, or otherwise. An important consideration here is to recognize the cruciality of Drummond's statement in light of the complexity that characterized budding Christianity. There were literally "Christianities" or various types of Christian groups back then.[11]

For my own understanding, then, I have come to the conclusion that there were, first, those who were "Gnostics" in terms of general disposition (representing diverse religious backgrounds and salvation systems); second, others who might be called "Gnostic Christians"[12] (some but not all of whom practiced gnostic*ism*, ranging from anti-flesh asceticism to libertine sensualism, including weird, magical, and occult rites); and third, others who can be appropriately designated as "Christian Gnostics."

It is the Christian Gnostics' vision of God, the universe, and human nature (that still survives in and among religious persons today) that concerns me here. This vital distinction is made even clearer by a modern Christian gnostic who says that "'Gnosticism' is not a heresy of the Church, but a 'heresy' of gnosis'"![13] Consider, if you will, the salvific irony of the paradoxical truth that though it was Gnostic*ism* that gave rise to the "alien God," it was the so-called alien God as the One True God (revealed in Jesus of Nazareth) Who gave humankind the gift of *gnosis.*

The previous use of the word *Christian,* as a descriptive adjective in front of "gnostic," is used advisedly because it is intended to suggest an inseparable relation between such persons, past and present, and the ethical-spiritual quality of life seen in the life of Jesus as fully incarnate, fully anointed by God, and fully committed not to gnosis per se but the Source of gnosis.[14]

Nonetheless, three kinds of gnostic Christians were conveniently designated by the Valentinian school of gnostic Christianity: the material-oriented *(hylikoi),* the mental-oriented *(psychikoi),* and the spiritual-oriented *(pneumatikoi).* On these ideas, one needs to take into account (1) that they refer to levels of spiritual understanding maintained by largely competitive gnostic sects; (2) that they existed in tension with an emerging conventional, episcopal (bishop-led) Christianity; and (3) that this form of leadership was eventually to develop into what we now know as Roman Catholic Christianity (led by a bishop *supreme:* a pope). This was characterized by a vast sacramental system (pan-sacramentarianism), with not two (baptism and holy communion) but seven sacraments.

The Gnostic Christian Myth—A Model Summary

The following seven-point simplified summary is

given here in the following form because it will help the reader to better understand just where the Gnostics of old were "coming from" in terms of their generally but variantly shared conception of the relation of the soul to Father-Mother God's universe.[15] It will also automatically tell you why, eventually, the entire official Christian Church rejected the Gnostics and why the Church Universal continues to be supersensitive to the use of the term *gnostic*—for some—regardless of its context.[16]

(1) There is an incomprehensible ("alien" or "unknown") *God* beyond all the gods as popularly conceived;

(2) Originally emanated souls through error, seduction, or rebellion "fell" from that God's pleroma (the *fullness* of the Inner Realm of God's Eternal Light) into lower realms or dimmer dimensions of light stretching into deeper darkness, as if descending into a spiritual "black hole" or beneath a type of astrodome of living death—the earth plane;

(3) A being less than God (called the Demiurge, also having other names) really but vainly created the physical universe, including the earth as a realm of ignorance, evil, and suffering;

(4) The Unknown God finally sent His prime Envoy of Eternal Light (the Messiah or Christ) into the realm of darkness to teach those souls trapped in the material world how to escape by awakening them to their true natures (divine "lights"), so that they could pierce the astrodome of (evil) matter and pass through all the intermediate dimensions or spheres to return to the pleroma of God;

(5) Rulers of ascending dimensions ("Archons") bar the Way and test the soul;

(6) Though faith is the preliminary key to spirituality, spiritual knowledge *(gnosis)* is its ultimate, indispensable aim and the key to spiritual liberation (salvation);

(7) A soul can succeed in its return to the pleroma only if it becomes as Jesus was—a "Christ" itself.[17]

As a general term, *gnostic* can refer to any or all Palestinian, Greek, Persian, or even far Oriental groups (probably including Hindus or Buddhists)[18] who advocated avenues to salvation that primarily emphasized "a world within" beyond the need for rigid use of rituals and external intermediaries. Though Christ remained central to their ideas of salvation, Gnostic Christians were those who were still advocates of a fundamentally dualistic conception of the universe.[19]

But Christian Gnostics were those to whom Christ not only remained central to salvation but to whom the following distinguishing conceptions were considered crucial: (1) that the universe was in fact created by that very so-called alien God whose existence the gnostic dualists affirmed; but (2) for Christian Gnostics the cosmos was not intrinsically evil, save deluded souls make it so; (3) that Jesus as indeed the Way, the Truth, and the Life did in fact teach and dispense gnosis to the few, or those who would receive it, but that it was finally open to all; (4) Paul of Tarsus bade us to see gnosis as one (but thoroughly treasured) component in a more complex system of spiritual gifts or virtues;[20] (5) that love (agape) as the ultimate divine virtue was even greater than *gnosis* and/or that *agape* was indeed the essence of *gnosis* (Mark 12:29-31, John 13:34, Cor. 13:2); (6) that indeed we can each become as Christ was; and (7) via John the Divine, we learn that we must at some time be born again, both physically and spiritually, in order to receive the glory that God gave to Jesus of Nazareth.[21]

Looking at things in this way enables one to understand both why such gnosis is given a distinctive place in John's gospel and Paul's epistles, as well as why it has never completely ceased to be a part of later Christian tradition no matter how subtle or bizarre its forms.[22] It also accounts in large measure for why no amount of ecclesiastical condemnation has been able to get rid of it. Drummond aptly recalls Rudolf Steiner's view that "we may class as Gnostics all the writers of the first Christian centuries who sought for a deeper spiritual sense in Christian teachings."[23]

To this we might add all the believers of all the ages who have sought to go beneath the surface of material and mental reality for the sake of achieving a more creative encounter, communion, or union with the spiritual "world within" that corresponds to the metaphysical universe.[24] But, as many persons know and others suspect, there is something distinctive about Jesus of Nazareth that makes the term Christian Gnostics important both for a look back at Christian origins and a look around at New Age forms of Gnosticism today. These Christian Gnostics correspond, incidentally, to those Valentinus called pneumatics, because they are led by the Holy Spirit (or what the Essenes called the "Holy Spirit of Truth").

Drummond notes that the Christian seer, Edgar Cayce, was once asked a very provocative question to which he gave an answer which reflects one that has rarely found acceptance in academic circles, but certainly the contrary in most esoteric religious circles. Cayce was asked (in reading 5749-14) whether Gnosticism was a "parallel" form of Christianity and compatible with the Christian vision his teachings reflected.[25]

Cayce said it was and implied that anything short of that vision, as occurred in early and later bureaucratic Christianity, indicates an attempt "to take shortcuts"; and he added, bluntly, that "there are none in Christianity!"[26]

It just so happens that this "parallel" tradition was not considered by Christian Gnostics to be the end-all and the be-all of human spirituality without some important qualifications. Futhermore, it cannot be overemphasized that the term *esoteric* is not intended to imply an attitude of spiritual elitism! One becomes radically aware of its highly elevated, intended meaning when one recalls Jesus' statement that "From everyone to whom much has been given, much will be required; and from the one to whom much has been entrusted, even more will be demanded"![27] If a so-called esotericist, therefore, tends to act like an elitist, then one can accurately conclude that such an individual is really an elitist "jerk" and not esoteric in the truest spiritual sense of the word.

Theologians and seers alike have told us that the problem of arrogance, conceit, and elitism did exist in probably all gnostic groups (e.g., I Cor. 8:1). However, what amounts to a virtual revelation to increasing numbers of Christians today is the fact that there were those in the earliest phases of the development of Christianity, especially Clement of Alexandria, who already knew that Jesus Himself had indeed taught on two levels of truth. This means that there was one level of teaching taking the form of parables and another level of teaching taking the form of mysteries.[28]

As many Christians know, Paul of Tarsus is acknowledged to have been the source of the primary impetus for the decisive thrust of Christianity toward a universal evangelistic movement. However, his Epistle to the Romans is typically regarded as a crucial theological letter in which he challenges the attitudes of Christians in Rome whom he found to be religiously but falsely proud due to their immersion in the empire's tradition of meritocracy. They were thereby tempted to apply that attitude to the new spiritual vision that Christianity had brought them. So, although Paul "knew" of a deeper dimension of Christian teaching which he describes in various ways among his epistles,[29] he yet tried to call would-be gnostics to accept the priority of God's Divine Grace in the quest-and-attainment process of salvation.[30]

Faith and Gnosis—In Harmony, Not Contradiction

Faith and gnosis are indeed intimately related and are capable of being conceived in several ways. First, their relation can be viewed as a spiritual continuum (or unbroken line) of spiritual development from childlike faith all the way to a mature knowledge of the spiritual realities of the Kingdom of God.[31] Second, they can be seen as in creative tension (a spiritual dialectic) in that along the way to a mature faith there may occur traumas in one's rethinking of inherited ideas and new experiences that seem to contradict each other. This dialectic arises because often there is a "digit of doubt" in faith that brings one into tension with gnosis as a deeper spiritual prospect. But, then, faith and gnosis can otherwise be experienced as a spiritual paradox. This means that there is a certain heightening of faith in any genuine gnostic experience, and there is a certain deepening of knowledge in any genuine faith experience. Recall that Paul of Tarsus could actually affirm these words: "I *know* in whom I have *believed.*" (II Tim. 1:12)

But, all in all, whether conceived of as a continuum, dialectic, or paradox, faith and gnosis are finally not intended to work against one another. Gnosis is intended to grasp, absorb, and cherish the essential truths of faith; and faith is intended to hunger and thirst for its fulfillment in gnosis. There is even a sense in which the relation of faith to gnosis can be experientially conceived in transitional terms. Here one may find oneself at different phases of one's spiritual evolution moving from a conception of the faith-gnosis relation as a continuum toward a dialectic and, finally, a living paradox.

Contrary to some ancient and modern (new age) thinking, therefore, faith and gnosis are not opposites in the practical spiritual sense. When conceived as part of a continuum (or an unbroken line), for example, faith is surely the door that leads to spiritual perception or an intuitive mystical understanding of what Jesus of Nazareth called the "mysteries of the Kingdom of God." (Mark 4:11) When conceived as a dialectic, of course, faith and gnosis would be characteristic of the conflict of consciousness any individual seeker might experience who trembles at the thought of being considered a heretic. Though one might not be dubbed a heretic by way of a formal "Inquisition," there is always the probability of being ostracized. Nonetheless, that initial conflict would also contain the prospect of developing into a synthetic understanding of the blessings of both faith and gnosis. Paul of Tarsus commits himself to a living paradox of faith and gnosis when he tells us: I *know* in whom I have *believed.*[32] This means that every experience of true faith is thus one of potential gnosis, and every experience of gnosis presupposes its actual beginning in an experience of true faith. Gnosis (spiritual knowledge), then, is the fulfillment of faith, as agape ("divine love" or "unconquerable good will") is the fulfillment of the Torah (the Law). Whichever way one may prefer to look at them, I myself want to make one thing clear. While I am undoubtedly trying to make the idea of gnosis more acceptable, I am certainly not trying to undermine or make irrelevant the idea of faith. For they are so intimately related and potentially inseparable; intimately related because the idea of a faith-gnosis continuum (as with Clement of Alexandria)[33] is primary for me; potentially inseparable because, with all the human claims to spiritual knowledge, there will probably always be ways of the Creator that are ultimately past finding out. Hence the notion in this work of "gnostic faith"—both a state of deepening spiritual consciousness *and* the experience in some human situations wherein one has to acknowledge that there are moments of agnosis (not knowing)!

Are You a Potential or an Actual Gnostic?

Shakespeare's assertion about the smell of a rose (in *Romeo and Juliet*) has retained over time a certain esoteric significance. For it is indeed difficult to deny Juliet's museful utterance that "That which we call a rose—by any other word would smell as sweet . . . "[34] So it was and is with the names given to the followers of Jesus over the centuries. Among such names, to state a few, there are "the Followers of the Way," "the Nazarenes," the *Christiāni* (Latin for "Christians"), "Gnostics," and others. Yet as it is with the rose, so it is with the term *gnostic,* with which I am certainly inspired but not intoxicated! The term *gnostic,* then, is important only insofar as these earlier persons who had "the gnostic spirit" deserve a lasting tribute for having introduced their contemporaries and subsequent generations to the possibility of experiencing (as I defined it briefly earlier) a radical spiritual freedom regarding the internalization of the spiritual intentions of the ancient mysteries[35] and especially the gnostic vision of eternity experienced by Jesus of Nazareth.

Having said that, let me say that you are a potential or an actual gnostic, if early in your life, if not recently, you have found yourself inclined (though still in a state of faith) to question from the deepest depths of your being the range of spiritual meaning of some of the very fundamental ideas passed on to you by your establishment (inherited) religion. It does not matter what your religion is (even beyond branches or denominations of the same), for, in any case, you *are* "gnostically" inclined. You are so because, without spiritually rushing to judgment about your particular religious tradition's entire treasury of ideas, you still hold *some* to be true yet realize that there must be deeper things to ponder—indeed, to *know*—concerning the nature of the Divine Reality, human nature, and human destiny.

Do recall Steiner's view cited earlier that "we may class as Gnostics all the writers of the first Christian centuries who sought for a deeper spiritual sense in Christian teachings." So, please, do not think that I have written this book so that you will become a gnostic merely for the sake of the name! In the end, the God of Eternity could not care less about the words "gnosticism" or "gnostic," but the Creator *is* concerned about your soul's possession of "the gnostic spirit" and ultimately your anointment with the *spirit of gnosis;*[36] for that is the point, the key, the reality to be experienced, affirmed—and demonstrated.

To be sure, there are gnostics in all the world's major religions—including the Native traditions (tribals) on all continents. Among the Australian Aborigines, for instance, early anthropologists encountered (whom I would call) "gnostic" beings whom they referred to as "Aboriginal men of high degree." Marlo Morgan's book, *Mutant Message, Down Under,*[37] though described as a novel by the *New York Times* (and dismissed as fraud by some), comes across to some individuals as helpful to their spiritual lives. Fraud or fiction, it is ironic that the work has the potential to impress the searching mind as a vivid and meaningful description of one modern woman's experience with living primordial wisdom, whether purely introspective or imaginative.[38] At any rate, both anthropologists and missionaries know that among the African Bantu and the Dogon (of West Africa) there are long-standing esoteric traditions regarding the cosmos, human nature, and human destiny. American anthropologist Paul Radin, who wrote a substantial essay on the esoteric rituals of Native Americans, saw what I (not he) would call gnostic conceptions and ways of being in the world among the shamans, whom he called "philosophers."

It so happens, however, that these gnostic dispositions and trends among all these religions tend to overlap with mysticism; for mysticism, as such, is a much broader term than gnosticism. It must be remembered, however, that there are mystics in some groups who not only give priority to faith but who also use rituals and other forms of worship that satisfy their inner hunger for deeper and more meaningful spiritual experience. Nonetheless, it is among the Hindus in India that we find the most radical fusion of mysticism and gnosticism, within the form of meditation called *jnana-yoga.*[39] The word *jnana* is, again, the very earliest form of the word *gnosis,* which itself stands beyond our general understanding of the word *knowledge.*

All this means that, while you may belong to one of a number of faiths in the world and you may find yourself worshiping or being religious in any manner that pleases you—and others—it is not impossible for you also to have the gnostic spirit. Thus if you are still searching for truth and are not afraid to follow the truth wherever it leads, then you are a potential gnostic. And if you have already made the extra effort it takes to sift out those things from your own tradition that need to be pondered—or repondered—for the first time in light of your ongoing spiritual experience because they no longer fit, *you are on your way!* Yet you are not an actual gnostic until you have become absolutely convinced that your own spiritual experience is the final court of appeal and that the truth that sets us all free lies within ourselves and not ultimately in sacred books or in the minds of bishops, ancient or modern! But whether you are just beginning to search or are beginning to "sift," once you have opened any one of your own soul's "doors of perception," you cannot close it again. Jesus in *The Gospel of Thomas* puts it this way: "Let him who seeks continue seeking until he finds. When he finds he will become troubled . . . "[40] Being such an individual, you must nonetheless be able to say, in the words of an old hymn, "I would be brave, for there is much to dare."

Still you are advised to be careful, for, as the Bible says with ominous wisdom, "There is a way that seems right to a person, but its end is the way to death."[41] Let yourself be consoled and assured, then, that "the souls of the righteous are in the hands of God";[42] moreover, the Son of the Living God has promised not only that you "shall *know* the truth and the truth shall make you free," but that "when the Spirit of truth comes [into your heart], he will guide you into all the truth."[43]

What Do Gnostics "Know"?

A question that continues to linger in the minds of skeptics and believers alike is "What do gnostics 'know'?" I will answer this directly.

(1) Gnostics "know" ("see" or "understand") that there is a larger picture involved in the process of moving from a state of moral and spiritual infancy—or degeneracy, if not, spiritual ignorance—into a state of spiritual enlightenment or truth than conventional sources of religion teach.[44]

(2) Gnostics "know" that *that* process of becoming spiritually enlightened can also involve being "born again" (physically and spiritually), and that while water

is the symbol of physical rebirth, spirit is the symbol of one's consciousness being raised from above in the metaphysical sense.[45]

(3) Gnostics "know" that the great world sages, including Buddha and Christ, taught persons on two levels of spiritual receptivity, corresponding to an exoteric mode of truth (ordinary perception) and an esoteric mode of truth (extraordinary perception); hence Mark 4:10-11, Matthew 13:10-11, and Luke 8:9-10.[46]

(4) Gnostics "know" that while the mysteries of the Realm of the Creator require that a given soul must be ready (deeply receptive) to perceive even higher truths, the essential saving message of the Creator is still contained in the parables or other forms taught by extraordinary masters of wisdom and compassion.[47]

(5) Gnostics "know" that all that the great teachers have been and demonstrated in relation to the Eternal applies potentially to all souls everywhere in the universe, both on the earth plane and in other dimensions of spiritual reality.[48] Ultimately, we are all the sons and daughters of the Creator.

(6) Gnostics "know" that the mysteries of the Realm of the Creator consist in cosmic truths that stand beneath, above, behind, and beyond all the dogmas of any particular religious faith, including Christianity itself as an institutional religion.[49]

(7) Gnostics "know" that there is the emanation of souls beyond the creation of bodies of intelligence in the universe; and that spiritual androgyny beyond the state of human sexual polarity is the ultimate state of spiritual being, consciousness, and bliss.[50]

(8) Gnostics "know" that there is a principle of reincarnation beyond solely one-time incarnations in the universe;[51] and that it is related to a law of compensation (karma or retribution), whose purpose is finally a positive and not a negative one.[52]

(9) Gnostics "know" that there is the universe as macrocosmos, and there is the human body as microcosmos; and that the human body is the real Temple of the Creator beyond the temples, churches, and mosques of the world.[53] There are, exoterically, on one plane of reality, faith, hope, and love, while on another, the esoteric, there are love, power, and wisdom; but love *(agape)* alone can permeate all planes—hence the gnostic cross.[54]

(10) Gnostics "know" there is the reality of mystic attunement beyond doctrines of blood-sacrificial atonement in the process of attaining co-creatorship; but that which the atonement rites symbolize is that same attunement; so they are to be appreciated, if not tolerated with utter seriousness.[55] There are, then, varieties of spiritual temperament; and the Creator is patient because millions still only "see through a glass darkly" (KJV).[56]

(11) Gnostics "know" there is indeed the Unknowable Creator (the "alien God" of anti-matter gnostics) in terms of the Absolutely Ultimate Reality that cannot be comprehended by human reason, but mysteriously that Reality can be "known" through the medium of childlikeness and through mystical experience when love is seen as "the life of the soul and the harmony of the universe."[57]

(12) Gnostics, in summary, "know" that no matter what happens in life, whatever the situation, the Holy Spirit of Truth can guide the soul into the straight path, even into unchartered waters of experimental faith, but always with a spiritual certainty rising in the soul.[58]

You need not be concerned with the fact that the broad selection of gnostic insights above are found in and among various traditions, thus leading some to say, "I've heard all this before!" For it is an essential part of the gnostic vision in a cross-cultural religious sense that it represents the universalization of timeless truths. This means that they apply to every one, potentially; and that, actually, they are *not* intended to be kept secret—for the sake of secrecy—but internalized by every being who is in a state of readiness to receive them.[59] The following words of Jesus of Nazareth have both an exoteric and an esoteric significance for all that I have just written: "... for nothing is covered up that will not be uncovered, and nothing secret that will not become known."[60] If you, the reader, can discern both the exoteric *and* the esoteric meaning of these words, you are more of a "gnostic" than you "know"!

Nuggets of Gnosis in the Teachings of Jesus, Paul, and John

The following is a selection of experiences in the life of Jesus of Nazareth and Paul of Tarsus and from John the Divine which will clearly illustrate to you the presence of the gnostic vision in their experiences with the Creator and with souls that they encountered. These experiences will both confirm the presence of the exoteric and the esoteric, thus also confirming that we are destined to come to a deeper understanding of the spiritual reality of God, human nature, and human destiny than traditional ecclesiastical frameworks have led us to believe. Moreover, as it appears on the far cover of MacGregor's book on *Gnosis,* we are destined to undertake "an evaluation of gnosticism as an integral aspect of Christian scripture."

The Holy Spirit as Wind and as Breath

Tradition has it that after the death and resurrection of Jesus of Nazareth the disciples, including the mother and brother (James) of Jesus, gathered in an upper room in Jerusalem to await the arrival (anointment) of the Holy Spirit. It is certainly one of the most important events in the entire history of the emerging Christian Church. Baptists, Pentecostalists, and Fundamentalist groups dearly recall this event in their lives and will even testify to its recurrence in some form in their individual experiences and during their evangelistic revivals over the years. Thus, in the Book of Acts, just before the Holy Spirit filled all those assembled there, "from heaven there came a sound as the rush of a violent wind"; and "divided tongues, as of fire, appeared among them, and a tongue rested on each of them." As a result they were all given the ability "to speak in other languages" before diverse receptive, sometimes hostile, audiences.[61]

No one interpretation of the meaning of the linguistic aspect of this event, however, has ever found universal acceptance. There is little disagreement, nonetheless, that, however one may wish to imagine what speaking in tongues *(glossolalia)* really is,[62] the Scripture does give the distinct impression that the disciples had the power to be understood by persons of sundry linguistic and cultural backgrounds. But this event's historical significance is not to be diminished, for it remains essentially an exoteric, external manifestation of the Creator's glory and power. Hearing, per se, thus plays a significant role through the medium of preaching in Christian missions and evangelism. Martin Luther thought that it is in itself a supernatural thing, in that the Living Word of God is transmitted via human *words* (as if on Providential wings) into the heart of the believer. However, hearing is still not the most glorious and powerful way through which to be led to spiritual transformation.

It is only when we turn our minds toward another account of the reception of the Holy Spirit by the disciples of Jesus that the esoteric perspective comes to light. Hence, in the (Christian gnostic) Gospel of John, Jesus does more than merely tell His disciples that the Spirit will be coming to them and that it will guide them into the truth of the things He has taught. John tells us that Jesus "breathed" upon them and said to them, "Receive the Holy Spirit." Notice that they received the Spirit from Jesus *directly*—and by a means practically unheard of or meditated on by run-of-the-mill believers, then or now.

But this manner of acting on the part of Jesus is highly resemblant of Oriental modes of blessing pupils or initiates under the auspices of gurus. In Hinduism, for example, part of the initiation process involves "the guru's transmission of spiritual power to the pupil . . . 'The disciple receives . . . Grace according to the impact of the [guru's] Shakti (or Creative Power) . . . where there is no impact . . . there is no fulfillment.'"[63] Hindu gurus have, therefore, long been associated with blessing disciples with an inflow of spiritual energy that accomplishes purification, enlightenment, and beatification.

Rather than regard this as a threat to the uniqueness of Jesus as the Christ, it were better to side with those who say that the very occurrence of this kind of event within a Christian framework shows the remarkable status and quality of the Christ Consciousness of Jesus. But we have to remember that "Christ in this perspective is more universal than the religion that possesses the name."[64] For this Spirit-dispensing and Spirit-in-breathing, indeed, has esoteric harmony with a mystery that finally transcends any particular religious tradition. You will recall my reference to the fact that even the work of Jesus as the Christ should not and cannot as a mystery be understood apart from all the other mysteries revealed in the ancient world antedating His coming.

The important thing is that this "breathing-on" or "inbreathing" experience that Jesus gave to His disciples in the Gospel of John could only have been accomplished by One who understood, who *knew*, not merely received, the glory and the power of the Creator. And it was a glory and power not to be merely manifested but to be now shared with the disciples. This event not only implies something more internal (or gnostic) in terms of the dynamics of spiritual transformation, but also implies that we, too, can become dispensers of such power in our intimate interpersonal relations with other human beings. Hence a very disturbing statement by Jesus to His followers—and to us?—was:

> Very truly, I tell you, the one who believes in me will also do the works that I do and, in fact, will do greater works than these . . . John 14:12

I say "disturbing" because, though it would surely be hard to find believers themselves who would dare to affirm that they can do what Jesus did, it would be even harder to find believers who would venture to say that they could do even *greater* things than Jesus! Yet, in this regard, it is affirmed by the gnostic Gospel of Thomas that we are even intended to become not merely *like* Christ, but more gloriously *as* Christ was. "Whoever achieves gnosis becomes 'no longer a Christian, but a Christ.'"[65] Thus Jesus says to His Father in prayer and praise, "Father, glorify me in your own presence with the *glory* that I had in your presence before the world existed . . . The *glory* that you have given me I have given *them,* so that they may be one, as we are one . . . "[66]

But we have to remember, however, that there are always levels of Christ Consciousness; and that there is no need to feign modesty about what the Creator expects us to manifest gloriously. As architect Frank Lloyd Wright is supposed to have said, "Honest arrogance is better than hypocritical humility"! Here, however, with the Christ Consciousness, one must avoid both honest arrogance *and* hypocritical humility and, instead, manifest honest humility. With no sense of undue self-depreciation, then, we are intended to accept that glory and to manifest it as spiritual power (and spiritual morality) to the world.

A science fiction motion picture I saw years ago, entitled *This Island Earth*, tells us much about what our attitudes should *not* be regarding the truth about ourselves in the most positive influential terms. Here one finds two earthlings having been complimented by an alien for the level of their scientific achievements. At once, one earthling, Dr. Adams, said to the other, "Be careful . . . [he, the alien] will flatter you to death." The alien answered, "The truth is never flattering, Dr. Adams"![67] In light of that statement, the following partial citation of the words of Jesus to the Pharisees applies to all of us: "Go and learn what this means . . . "[68]

Continuing in this spirit and that of the Gospel According to John, a longtime dear friend of mine, Dr. Peggy Tyler, a Christian and an educator who has had advanced training in Transcendental Meditation, once told me of a rather quiet but impactful gnostic moment she experienced. She was in a restaurant where from her booth she noticed a man sitting alone at the bar, looking rather sad. However, he had not in turn noticed her. Experimentally, she sent him through the eye of her soul a blessing of peace. Unbelievably, the man turned and looked at her and smiled, as though he had conscious knowledge of having received the power of the good will (or Good Will Power!) she had transmitted to him. Truly, we do not need to be (falsely) modest about our spiritual powers, as long as we "know" the Source of such powers! I am sure there are readers of this book who know exactly what I am saying in this regard from their own spiritual experience.

Faith as Hearing and Gnosis as Seeing

How many times have you heard a minister or evangelist say, "We walk by faith and not by sight"? Even Jesus said to the doubting Thomas, "Blessed are those who have not seen and yet have come to believe."[69] In fact, it has been the predominant view of Protestant churches the world over that we are saved by faith *only*. Christians who believe this are in basic agreement with the Protestant reformer, Martin Luther, who, they say, was only keeping true to what Paul of Tarsus had said much earlier (Romans 1:17, 3:28).[70] "Hearing," then, as a religious idea refers both to the act of having something sacred revealed to you about your salvation; and it refers to the act of responding receptively to the saving truth that has been heard. The very Ten Commandments of Judaism are preambled by the Hebrew word *Shema*, which means "hear"; and *the Shema* (Deut. 6:4-5) is the affirmation of the faith of Israel in the Living God who said: "Hear, O Israel: the Lord is our God, the Lord alone. You shall love the Lord your God with all your heart, and with all your soul, and with all your might." There is no need, however, to show irreverence or lack of compassion toward those who, through hearing what Jews or Christians consider the Divine Word, have lived their lives within such an authentically meaningful religious perspective. Jesus of Nazareth gave us an example of the hearing/seeing distinction while talking compassionately to a group of believing Jews: "I declare what I have *seen* in the Father's presence; as for you, you should do what you have *heard* from the Father."[71]

Yet it remains vital to any individual seeking "for a deeper spiritual sense in Christian teachings" (Steiner) to realize that the hearing/believing perspective is essentially an exoteric one. For consistent with the distinction Jesus Himself made between teaching through parables and knowing through mysteries, there *is* an esoteric view. That view is also based upon faith but includes a vision of reality that reflects a faith beyond faith. Sometimes I like to call this "gnostic faith." It is intimately radical faith *becoming* knowledge, and it is ultimately mature faith that is *prevalent* knowledge (gnosis). But it is, practically, an experiential gnostic vision of the nature and meaning of the Creator, human nature, and human destiny.

In the examples that follow, I shall show you that there are in fact golden nuggets of gnostic visions scattered throughout the Hebrew Scriptures and the New Testament. But, for now, I call your attention to the fact that, because Paul, as did Jesus and John, *knew* this rather early, "gnostic Christians" and "Christ-conscious gnostics" read the words of Paul of Tarsus on both the exoteric and the esoteric levels of understanding.[72] But these gnostics were all convinced that Jesus Himself had taught them by word and example, so that gnosis as a mystery goes back to the very founder of Christianity. Thus Jesus said the following three things:

> Blessed are the eyes that *see* what you *see!* For I tell you that many prophets and kings desired to see what you see, but did *not* see it . . . [73]
>
> And why do you not judge *for yourselves* what is right?" [as if they could *know* what was right!]
>
> " . . . and you will *know* the truth, and the truth will make you *free.*"[74]

Perhaps the most exquisite illustration of faith beyond faith that has become *a saving gnosis* appears in that ever-mysterious and ever-fascinating Scripture, the Book of Job. Job is a sacred and esoteric Scripture that has evoked massive commentary. Carl Jung, whom many consider to have been a mystical psychologist, if more, a modern gnostic,[75] wrote on this mysterious figure in his *Answer to Job.* Having no absolutely verifiable author or date, according to critical scholars (but probably written sometime during the second half of the pre-Christian millennium), the Book of Job was yet said by Edgar Cayce to have been written by the same soul who appeared as Jesus of Nazareth in Judaea. (See reading 262-55.)

In considering Job's radical experience of natural evil, it is important to notice that after Job had endured all the intellectual explanations and judgmental rationalizations regarding his suffering from his critics, Job himself approached the threshold of arrogance with his Creator. And, in this case, many have noted that Job's apparent "honest arrogance" with his Creator found more favor than Job's opponents. For Job, the Creator understood, was an absolutely frustrated but honest believer, not an absolutely frustrated unbeliever or, like his opponents, a bunch of hypocritically humble believers! As Will Herberg has so aptly put the matter:

> Not unbelief but indifference, not atheism but taking God for granted, is the ultimate sin . . . not skeptical questioning, not even passionate denial of God, is so displeasing to him as the lukewarmness of conventional piety.[76]

Job, therefore, contends with the Creator over what seems his unmerited suffering: loss of economic sustenance, loss of family, the endurance of boils all over his body, etc. In fact, at one point, his wife's frustration reached its apex, and she said that he should just curse God and die![77] Having, therefore, heard Job's complaints to his tormentors and concerning God's ways with a mortal,[78] the Creator verbally threshes Job with a barrage of "cosmic questions" totally beyond not only Job's but all human power to answer. Thoroughly humbled by the experience, something deeply esoteric happens in the mind of Job in stark contrast to his earlier state of spiritual consciousness when he said,

> If I go forward, he is not there; or backward, I cannot perceive him; on the left he hides, and I cannot behold him; I turn to the right, but I cannot see him.[79]

For now, something causes him finally to utter these astounding words: "I had *heard* of you by the hearing of the ear, but now my eye *sees* you."[80]

I hold that these words are the key to the entire book of Job, which is a gnostic allegory of the odyssey of the soul in need and in search of a direct vision of the Creator. For, thereafter, Job was truly in a new and higher state of spiritual consciousness, prototypical of the Christ Consciousness.

It must be pointed out, however, that a direct vision of the Creator in Christ-conscious gnostic terms does not mean that one should be able to claim to have seen God as if the Creator could be confined to a particular form or manifestation. For John the Divine tells us that *"No one has ever seen God"* (1:18)! This has serious esoteric implications for Moses' having encountered God's Presence in Exodus 33:18-23;[81] and Jesus' statement, "If you have seen me, you have seen the Father." (John 14:9) Do you, the reader, now perceive the answer to these matters? For "God is Spirit," and what the soul in its own Inner Eye can "see" without form is greater and more convincing than what the physical eye can see with form. Thus, if by now you have begun to perceive the inner meaning of the forgoing at a *gnostic* level of spiritual understanding, no one needs to explain to you two other sacred utterances of Jesus: "Blessed are the pure in heart, for they shall see God" (Matt. 5:8);[82] "The kingdom of God is not coming with things that can be observed . . . For, in fact, the kingdom of God is within you" (Luke 17:20, 21).

By way of analogy we receive a dramatic illustration of this form of seeing in the national bestselling book and in the cinematic form of the story, *Contact,* based on an earlier original story by the late Carl Sagan and his wife Ann Druyan. The remarks that follow combine both the book and the film.

Actress Jody Foster's character, Ellie Arroway, has spent her life from early childhood dreaming of discovering that there is intelligent life among the stars. During the movie, the heart-pounding momentum reaches its apex when Ellie with traumatic impact has apparently just been transported to the star Vega in the constellation of Ursa Major. This was accomplished by way of a highly sophisticated device built from astrophysical plans sent to earth by unbelievably advanced extraterrestrials. The mystery looms because, afterward, Ellie is quite certain of having had a cosmic, transcendental experience at Vega (including a meaningful encounter with her "deceased" father). But scientists insist that her transporting device had actually failed and that all witnesses to it swear that she never really left the launching station! The growing, knelling criticism mounts as one of her major doubters says,

> "You come back one nanosecond or something after you leave, so to any neutral observer *you never left at all.*"[83]

Yet at a climactic hearing before an international committee and before hundreds of seated observers, Ellie, with *gnostic*-like intuitive conviction, is totally unable to deny the truth of her experience, even while tearfully admitting to her questioners that, as a radio-astronomer and in scientific terms, what happened to her is practically impossible.

While the novel was probably written to inspire a variety of opinions, scientific, religious, and philosophical, I perceive that the motif of persistence in Ellie's search has powerful, symbolic spiritual significance. As Richard Bach says it, "You are never given a wish without also being given the power to make it true. You may have to work for it, however";[84] or, as Ellie herself at last came to discover,

> " . . . sooner or later you'll find it. It's already there. It's inside everything. *You don't have to leave your planet to find it.*"[85]

I also perceive that, as with any ultimate dream, the intensity of one's conviction must be great enough to die for (so said Martin Luther King, Jr.). Thus Ellie was willing to take such an utterly dangerous journey, even with the prospect that, returning fifty years later, she could probably only return to a world without those she loved and who loved her. It also seems that the technicians' failure consisted in not realizing that the extraterrestrial device was probably not meant to serve as a corporal transporter but as a *consciousness* transporter—if by "transporter" one might mean a consciousness transformer! Ellie's *body* may never have been intended to leave this dimension, and that is why her material transporter was viewed by so many witnesses as a failed launch. Even to say that it was a consciousness transporter need not mean that her consciousness left her body, but that the height, depth, and breadth of consciousness (i.e., Cosmic Consciousness) she experienced had brought her into transcendent attunement with a realm beyond time and space (it appeared that eighteen hours of static had been recorded on Ellie's video unit); but it was a realm or dimension where, for Ellie, beyond all other things, love did endure. As I said earlier, love permeates all dimensions. One receives, then, both from the book and the film that in the life of the Vegan extraterrestrials there was no rigid line of separation of science and religion, consciousness and reality, life and love.

> Speaking for herself—but also, she thought, for most Americans—the discovery had strengthened her belief in God, now revealed to be creating life and intelligence on many worlds . . . [86]

Without attempting to go into other breathtaking scenes in the book and film and their possible religious implications, I shall merely add the following remarks that relate Job, "Ellie," and the early gnostics. For the gnostics—Christian, "Christ-conscious," and non-Christian—the esoteric meaning of the so-called resurrection of Jesus of Nazareth was not something essentially related to psychobiological resuscitation but rather something related to metaphysical-intuitive gnosis of things beyond the realm of scientific proof.[87] Both the gnostic Gospels and the gnostic aspects of the New Testament Gospels support the spiritual perspective that there is a depth of understanding available to the *know*ledgeable soul that transcends the need for material manifestations that "prove."[88] Consider the boldness of this remark made to Roman Christians, who were still incarnate:

> But you are not in the flesh; you are in the Spirit, since the Spirit of Christ dwells in you."[89]

Earlier I mentioned the Christian gnosis of John the Divine, alongside Jesus and Paul of Tarsus. He, too, was among the very first Christian gnostics ("those who know"), just as Jesus could say to His believers, "I declare what I have seen,"[90] John could say, " . . . we declare to you what we have seen . . . " What did he and Paul and others "see," "know," or "understand"? They had directly experienced a vision of the complex process of the redemption of souls by the Power of the Eternal Divine. In and through their own processes of soul development, they had been raised to a level of love, power, and wisdom so great that they knew that when you have truly "seen" God, you do not need to question God's ways or to defend yourself against God, as Job did.[91] And this is also the real meaning and context (life's trials) of the Oriental saying, "Those who know do not speak, those who speak do not know." Thus there can be no true Christian gnostic who has ever had to ask the question, "Why me?" For if one absolutely insists upon an answer and if an answer were given from above in the light of one's entire cosmic reincarnational biography, the answer might very well be, "Why not you?"

Christ as Advocate and the Father Who Himself Loves You

Just how long has it been since you heard about or took seriously the idea that even with God—you need a *lawyer?* If you are one of those persons who believe that only through atonement rituals or a Savior-God or other intermediaries can you approach God, then the concept of Christ as the atoning Advocate probably still has literal meaning to you. You are, of course, not by any means alone. For there are millions who continue to associate the advocacy role of Jesus with the idea that, after Eden, the Creator was either desirous of destroying humankind because of its inherent sinfulness, or the Creator, though unwilling, was obligated to do so because "the wages of sin is death"[92] and the Creator's justice demands satisfaction.

The term *advocate* means "a person who argues . . . pleads in another's behalf; an intercessor," even a "lawyer"![93] For various sectors of fundamentalist Christianity, Jesus thus stands or sits near the Heavenly Father as the great Advocate, Defender, and Intercessor in order to plead humankind's case for forgiveness, leniency—indeed, being saved. Humankind, it is believed, is not and can never be worthy of salvation. Moreover, it is the fact that Jesus shed His blood that is inseparable from His advocacy, for "without the shedding of blood, there is no forgiveness of sins" (Heb. 9:22).[94] In this most commonplace (exoteric) frame of reference, believers everywhere have followed a biblical saying that merely reflects the effort to couch something spiritually and inexpressibly wonderful in ritual language: " . . . if anyone does sin, we have an *advocate* with the Father, Jesus Christ the righteous; and he is the atoning sacrifice for our sins, and not for ours only but also for the sins of the whole world."[95]

Of course, when this conception is taken to its most far-reaching conclusions, it becomes associated, as it has, with the idea of the Eternal Divine's use of hierarchies of intermediaries between God and ourselves. To be sure, the universe seems virtually to bubble with Grace, and many tend either to think that they have been instantly saved by that one act of Jesus or that Jesus' mother, if not a host of other lesser but also interceding saints, will guarantee their final entry into the Kingdom of Heaven. But as it was said earlier, this basically exoteric perspective should become no pretext for intolerance on the part of those of us who understand things differently. For the commonplace perspective (of the saving advocate) has served to comfort and inspire believers throughout many ages.

Unfortunately it has also established barriers not only between believers and nonbelievers, but also among believers themselves who continue to have diverse conceptions of what role Jesus plays essentially in behalf of humankind's salvation.

Yet the inner meaning, therefore, of all the metaphors

that are used of Jesus' role in opening the way for our salvation (and there are many) is contained in a single biblical verse found in the Gospel of John (16:26-27): " . . . and I do *not* say to you that I will ask the Father on your behalf; *for the Father himself loves you . . .* "[96]

One needs to recall that of all the Gospels, John's often uses the exoteric and the esoteric in combination, even juxtaposition.[97] The use of the idea of Christ the Advocate, therefore, refers to and reflects the way in which the earliest Christians, who were fundamentally Jewish in background, sought creatively to link the spiritual freedom they had found through Jesus' vision, with their tradition of *atonement* cleansing through the sacred sacrifice of animals. Hence John the Baptist calls Jesus "the *Lamb* of God who takes away the sin of the world!"[98]

Nonetheless, the esoteric truth is that in the biblical verse above this, Jesus is telling His disciples that the time is coming when they will come to realize that they do not even need Him to speak in their behalf before God, because "the Father himself loves you." Once the cosmic truth of this metaphysical mystery has enlightened the soul, it also at once engulfs all that we have heard or envisioned regarding the Pattern and the Power that was in Christ. And our level of acceptance, understanding, and appreciation of what His self-sacrifice could mean to us personally is also raised to another level of superconscious awareness in ethical-spiritual terms.

Exoterically, then, we are saved by a human Sacrificial Lamb (i.e., Jesus of Nazareth crucified); and esoterically we are saved by perceiving Jesus as the Cosmic Pattern, and the Christ Consciousness in Him is that Eternal Power that can empower us at last to accept the ultimate challenge He offers us: "If any want to become my followers, let them *deny themselves* and take up *their* cross and follow me."[99] Jesus "saves" humankind, as such, by showing us—by being—the Pattern; but we must continue to demonstrate the Pattern through the same Power that was within Him. It makes perfect spiritual sense, then, that in John's Gospel (8:12), Jesus says, "*I* am the light of the world," and that in Matthew's Gospel (5:14), Jesus says, "*Ye* are the light of the world"!

Moreover, here is something else very challenging to ponder. Though religious tradition through the concept of the Trinity has directly associated Jesus of Nazareth with the idea of the redeeming Advocate, the Gospel of John enables us to perceive the vital link between the sustaining Advocate as *Spirit* and "the Father [Who] Himself loves you." For in that Gospel two astounding things are made clear. One is that we are not intended to hold on to the "apron strings" of Jesus as Redeemer: "It is to *your* advantage that I go away, for if *I* do *not* go away, the Advocate, will not come to *you*." (John 15:7) In gnostic terms this means that Jesus did not come to save humankind, as much as He came to show humankind *how to be saved!* And, again, as if to summarize all this, Jesus tells us that "when he [the Advocate, the *Holy Spirit*] comes, he will prove the world *wrong* about sin and righteousness and judgment . . . "[100] This should give us all much to ponder.

But, finally, because "the Father himself loves you," the manifestation of the Christ Consciousness in Jesus of Nazareth is in fact a gift. And this truth that it is indeed a *gift* is stated by Jesus in a chapter and verse not too far away from John 3:16 ("God so *loved* the world . . . "): "If you knew the *gift* of God, and who it is that is saying, 'Give me to drink' you would have asked *him*, and *he* would have given *you living* water" (John 4:10; italics added). The reality of Jesus as a gift to the human race has the power to inspire us to develop feelings of deep and everlasting gratitude to the Giver of the gift, convicting and unbearable shame for ignoring the gift for so long, and unspeakable and comforting joy for finally accepting the gift. When Jacob Needleman finally began to sense a deeper dimension of meaning to the mystery of Christianity, that somehow the immensity of the sacrifice of Christ required a response, his interviewee, Metropolitan Anthony, answered with these words:

> You ask what in yourself can respond to the sacrifice of God? But this sacrifice, as you call it, is *love.* What is the proper response to love? . . . The proper response to love . . . is to accept it. There is nothing to *do*. The response to a gift is . . . to accept it. Why would you wish to *do* anything?[101]

"I Know He Shall Rise on the Last Day"/ "He That Believeth in Me Shall Never Die"

In the first statement, Mary, sister of Martha and Lazarus, was speaking from within a traditional framework of thought—an (exoteric) "general resurrection" (John 11:24), i.e., that the "dead" actually "rise"; in the second statement, Jesus spoke of the immortality of the soul, which needs no body. That, as a general phenomenon, the so-called dead neither "rise" nor are "raised' in order to re-live is a truth that has been right before our eyes for centuries in Matthew (22:31-32) and in Mark (12:26-27) and in John (11:24, 26). But, because of bedrock but static doctrine, it has remained hidden from so many conventional "eyes" that continue to believe that every human being is essentially both soul-and-body (cf. Matthew 10:28a). Note that both Abraham and Moses were of old declared to be "dead" (Deut. 34:5-6; Hebrews 11:8, 13: "These all died . . . "), yet Jesus speaks of the God of Abraham and others in the present tense; and Moses appeared fully alive with Jesus and Elijah at the Transfiguration (Matthew 17:3). The tension, therefore, between the exoteric and the esoteric reaches its peak when we are told that those who perished in the Great Flood (or, as it were, in the *Titanic)* are still alive and expected to strive to live in other spiritual realms, as others in Christ live here in the flesh, with spiritual understanding (see p. 164, #2; esp. chapter 8, p. 197). Do you dare meditate on what all this implies about the nature of God's love? This text is accepted by some and not accepted by others as biblical proof of a realm called purgatory. Whatever else one may think, it is clear that the sufferers of the Flood were still alive, somewhere; and that God had not forgotten or forsaken them. Besides, the esoteric meaning of the idea of purgatory is not fundamentally about Roman Catholic mediation or intercession regarding not-yet-savable discarnate human beings (though Mother Church is to be revered, after all, for this "purgatorial" insight). It is, rather, symbolic of the breadth and length and height and depth of the Creator's divine love and how far the Creator will go to bring us Home. A Christian hymn refers to the unfathomably compassionate God as, "O Love that wilt not let me go." And Paul of Tarsus said:

> For this reason I bow my knees before the Father, from whom every family in heaven and earth takes its name. I pray that, according to the riches of his glory, he may grant that you may be strengthened in your inner being with power through his Spirit, and that Christ may dwell in your hearts through faith, as you are being rooted and grounded in love. I pray that you may have the power to comprehend, with all the saints, what is the breadth and length and height and depth, and to know the love of Christ that surpasses knowledge, so that you may be filled with all the fullness of God.[102]

Learning from Moses and the Prophets/ "Though One Rise from the Dead"

Parable and mystery as two layers of spiritual understanding are always intimately related. Every parable is potentially a gateway for the revelation of a mystery; and every mystery is actually what one "sees," should one pass from a lower to a higher plane of understanding. Here, the mystery is especially important in light of a famous theologian's remark that Christianity stands or falls on the basis of the authenticity or inauthenticity of the resurrection of Jesus Christ.[103] Briefly, the parable (Luke 16:19-31) tells us about a postmortem encounter of the patriarch Abraham with a rich man, now in utterly hellish misery due to his callous earthly treatment of a poor man. Abraham is implored to send the poor man now residing in a heavenly place ("Abraham's bosom," KJV) to warn the rich man's brothers not to end up where he is.

But Abraham says something that should prove quite shocking to those whose sensibilities are only concerned with being resurrected to Eternal Life. Abraham tells him that his brothers have already heard the Divine Message through Moses and the prophets; and that even the miraculous reappearance of the poor man to warn the rich one's family would do no good. Abraham said, "If they do not listen to Moses and the prophets, neither will they be convinced even if someone rises from the dead."[104]

Do you see the relation between this mystery and the foregoing one? Few Christians have seen that the same statement could, therefore, apply to the conventional belief in the so-called resurrection of Jesus Himself! Indeed consider what human beings have done since the miracle of Jesus' "rising from the dead." Wars, class struggles, caste systems, slavery, sexism, etc.! Were they—have we—really been convinced at the level that so many of us profess? We need to ponder what Dostoevski said about "*miracle,* mystery, and authority."[105] Thus a resurrection of Jesus or anyone else has not been ultimately convincing for millions as an ongoing inspiration for cultivating the holy life. For it is only the living out (by example) of the spiritual values of the sages and the prophets that can do that. Jesus proved this when He said, "If I am not doing the works of my Father, *then do not believe me.*"[106] The souls of men and women—and children—are influenced by miracles only in the short run; in the long run they are decisively influenced by living, ethical-spiritual examples of what they have been taught. In the entire stretch of human history, I do not believe there has ever been a more powerful and inspiring miracle than to discover that an apparently extraordinary human being, ethically and spiritually, is in fact what he or she seems to be.

Space will not allow for an elaboration of so many other instances of the twofold nature of Scripture. In the ones given above, do notice that oftentimes the outer meanings and the inner meanings of spiritual teachings appear side by side. Whether in esoteric or exoteric form they all have radically deep spiritual significance for the nature and destiny of the soul.

This chapter closes with a fervent wish that you will resolve to examine for yourself the actual Scriptural passages included that contain such nuggets of gnosis. These nuggets can also be helpful to Study Groups interested in contemplative and meditative readings not only from the Jewish and Christian traditions but those of other religious traditions East and West.

For in the individual effort to move from a simplistic and uninformed faith, some have dived into deep waters without their spiritual life jackets. Professing to have gained wisdom, they do not realize that without a solid foundation in the richness of humankind's cumulative, sacred oral and written heritage, it is quite easy to confuse the mere assimilation of occult information with spiritual illumination. Putting aside, therefore, one's quite understandable hypersensitivity toward systems of religious authority and, instead, letting the various sacred Scriptures speak for themselves to you requires an act of great courage. It is rather ironic that it took, perhaps, Europe's most notorious atheist to tell us that "more than having the courage of one's convictions is to have the courage to change one's convictions" (Nietzsche); but more than having the courage to change one's convictions is for one to make sure one knows and understands that from which one is changing and into what one is changing.

Thus when we go back and rediscover what was originally there in our own respective religious heritages, from which so many interested in the esoteric truths have come, it is often found that the baby has been thrown out with the bath water; and that hidden within the tradition one has left is a treasury of wisdom[107] also left behind, but something that could have helped one move on more easily—more comfortably—in spirit and in truth.

A Gnostic Mystery: Peter the Rock and the Rock as Christ

A simple spiritual pun has become over many centuries the source of ardent controversy regarding the meaning that the speaker, Jesus, intended. When Jesus praises Peter and notes that God the Father has directly revealed to him who Jesus really is, Jesus adds these words: "And I tell you, you are Peter [Gk. *Petros*], and on this rock [Gk. *petra*] I will build my church, and the gates of Hades will not prevail against it. I will give you the *keys* of the kingdom of heaven, and whatever you bind on earth will be bound in heaven, and whatever you loose on earth will be loosed in heaven."[108]

The Roman Catholic Church has insisted throughout its history that this is a valid and authentic affirmation of Jesus' intention to ordain that Peter assume the papal—and universal—leadership of all subsequent Christian communities. That ordainment also includes the authority of all subsequent popes to act in place of Christ on earth regarding matters of faith and morals that might affect the destinies of human beings ranging from rulers to ordinary citizens, from priests, monks, nuns, and all other members of the Christian church at large.

Protestant churches, to the contrary, generally insist that the "rock" that matters here is not really Peter himself, but the content of Peter's own words (i.e., the Petrine Declaration): "You are the Messiah [in Hebrew; *Christ* in Greek], the Son of the living God" (Matt. 16:16). In a word, the endurance and invincibility of the Church Universal depends on its faithful recognition of Jesus as the messianic "Rock" of Ages. While we cannot dogmatically claim to be able to turn back the clock and be sure what Jesus really meant, it is valuable to ponder the fact that the Protestant view is in harmony with two very important spiritual prophecies regarding God's ultimate intentions for Israel and for everyone else.

First, the "Rock-as-Christ-and-not-Peter" and/or "Christ-as-the-Rock-that-is-not Peter-the-Rock" is in essential harmony with the original calling of Israel not to be an empire, or even a nation, in the modern nationalistic sense of the word. Indeed scholars have aptly noted that Israel herself is not even listed in her own Table of Nations in the Hebrew Scriptures (Tanakh)! Instead, this is what God told Moses he was to say to Israel in terms of her ultimate spiritual destiny *in* the world: " . . . you shall be for me *a priestly kingdom* and a *holy* nation" (Exodus 19:6; italics added). This almost incredible statement, that would be a radical spiritual-communal goal for any people, was to become a part of the same vision seen in the Epistle of Peter: " . . . ye are . . . a royal priesthood, a holy nation . . . " (I Peter 2:9) Although it is not certain to what extent we can associate the apostle Peter with the Epistle of Peter, the presence of this theme there is highly indicative.

Second, the "Rock-as-Christ-and-not-Peter" interpretation is in essential harmony with the vision of the prophet Jeremiah, when he spoke of a new covenant that God would make with Israel:

> . . . this is the covenant that I will make with the house of Israel . . . I will put my law within them, and I will write it on their hearts; and I will be their God, and they shall be my people. No longer shall they teach one another, or say to each other, "Know the Lord," for they shall all know me, from the least of them to the greatest . . . [109]

Your Attitude and the Keys to the Kingdom of God

Whatever else experiential faith may be said to be, it is the simplest initial spiritual response to the presence of the Divine in human life. Even the little baby in his/her crib who looks up at a human mother is commencing to look into the face of God under the form of that loving and hopeful mother. Although the poet Alfred Joyce Kilmer (1886-1918) was right to say that "only God can make a tree," it is also true to say that of all the wonders that God has made it is you and I, male and female, who most exquisitely reflect in uniquely composite form the image of God *(imago dei)*. As infants, you and I began our journey of faith in the arms of our mothers—and bilaterally, though not as often initially—in the arms of our fathers. More often than not, our parents hoped that you and I would increase "in wisdom and stature, and in favor with God and [humankind]" (Luke 2:52). And even now, you and I must eventually maintain, or return to, but certainly nurture a childlike faith in the Eternal Mind in order to continue to have access to and to receive God's amazing saving grace. But there is a persistent paradox here. It consists in the fact that while it would seem that we had, eventually, to cast aside our childhood faith as something childish, the fully functioning spiritual man or woman really needs to retain that childhood faith, while at the same time learning more realistically to face the challenges of adulthood.

Psychologists of religion know that this paradox can engulf both the claims of atheism and theism. For the former, Sigmund Freud could claim that childhood reminiscences reflect the neurotic urge of individuals to return to our mothers' wombs as an expression of the desire to escape reality (the Reality Principle). Add to this the childish desire to escape the shock of suffering and dying by remaining bonded to the prenatal bliss of our mothers' wombs (the Nirvana Principle). But it has also been noticed that Jesus of Nazareth urges us to take on the very attitude of a little child as the one indispensable attitudinal key to salvation and without which there is absolutely no hope for entering the Kingdom of God (Mark 10:15).

Paradoxically, therefore, both Freud and Jesus are right, only because there is the necessity here to distinguish the reality of childishness (I Corinthians 13:11) and the reality of childlikeness (hence Mark 10:15). Childlikeness (for Jesus) is synonymous with humility, sincerity, simplicity and especially vulnerability (a term which will recur later). Childishness, on the other hand, is synonymous with selfishness, self-delusion, self-pity, self-protectiveness, and self-indulgence.

In summary, the hidden meaning of the keys to the Kingdom of Heaven that Jesus promised to Peter thus requires a twofold realization. First, it refers to the priority of your having a thoroughgoing attitude of childlikeness (humility, sincerity, simplicity, etc.) before God, in order for you to be worthy of receiving those keys. And this is true even while we are free to continue to have an attitude of dignity before other human beings. This point cannot be stressed too often. The use of the word *keys* and not *key,* as though it were one key to the understanding of all things, is appropriate since, as the saying goes, a single key that fits all locks usually turns out to be a false key.

Second, the word *keys* refers to something that I do not believe has occurred to those who are more interested in ecclesiastical authority than in personal growth through the guidance of the Holy Spirit of Truth (John 14 and 16). That "something" is what Jesus called "the mysteries of the Kingdom of Heaven." Jesus mentioned this to His inner circle of disciples,[110] and it was not intended to refer to Peter's unique leadership of the vast church bureaucracy that was later to engage the minds of so many of the Christian churches. The vital signal of the spiritual connection between the keys and the mysteries that transcend bureaucratic ecclesiastical tradition is contained in the very same passages above. They happen to add that "whatever you bind on earth will be bound in heaven, and whatever you loose on earth will be loosed in heaven" (Matt. 16:19, 18:18). For this is Jesus' affirmation of one of the timeless cosmic spiritual principles of practically all the esoteric traditions known to humankind: "As above, so below"![111]

The wonder of this statement is that it has Kabbalistic kinship with the mysteries found in the New Testament itself; and it is also intimately related to Jesus' expression of impatience with the *exoteric* naiveté of Nicodemus (as a "teacher of Israel") who, Jesus thought, should not have been confused about the mystery of rebirth as reincarnation.[112] But the mystery does not involve the typical exercise of priestly monopoly of the knowledge of sacred things in the dogmatic or in the liturgical sense. Rather it is a knowledge that begins with a small inner circle of the friends of Jesus and expands outward, eventually to encompass a gradually and variously receptive popular audience of blessed believers who have not yet seen.[113] In Peter's case, you have to take into account his process of growth both in relation to his tension with Paul of Tarsus over circumcision and the vision of universal love that God gave him about making false distinctions concerning what is clean or unclean in spiritual terms.[114]

But, later, it is in the very epistle attributed to Peter that certain mysteries do appear. This means that Jesus in the long run did indeed keep His promise to Peter in terms of the understanding of the "keys" above. For here are some examples of the mysteries of the Kingdom found in the Epistle of Peter:

(1) The Creator's wish is that no soul will be lost (II Peter 3:9; John 3:16-17). This should immediately make us aware that the Creator must have made arrangements for souls not ready to enter into Paradise after any one lifetime opportunity to have more than a one-life chance to come to the knowledge (gnosis) of the truth.

(2) The Creator's love is bottomless, in that even those who died in the great Flood (or who in their incarnate histories missed out on the opportunity for gnosis) can yet have the opportunity to follow the example of Jesus in other spiritual dimensions (I Peter 3:18-20, 4:6). If this is not "Amazing Grace" or "Love Divine, all loves excelling," what is?

(3) The Creator's will is that the "Church" be composed

of persons who each know themselves to be in a royal, holy, priestly state of spiritual consciousness in fulfillment of the destiny given to ancient Israel (I Peter 2:9; Exodus 19:6). This state of spirituality corresponds both to the call of Israel to become a holy priesthood, or community of priests, to the prophecy of Jeremiah (31:31-34), and to the words of Jesus Himself that the time had come to worship the Creator "in spirit and in truth" (John 4:24).

(4) The Creator's power is so great that even after aeons have elapsed, and it should happen that "the heavens will pass away" or be "dissolved," the cycle of renewal will continue (II Peter 3:10, 12, 13); so that even the spiritual states of "death" and "hell" will be no more (Revelation 20:14; *esoterically,* here and in Matthew 2:11: "fire" symbolizes Agape, the Creator's abysmal love).

These are some of the keys that Jesus gave to Peter (and to us, probably via Peter's own disciples, who gave us the books, the "Epistle[s] of Peter"). These keys, therefore, have little to do with ecclesiastical keys of control over the Sons and thc Daughters of God. This is indeed why Jesus uttered another statement which has yet to resound in the minds and hearts and souls of millions, clergy and laity: "But you are not to be called rabbi, for you have one teacher, and you are all students. And call no one your father on earth, for you have one Father—the one in heaven."[115]

Endnotes

1. For the heart as the source of moral evil, see Mark 7:21-23.

2. No less than sixteen characteristics of Gnosticism are noted by the scholar, T.P. van Baaren; for a convenient listing, see Erwin M. Yamaguchi, *Pre-Christian Gnosticism: A Survey of the Proposed Evidences* (Grand Rapids, Michigan: Baker Book House, 1983), pp. 14-15. For a brief but perceptive

commentary on those sixteen items of "Van Baaren's List," see Geddes MacGregor, *Gnosis: A Renaissance in Christian Thought* (Wheaton, Illinois: The Theosophical Publishing House, 1979), chapter 4. For a convenient readable summary of "Gnosticism and Neo-Gnosticism" or "Gnosticism Today?" see David R. Fideler, "The Passion of Sophia: An Early Gnostic Creation Myth," in the first issue of *Gnosis: A Journal of the Western Inner Tradition* (Fall/Winter, 1985), pp. 16-22; also Vanessa Weber, "Modern Cults and Gnosticism: Some Observations on Religious and Totalitarian Movements," chapter 2 of David A. Halperin, ed., *Religion Sect and Cult* (Boston, Mass.: John Wright/PSG Inc., 1983). For the advanced reader, it is hard to surpass the skill and insight of Ioan P. Couliano (tr., Hillary W. Wiesner), *The Tree of Gnosis: The Untold Story of Gnostic Mythology from Early Christianity to Modern Nihilism* (HarperSanFrancisco, 1992).

3. Gnosticism is truly ageless in the larger scheme of earthly religious experience, should one consider the wisdom of the sages, both East and West. Much of Western scholarship prefers to view it as a movement no earlier than the first three centuries A.D. A brief scholarly and quite readable summary of its origins, nature, and issues is presented by Charles W. Hedrick, "Gnosticism: The Religion of the Alien God," *The Fourth R* (November 1990), pp. 1-7. Others, West and East, say that as a spiritual disposition it reaches far into the time before Christ (even into pre-Christian Judaism); and especially if *jnana-yoga* (India's classical form of *gnosis,* earlier than the sixth century B.C.) is taken into account. The reader should note that the (English) *kno*wledge and the (Greek) *gno*sis both have common origins in the Hindu (Sanskrit) word *jna*na, that is, (mystical intuitive) *knowledge.*

4. The relation of Love and Wisdom can be seen as analogous to that of energy and matter in the formula of Einstein (see Jon Robertson, *The Golden Thread of Oneness,* p. 30). Love is the divine energy that keeps the universe in harmony; and Wisdom, the material manifestation of the best behaviors and courses of action in all worlds; but ultimately they are spiritually coinherent. I have also referred to Love and Wisdom in other ways in this work.

5. No less than seven times, what the Eternal One did was conceived to have been "good"; see Genesis 1:4, 10, 12, 18, 21, 25, 31.

6. Hence, the historical-symbolic significance of the Book of Job; cf. Ecclesiastes, chapters 3 and 6.

7. Note the words of Jesus at the end of His exoteric (Matthew 22:30)/ esoteric (Matthew 22:31-32) rebuttal to the Sadducees: "You are wrong . . . " (Matthew 22:29); " . . . you are quite wrong" (Mark 12:27); see pp. 155-156 in this book. How many clergymen have asked themselves just why "the crowd . . . were astounded at his teaching," if Jesus was not saying that a general resurrection was not necessary.

8. See "Schuon's *The Transcendent Unity of Religions:* Pro," *JAAR* (Dec. 1976), p. 723.

9. Richard Drummond, *Unto the Churches* (Virginia Beach, Virginia: A.R.E. Press, 1978), p. 73. Italics added.

10. There are also gnostic insights in Matthew, Mark, and Luke. Geddes MacGregor, *op. cit.,* p. 18, note #2, notes that Clement of Alexandria "put forward a 'true *gnosis*' against the 'false *gnosis*' of the heretics. He called his perfected Christian 'the gnostic' and denied to the heretics the right to the name." Clement's views are admirably treated by Salvatore R.C. Lilla, *Clement of Alexandria: A Study in Christian Platonism and Gnosticism* (Oxford University Press, 1971). Unlike Clement, I think that some of his "heretics"

deserve to be called "gnostic Christians" in contrast to those, like Clement himself, whom I have called "Christian gnostics" in this book. Drummond allows the term "Christian Gnostics" for both groups above, but sees worthy of criticism "some of the Christian Gnostics for a generally negative view of the world of matter," *op. cit.*, p. 71; see also "The Christian Gnostic Myth: A Model Summary," p. 126 in this book. The highly learned Church Father, Origen, and other Church Fathers were *anti*-gnostic in the face of false pagan gnosis; but that a few of those Fathers, as Christians, were themselves also gnostic in orientation was largely ignored in subsequent history.

11. For a brief, credible summary of what happened back there after the resurrection, see Father Sylvan, in Jacob Needleman, *Lost Christianity*, pp. 194-195.

12. For general Christian readers who may wish to explore the foregoing *gnostic* issues in quite readable sources, see Elaine Pagels, *The Gnostic Gospels* (New York: Random House, 1979), pp. xix-xx, 13-15, 28-47; *The Gnostic Paul* (Philadelphia: Fortress Press, 1975); Geddes Macgregor, *Gnosis;* and Drummond, *Unto the Churches*, pp. 59-76, especially p. 70ff.

13. Father Sylvan, in Needleman, *op.cit.*, p. 195; italics added. Father Sylvan's subtle distinction also applies to the dialogue between East and West (p. 143). Like MacGregor (see endnote #3 above), he also commentates with keen insight on several key doctrines of the dualistic gnostics (pp. 196-207).

14. The use of the word *gnostic* in general and as a descriptive adjective in the phrase "gnostic Christians" means that, among such, there were those who thought that the sufferings of Jesus were all illusory; that they could not be held accountable for their sexual behavior, and that only a limited number of souls could finally escape the astrodome of darkness, ignorance, and death.

15. Described by one critic as something for "the religious and mystic mind," I have read no better source telling where the Gnostics were really "coming from," in terms of how very disturbed they were with the nature of earthly existence, than Jacques Lacarriere's *The Gnostics* (tr., Nina Rootes, San Francisco, California: City Lights Books, 1989).

16. The reader might find it interesting to consider what follows in comparison to the extremely important chapter on Creation (reflecting Edgar Cayce), entitled "Philosophy," in Thomas Sugrue's *There Is a River*, pp. 305-322. Note that the words "Certain souls became bemused with their own power and began to experiment with it" (p. 310) can be symbolically related to other themes, such as (1) the "devolution" of the Great Chain of Being; (2) the "Error" of Sophia and her arrogant son (Yaldabaoth), who thought he was God; and (3) the rebellion of Satan and his angels (the "War in Heaven," Revelation 12:7-9).

17. Generally, it was not conceived among Gnostic Christians either that every soul possessed a spark of Eternal Light or that everyone could be saved. Such Gnostics could always point to Matthew 7:14: "For the gate is narrow and the way is hard, that leads to life, and those who find it are few . . . "

18. According to Hans Jonas, a well-known expert on Gnosticism, "the systems compounded everything—Oriental mythologies, astrological doctrines, Iranian theology, elements of Jewish tradition, whether biblical, rabbinical or occult, Christian salvation-eschatology, Platonic terms and concepts . . . " (*The Gnostic Religion*, 2nd ed., rev., Boston, Mass.: Beacon Press, 1963), p. 25. Comments on Jonas and an allusion to the Buddhist element are in Pagels's *The Gnostic Gospels, op cit.*, pp. xxi, xxx-xxxi.

19. Dualistic (Spirit is good; matter—the entire manifest universe—is evil). In this group some (especially early Church Fathers, such as Irenaeus, Clement of Alexandria, and Hippolytus) have placed Valentinus, a teacher in Rome; Marcion, an ascetic leader; and Basilides, a teacher in Alexandria (Drummond, *Unto the Churches, op. cit.*, p. 64). Although both Drummond and Pagels have noted the unique place of Valentinus and/or the Valentinian gnostic system, Drummond and Fideler emphasize Valentinius's association with the text, the *Gospel of Truth* (p. 67ff.), a text which might well be worthy of canonization; and Pagels, *The Gnostic Gospels*, p. 31, refers to Valentinian Gnosticism not only as "the most influential and sophisticated form of gnostic teaching, and by far the most threatening to the church," but also one that "differs essentially from dualism," emphasizing "the oneness of God." On Valentinus, also see Stephan A. Hoeller, "Valentinus: A Gnostic for All Seasons" (*Gnosis: A Journal . . .*), pp. 23-26.

20. It should become increasingly apparent that in my use of the formula "Gnosis = Agape + Sophia," I am not in contradiction to Paul, insofar as *agape* has absolute priority since it is the essence of *gnosis;* cf. I Corinthians 13:2.

21. Esoterics are not inclined to accept a metaphorical meaning of John 3:3; see the double meaning of the words "born again" in my article, "Reincarnation and Christianity," *World Faiths Insight* (February 1988), especially pp. 17-26 and 57.

22. See, e.g., Harvey Humann, "The Great Heresy," *Venture Inward* 5:4 (July/August 1989), pp. 18-21.

23. Drummond, *Unto the Churches, op. cit.*, p. 60.

24. MacGregor, *Gnosis, op. cit.*, chapter 5, especially pp. 53-56.

25. It is noteworthy that the phrase "a parallel claim" with reference to the rise of the Gnostics also appears in *The Common Catechism* (eds., Johannes Feiner and Lukas Vischer, New York, N.Y.: The Seabury Press, 1975), p. 23. As it was, faith aimed "to give hope" to humankind, and *gnosis* aimed "to give direction to [its] thinking" *(loc. cit.)*.

26. See Drummond, *Unto the Churches, op. cit.*, p. 59.

27. Luke 12:48.

28. Matthew 13:10-11; Mark 4:10-11; Luke 8:9-10. Clement of Alexandria used these verses of Scripture (among others) in his treatment of *gnosis;* see Lilla, *Clement of Alexandria, op. cit.*, p. 147.

29. For example, I Cor. 2, especially 3:2; cf. Heb. 5:12-14.

30. I Cor. 8:1; Romans 11:6. The seer, Edgar Cayce, also included the role of grace in his readings: e.g., 987-4 (here: "ye *grow* in grace . . . "); it is also linked to the "fruits of the spirit of truth," corresponding to Galatians 5:22-23; other indications are readings 2977-2, 2936-2, 3138-1, 3003-1, 3684-1, and 2828-4.

31. The "Kingdom of God" as used by Jesus of Nazareth refers both to God's eternal sovereignty in all universes and their related spiritual dimensions *and* to a state of spiritual consciousness that corresponds to what has been called "heaven"—hence the phrase "the Kingdom of Heaven" *and* His saying "The Kingdom of Heaven is within you" (Luke 17:21 KJV).

32. II Timothy 1:12.

33. Although "faith" in Clement is rather complex, its relation to gnosis is quite harmonious; and it is, as I seek to demonstrate throughout this work, inseparably related to the esoteric interpretation of Scripture; see Lilla, *Clement of Alexandria, op. cit.*, pp. 136-142, 154f.

34. Act II, Scene 2, lines 43-44.

35. That is, for most Western esoterics today, the mysteries going back to ancient Egypt and ultimately to a lost continent called Atlantis. This matter will not be discussed in this present volume.

36. The "gnostic spirit," of course, refers to that restless but positive hunger within that drives you to ask, to seek, to knock, regarding both your life needs and the perception of things that Paul of Tarsus calls "the depths of God." But it is the *spirit of gnosis* ["the Spirit of truth" (John 14:17) that requires "anointment" (John 20:22) in order for us to receive "the Spirit that is from God, so that we may understand . . . " (I Corinthians 2:10, 12)]

37. New York, N.Y.: HarperCollins, 1994.

38. One of Morgan's most intriguing moments in the book is her allusion to how the Aboriginals viewed the person of Jesus of Nazareth; see *ibid.*, p. 126.

39. See Parrinder's *Upanishads, Gita and Bible*, chapters 3 and 8.

40. Pagels, *The Gnostic Gospels, op. cit.*, pp. 127, 172; note #33.

41. Proverbs 14:12, 16:25.

42. Wisdom of Solomon 3:1.

43. John 8:32, 16:13. Italics added. The former verse influenced decisively the thinkers Tolstoy and Mahatma Gandhi. Knowing that so many befuddling concepts of God existed, Gandhi said that if he had to make a choice between God and Truth, he would choose Truth. For him (and others, no doubt) pursuing the Truth can only lead to the Reality of the One True God.

44. More than one seeker with the "spirit of gnosis" has continued to be fascinated in this regard by the words of Jesus to His disciples: "I still have many things to say to you, but you cannot bear them now. When the *Spirit of truth* comes, he will guide you into all the truth" (John 16:12-13). Italics added.

45. See John 3:3, 5 (RSV) and the word *above* in its accompanying gloss; also Beane, "Christianity and Reincarnation," *op. cit.*, pp. 21-22.

46. In Hinduism and Buddhism this tradition is called "The Doctrine of the Two Truths."

47. On *perceiving* see especially Mark 4:12, which completes v. 11. There is indeed a Buddhist parable of the "Lost Son," which corresponds (but with significant and instructive differences) to the Christian parable of the "Prodigal Son" (Luke 15:11-32); see Wm. Theodore de Bary, ed., *Sources of Indian Tradition* (New York, N.Y.: Columbia University Press, 1964), pp. 162-166.

48. See John 14:12; Hebrews 6:1-3.

49. For an example of another "mystery," see pp. 159-165 in this book; esp. p. 163: "As above, so below."

50. Spiritual androgyny here does not refer to physical bisexuality per se, but is rather a symbol of the soul's radical spiritual communion with God in a gnostic sense: a high integration (in degrees) of male and female forces, values, and behaviors.

51. See my article, "Christianity and Reincarnation," *op. cit.*, p. 26, note #2.

52. "Karma-Nemesis is a synonym of Providence, minus design . . . it is not therefore Karma that rewards or punishes, but it is we who punish ourselves." H.P. Blavatsky (*The Secret Doctrine*, Vol. II), cited in Beane, "Karma and the Law of Love," p. 39.

53. See I Corinthians 3:16, 17; 6:19; cf. John 2:19.

54. See I Corinthians 2:6-13, 13:1-13; and chapter 7.

55. See Hebrews 8:11-13; cf. 8:5; see also p. 176 and chapter 3 in this book.

56. I Corinthians 13:12 KJV; NRSV states, "for now we see in a mirror [or 'in a riddle'], dimly."

57. See Colossians 1:16, 2:2; Romans 8:38-39; and chapter 9.
58. John 16:13; cf. Isaiah 30:20-21.
59. See, e.g., Matthew 11:11-15; cf. 13:13-17.
60. Matthew 10:26.
61. Acts 1:12-14, 2:2-12.
62. For example, the human vocal system's traumatic response to becoming a medium of divine power (the Holy Spirit); temporary (but positive) angelic possession; an inexplicable (miraculous) mass psychic phenomenon, etc.
63 . W.C. Beane, *Myth, Cult, and Symbols in Śākta Hinduism* (Leiden, The Netherlands: E.J. Brill, 1977), p. 244 and note #97.
64. John Van Auken, *Edgar Cayce's Approach to Rejuvenation of the Body* (Virginia Beach, Virginia: A.R.E. Press, 1996), p. 81.
65. Pagels, *op. cit.*, p. 134; see also Matthew 10:24-25; cf. Colossians 1:19 and Ephesians 3:19, where what Paul says of Jesus, Paul also says of us! Martin Luther, in a rather non-gnostic but certainly a sincere moral sense, also said that every Christian was to become a "Christ" to his or her neighbor.
66. John 17:5, 22; cf. 1:14.
67. Earthling Faith Domergue (Dr. Adams) being responded to by alien Jeff Morrow. Screenplay by Franklin Coen and Edward G. O'Callaghan; based on a story by Raymond R. Jones.
68. Matthew 9:13.
69. John 20:29. It is interesting to notice that in a gnostic spiritual perspective, the commonplace but profane remark, "Seeing is believing," contains a spiritual truth; but, at the same time, from a sacred and esoteric perspective, "believing" is not necessarily the same as "seeing."
70. The "gnostic" Paul is yet frequently present, as in the alternative interpretations of Galatians 2:20, where, for instance, the verse can be translated either as "I live by faith *in* the Son of God," or "I live *by the faith of* the Son of God."
71. John 8:38. Italics added.
72. Hence, Elaine Pagel's *The Gnostic Paul* (Philadelphia, Pennsylvania: Fortress Press, 1975).
73. See Job's words, p. 147 in this book. Italics added.
74. Luke 10:23-24; 12:57; John 8:32. Italics added.
75. See Robert A. Segal, *The Gnostic Jung* (Princeton, New Jersey: Princeton University Press, 1992), especially Jung's response to Martin Buber's criticism (pp. 155-163); and Jung's own comments on being called a "gnostic" (pp. 163-166).
76. Will Herberg, *Faith Enacted as History: Essays in Biblical Theology* (Philadelphia, Pennsylvania: The Westminster Press, 1976), p. 74.
77. Job 2:9.
78. Job 16:20-21.
79. Job 23:8-9.
80. Job 42:5. Italics added. This language is reminiscent of Plato's "eye of the soul"; and it reminds us of my earlier reference to extraordinary perception in Hindu and Buddhist traditions (see notes #46 and #81). Carl Jung was a veritable expert on gnostic mystical symbolism. But his analysis of the Book of Job was too consumed by his estrangement from its portrait of what he considered an arbitrary god (Yahweh). It did not, therefore, allow him to plumb the depths of its potential for revealing the "mystery" of evil and suffering hidden in chapter 42:5, which he cites but, apparently, did not "see";

see Jung's "Answer to Job," in Campbell, *op.cit.*, p. 546.

81. To "see" the "Face of God" as Infinite Light Energy with positive, beatific consequences would require a radically advanced state of the Christ Consciousness. Krishna had to prepare the warrior Arjuna to "see" his Cosmic Glory in Bhagavadgita, chapter 11:8—"A celestial eye I'll give thee"; and in the Buddhist faith there is such a thing as the "Omniscient Eye"; see Kramer, *World Scriptures*, pp. 69, 76.

82. For a potentially meditative link between the "heart" and "seeing" as a form of knowing, there is Proverbs 23:26: "My child, give me your heart and let your eyes observe my ways."

83. Carl Sagan, *Contact*, p. 389.

84. Richard Bach, *Illusions*, p. 120; cf. Jesus on persistence vs. persecution—concerning the wish for or the dream of salvation: "the one who endures to the end will be saved" (Matthew 10:22).

85. Sagan, *op.cit.*, p. 431. In connection with Ellie's words but in a nonastronomical, spiritual sense, consider these selections from among the following biblical passages:

> Deuteronomy 30:11-14: "Surely [what] . . . I am commanding you today is [not] . . . too far away. It is not in heaven, that you should say, 'Who will go up to heaven for us, and get it for us so that we may hear it and observe it' . . . No, the word is very near to you . . . in your heart . . . "
>
> The Gospel of Thomas (in J.M. Robinson's *The Nag Hammadi Library in English*, rev. ed., HarperSanFrancisco, 1988), p. 126: "If those who lead you say . . . 'See, the kingdom is in the sky, then the birds will precede you' . . . Rather, the kingdom is inside of you, and it is outside of you."
>
> Luke 17:20-21: "The kingdom of God is not coming with things that can be observed . . . For, in fact, the kingdom of God is among [or within] you."

86. Sagan, *op.cit.*, p. 410. In the novel a multinational team ventured to Vega.

87. See Drummond's commentary on this in relation to Edgar Cayce's insights in his *Unto the Churches, op. cit.*, chapter 9; and *A Life of Jesus the Christ*, chapter 13.

88. In the Greek, "knowledgeable" is *gnostike.* For *gnosis* as used by Paul of Tarsus, and *gnostikos* and *gnostike* as used by Clement of Alexandria, see Drummond, *Unto the Churches, op. cit.*, pp. 62-63. Bear in mind that Clement was a "Christian gnostic."

89. Romans 8:9; see what for many usually turns out to be an astonishing surprise in the Bible; i.e., I Peter 3:18-20, and in special relation to Romans 8:9 see I Peter 4:6.

90. I John 1:3.

91. See Job, chapters 16, 23, and 29.

92. Romans 6:23.

93. Note the French: *avocat* (barrister, lawyer).

94. Both the Gospel of John and the Epistle to the Hebrews abound with exoteric and esoteric teachings. Compare Hebrews 9:22 with 7:11-13 and 5:1-3. For the Melchizedek-Jesus reincarnative connection, see Glenn Sanderfur, *The Lives of the Master* (Virginia Beach, Virginia: A.R.E. Press, 1988), chapter 8; and my "Reincarnation and Christianity: Problems and Prospects," *op. cit.*, p. 24; also Cayce in Drummond, *A Life of Jesus the Christ*, pp. 4, 11; cf. pp. 165, 167-168.

95. I John 2:1-2. Italics added. Here the Greek word *parakletos* is used: literally, "called to one's side, i.e., to one's aid . . . It was used in a court of justice to denote a legal assistant, counsel for the defense . . . "; but "generally, one who pleads another's cause, an intercessor, advocate . . . " *Vine's Expository Dictionary of Biblical Words*, eds., W.E. Vine, M.F. Unger, and W. White, Jr. (Nashville, Tennessee: Thomas Nelson Publishers, 1985), p. 111.

96. Italics added. Esoterically Jesus is, therefore, neither defense lawyer nor prosecutor (John 3:17; 5:45: "Do not think that I will accuse you before the Father . . . ").

97. John 5:25-29 (note v. 24); 11:25-26.

98. John 1:29. Italics added.

99. Matthew 16:24. Italics added.

100. See John 16:7-8. Italics added.

101. Needleman, *Lost Christianity*, pp. 30-33, especially p. 33.

102. See Ephesians 3:14-19; and II Peter 3:9; cf. Hosea 11.

103. This is a discouraging criterion of exoteric theology; "a pity," says Thich Nhat Hanh, *Living Buddha, Living Christ* (New York, N.Y.: Riverhead Books, 1995), p. 35, "because we can appreciate Jesus Christ as both an historical door and an ultimate door."

104. Luke 16:31. Italics added.

105. See the opening of chapter 9.

106. John 10:37 (in part). Italics added. His opponents were yet urged, though they did not believe Him, to believe in the implications of His deeds in consideration of His authenticity (10:37, in full).

107. Such is the case of devout Jews whose exposure to the mysteries of the Kabbalah has led them to rediscover a new (i.e., esoteric) dimension of depth in Judaic spirituality; for such insights, see Daniel Redwood, "The Kabbala Tradition" (Interview: Rabbi Morris Gordon), in *Venture Inward* (July/August 1992, Vol. 8, No. 4), pp. 20-22; for further reading, see Gershom Scholem, *On the Mystical Shape of the Godhead: Concepts in the Kabbalah* (New York, N.Y.: Schocken Books, 1991); and Adin Steinsaltz, *The Thirteen Petalled Rose* (New York, N.Y.: Basic Books, Inc., Publishers, 1980).

108. Matthew 16:18-19. Italics added.

109. Jeremiah 31:33-34.

110. See Matthew 13:10-13.

111. See Huston Smith, *Forgotten Truth: The Primordial Tradition* (New York, N.Y.: Harper & Row, 1977), especially chapter 4: "The Levels of Selfhood." This celestial-terrestrial correspondence is not under the exclusive control of the ecclesiastical bureaucracy of any world religion, secret order, or religious cult. We do indeed live in an "unobstructed universe."

112. See John 3:1-11. Notice the use (in verses 10 and 11) of the words *understand, know,* and *seen;* also see Matthew 17:1-13; cf. Beane, "Christianity and Reincarnation," *op. cit.*, pp. 21-22.

113. See John 20:29. Even John 20:23 is not a power ultimately intended only for the few, in that the Holy Spirit to which that authority is inseparably linked (20:22) is itself intended for all.

114. See Acts 10:1-33, especially v. 13-15; Galatians 2:11-14; and Romans 2:29.

115. Matthew 23:8-9.

7

Faith, Hope, and Love: The Gnostic Cross

The Gnostic Cross

The Meaning of the Figure

This section of the book has been so entitled for the sake of encouraging you to consider that there is an esoteric underside to the three things alone (faith, hope, love), which Paul of Tarsus says endure forever;[1] to certain key doctrinal conceptions held sacred and unalterable by many; and to other fundamental ideas whose function can take on an "experimental" meaning that crosses the boundaries of religious tradition.

At the top of the Gnostic Cross is Spirit, the Absolutely Ultimate Reality, which is the original Ground of Being and the Emanating-Source of the Pleroma (the Fullness of the Inner Realm of Eternal Light), which in turn reveals itself as Theos (God; divinity) under many forms.

At the foot of the Cross is Anthropos, the symbol of

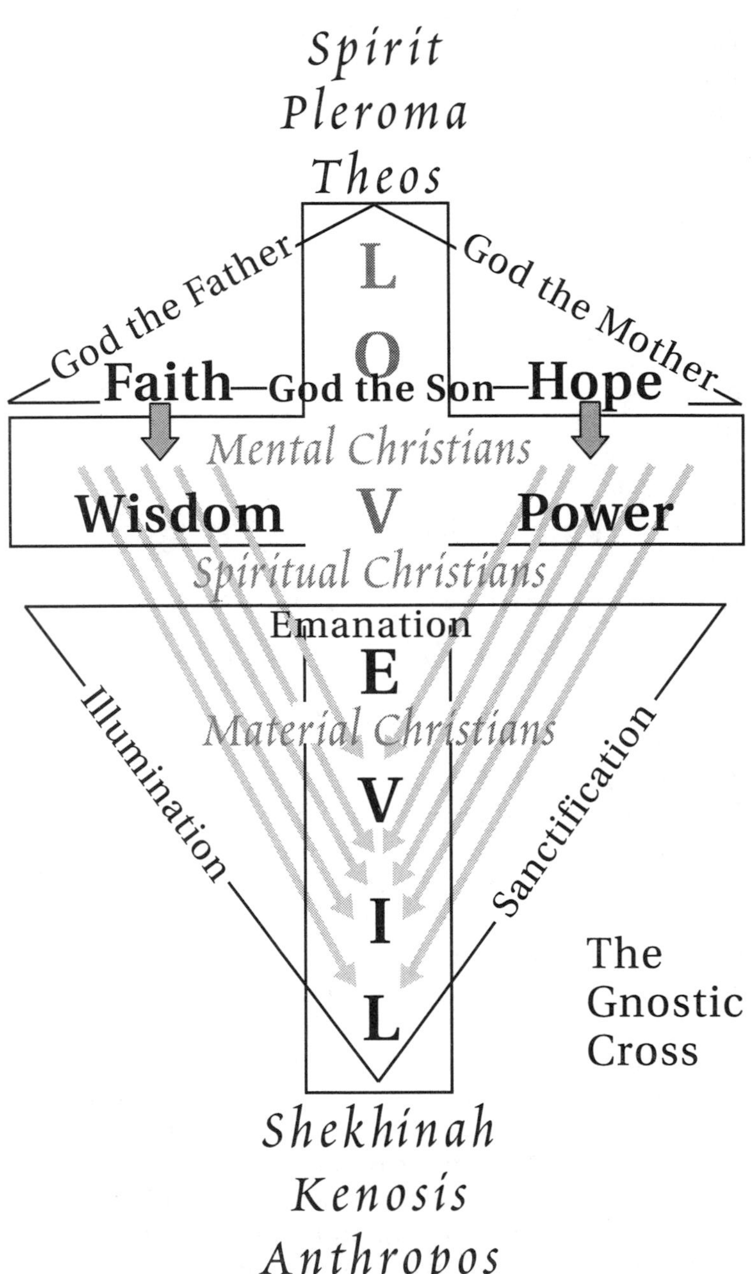
Spirit
Pleroma
Theos
L
O
V
E
God the Father
God the Mother
Faith
God the Son
Hope
Mental Christians
Wisdom
Power
Spiritual Christians
Emanation
Material Christians
E
V
I
L
Illumination
Sanctification
The Gnostic Cross
Shekhinah
Kenosis
Anthropos

God the Son incarnate; also individual and collective humankind, which corresponds to Theos, as Kenosis corresponds to Pleroma, and as Shekhinah corresponds to Spirit.

It is Pleroma which underwent a decisive Kenosis (Emptying), i.e., incarnation of its Glory into the realm of human nature and through which the Shekhinah (the "Presence" of Theos) makes truth known to humankind (Anthropos); inherently male-female souls; beings in whom the intimate (essential) and the ultimate (quintessential) dimensions of the character of the Creator meet; beings in whom the experience of cosmic (universal) values means co-creatorship and companionship with the Creator.

At the upper left end of the horizontal dimension of the Gnostic Cross stands Faith and at the right end, Hope; at the lower left end of the horizontal dimension stands Wisdom, and at the lower right end of the horizontal dimension stands Power. Hence Wisdom is the depth-dimension of Faith; and Power is the depth-dimension of Hope. These Faith-Wisdom and the Hope-Power dimensions are both "crossed" by the presence of the very essence of the God-Force (Love), which, altogether in the esoteric sense, constitute the overt and the covert, the revealed and the hidden, Reality that pervades our spiritual experience in Time and in Eternity.

The upper triangular field of the Cross takes the form of the cosmic nuclear trinity: Father, Mother, and Son;[2] the lower triangular field of the Cross takes the form of the cosmic salvific process: Emanation, Illumination, and Sanctification.[3] The two triangular fields intersect exoterically and esoterically as God the Father engendering Emanation-Creation; as God the Mother engendering Sanctification-Redemption; and as God the Son engendering Illumination-Revelation.

The Material Christians (worldly focused adherents)

are those who are ambivalent about Jesus of Nazareth's vision of God and who are strongly inclined to associate religion with personal security, economic success, and "the good life"; those who, like the early Peter, would make dwellings for God's outstanding messengers rather than perceive the meaning of God's Holy Light;[4] those who are not yet fully prepared to mean what they say when they affirm "Not my will, but Thy will be done."

The Mental Christians (denominationally focused believers) are those who are primarily focused on Jesus of Nazareth as a Savior-God, who has died in our place; and who are orientated toward the pursuit of the life of faith, hope, and love; but who are unable to perceive the esoteric dimensions of doctrines, creeds, and rituals; who cannot yet universally celebrate the sacrament-of-sacraments (the Lord's Supper) together without reservations; hence the presence of much separatism among various groups, all claiming to be committed to "One Lord, One Faith, One Baptism."[5]

The Spiritual Christians (transdenominationally focused perceivers), those who know that Jesus came not to die in our place but in our behalf; that the only enduring anointment is a spiritual one (the Christ Consciousness); that Faith is the gateway but gnosis is the pathway; the body is the only true temple of God; the Source lies ultimately beyond religious symbols; true worship is in spirit and in truth; holiness, not happiness, is life's final aim.

Emanation is spiritual creation (mere "creation" to non-Gnostic believers), the pouring forth of myriads of souls from the Maternal Womb of the Pleroma aeons before the stories of creation were told or written in the sacred books of humankind. It is the Spirit that was in souls before they became fused with matter; it is the original beaming out of sparks of cosmic creative intelligence into galactic playgrounds for adventures in Faith,

Hope, and Love; yet ultimately adventures in Wisdom, in Power, but—always—Love.

Illumination, known as revelation to mental and material Christians, is the process or the state of having one's spiritual eyes opened; to see, to know, to understand things that even prophets, priests, and rulers have not perceived—the deep things of God—things that ultimately transcend sacred words, rituals, and gestures; it is the interiorization of all that they intend; it is the mergence of Faith and reason, the marriage of Love and Wisdom. It is spiritual enlightenment—the Light of Gnosis.

Sanctification: considered among all Christians to be essential to salvation (redemption); a lifelong process of anointment by the Holy Spirit of Truth, that comes in degrees; a thing that makes one holy, dissipates the profane, lures the doubtful and the unknowing (the agnostic); encourages the fearful and disheartened, and unites the disunited; it is the way that the Creator finally lures the soul back to its point of origin for the sake of new explorations in and outside of the Pleroma.

The vertical LovEvil is the point of the intersection of sanctifying-redemptive Love of God and the astrodome of Evil incarnate and discarnate forces. The continuum of Love and Evil marks the intention of the Incarnation of the Christ-Spirit in Jesus of Nazareth to conquer Evil through the R-a-y-s-of-L-i-g-h-t penetrating it and descending to the foot of the Cross, which also marks the sanctification of souls in the world.

Love (agape) is the ethical form in which Spirit manifests itself in all dimensions in the Great Chain of Being; it is the ultimate goal of the Torah itself; it is the beginning and the end of the Creator's infinite purpose; it is the essence of the God-Force in resistance to which weird patterns of Evil have been spawned, which only Love's "Power" to endure can finally transform into the obsessingly beautiful and glorious unfolding Pattern which the Creator gave us as the very First Gift at the Nativity. As one hymn truly says, "Love came down at Christmas"!

Evil is a singular or collective force which obstructs the Good in the universe, is harmful to the image of God in human personality; can take on subtle and terrible concrete reality; and thrives on fear, alienation, violence, and death. It has not one supreme but many angelic and human personations (exoterically taken for "one" archangel: Lucifer-Belial-Satan-Iblis); yet only if the "I" (egoism) is taken out of E v "i" l can Love look backwards (e v o L) and see its final victory over spiritual darkness—over all things.

Thus the portrayed R-a-y-s-of-L-i-g-h-t falling from the Gnostic Cross mean that dualism is not the answer to the cosmic predicament (human pride, error, sin); that only an all-inclusive, holistic Love, "bathing" the body and soul of humankind in time with the beams of the Light of Eternity, can guarantee the manifestation of the breadth, depth, and height of the Creator's Grace; so that the Realm, the Power, and the Glory of the Creator will become all-in-all to all.

At the foot of the Gnostic Cross is the Shekhinah (the "Presence" of Spirit in the world, the Holy Spirit, the Holy Spirit of Truth); then there is Kenosis, the emptying of the essence (agape) of the Pleroma into the souls of men and women for the sake of co-creatorship, companionship, and compassion, for the sake of the suffering, and for sacred worlds in the making. Anthropos (the Original Being emanated into the image of the Creator) is the one (Christ) *and* the many (humankind) who correspond to Theos, as Kenosis to Pleroma, as Shekhinah to Spirit.

❊ ❊ ❊

The Faith That Becomes Wisdom

While faith is the key that opens the doors of eternity for the sake of the souls exploration of both the fact that God is and what God can do, wisdom *(Sophia)* is that aspect of Gnosis which refers to the ways in which the Holy Spirit guides the soul in its relation to this world—and other worlds. On earth, wisdom is the application of Gnosis to the resolution of problems and the fulfillment of the needs in everyday life. Thus it should come as no surprise, then, that Jesus could say, "Wisdom is vindicated by her deeds."[6] Yet faith must eventually become wisdom, just as a child cannot for too long subsist only on the milk of its mother. It is also no wonder, therefore, that wisdom is portrayed in Hebrew poetic wisdom-sayings as female.

Still wisdom does not totally replace faith, as much as it continues to absorb from faith a distinctive element that some would say reflects a certain naiveté. That naiveté is, however, the very precious element that has always accompanied it—humility. The case of the newly baptized Burmese Christian, mentioned by Agnes Sanford, starkly illustrates the nature and the association of humility with simplicity, sincerity, etc., as mentioned before. Wisdom thus encompasses humility, and wisdom is the nurturing aspect of Gnosis. It nurtures the mind and the heart through the Spirit's driving the individual soul into the wilderness of problems, relationships, and associations related to family, job, and diverse allegiances related to government, community service, and personal creativity.

But wisdom is necessarily a hard teacher. For the God-given gift of human free will is fraught with such angelic or demonic potential for good or evil. The gift is sometimes referred to as the good-inclination and the evil-inclination; but, unresolved, it is certainly what oftentimes likens us to a chariot being driven by a certain wild man, named Oedipus, to the crossroads in Thebes. Thus the soul—even as its own charioteer—needs the Eternal Divine as its Master. This image of being in control yet over*seer*ed by the Eternal Divine is presented to us in one of India's mystical scriptures, *The Katha Upanishad,* wherein:

> . . . the body is the chariot. The road over which it travels are the sense objects. The horses that pull the chariot over the road are the senses themselves. The mind that controls the senses when they are disciplined is represented by the reins. The decisional faculty of the mind is the driver, and the master of the chariot, who is in full authority but need not lift a finger, is the Omniscient Self.[7]

This image is represented as living ritual action in the classic Hindu text, *The Bhagavad-Gita.* Therein, on the battlefield, Lord Krishna is the driver of the chariot of a warrior in whose own heart wages a war between the karma of attachment and the karma of detachment. It is the latter form of disinterested involvement in Hindu gnosis that commends itself to the individual who would simultaneously be in the world, yet overcome it.

Thus the Spirit lures the mind into a host of situations ripe with opportunities for growing through temptation, gaining through suffering, and learning through entrapments. Gradually, one begins to move, for example, from being merely a mental Hindu toward a spiritual Hindu, a mental Jew toward becoming a spiritual Jew, a mental Christian toward becoming a spiritual Christian.[8] Ultimately, one gravitates from being a mere mental adherent to any particular cult or religion, toward becoming a spiritual citizen of the universe. Wisdom, then, is the extension of faith into the Realm of God for the sake of becoming in turn an extension into the realm of humankind—its daily affairs. Only an individual so nurtured by gnostic wisdom could ever survive without negative karma on Wall Street, wheeling and dealing, yet somehow primarily yearning for and yielding to the lure of eternity during some of the most concrete and entangling moments in life. Wisdom is, finally, faith's acknowledgment that it is not an end in itself but a means to a more glorious end—the experience of the even Higher Wisdom of the Creator.

The Hope That Becomes Power

As faith, then, finds its ultimate fulfillment in a state of spiritual ac*know*ledgment along the faith-wisdom continuum, hope, too, finds its ultimate fulfillment in a state of spiritual em*power*ment along the hope-power continuum. As one of the last things held back in Pandora's box, hope is naturally one of the things that Paul of Tarsus could name as having eternal value. For without hope the world would surely fall into despair and come to a tragic end. But is the loss of hope in the human heart due only to external life circumstances, thus giving rise to bad attitudes; or are bad attitudes the cause of the loss of hope, thus due to internal life circumstances?

A preeminent Catholic philosopher, Jose Pieper, author of the book *Hope and History*, shares with us some engaging insights into the nature of hope. First, he tells us, "Nobody *must* hope. One can also refuse to do so; one can refuse fundamental hope and reject it." Second, he says that all the things that happen in our lives, good or bad, do not really make up our spiritual history. Rather "the really *crucial* thing is what we ourselves make of all this!"[9] Third, we are told that though hope is inseparable from the experience of utter disappointment, it can become a source of learning.[10] Lastly, he cites a stunning statement by Gabriel Marcel, who said, "'The only genuine hope is one directed toward something that does not depend on us.'"[11] Pieper's "hope" is ultimately rooted in Divine Providence; but it is characterized by a perpetual openness "to the possibility of a fulfillment that surpasses every preconceivable human notion."[12]

My response to these insights is rather mixed. For I am convinced that, even in purely secular terms, one *must* indeed hope—even if it is the "hope to die" that can occur when one's fondest hopes have recurrently, then absolutely, failed to materialize.[13] Again, here is a peculiar but positive irony: that though in mythology hope remained tragically in Pandora's box, in Christian theology, through the vision of Jesus of Nazareth, it can remain thoroughly embedded in the human heart instead, especially if it is a human hope that has been enshrouded by God's Eternal Hope.[14] Another point to be made is that that "something" (of Marcel), for the Christ-conscious gnostic, can only be the God of Eternal Mind, through whose manifestation in Jesus of Nazareth, hope itself was finally liberated from Pandora and given to faith *(Pistis)* and love *(Agape)*.[15]

If, as the saying goes, "Hope springs eternal in the human breast," then there must be the need for us to reorientate our attitudes toward Eternal Life-circumstances (the Realm of God) for hope to spring eternally. This is for the sake of attaining the hope-against-hopelessness that Paul of Tarsus knew the Christ Consciousness causes to spring eternally.[16] Notice that Paul, in full, says that "our hope faileth not because the love of God is shed abroad in our hearts by the Holy Spirit."[17] Let us recall that where there is hopelessness there is also the absence of spiritual Power, for spiritual Power is the end of the hope-power continuum. We need not hope for what we already have the power to have or to be. Hope, like faith, for reasons ultimately hidden in the Eternal Mind, is being required of us on earth at this stage of our spiritual evolution. But we can say that whatever else hope's aim may be, it is certainly to attune us to the Ultimate Power that purifies us and enables us to endure under fire with patience.[18]

There can, therefore, be no hard work without hope; there can be no meaningful relationships without hope; there can be no parenting without hope; there can be no multicultural enrichment without hope; there can be no healing without hope; there can be no world peace without hope; there can be no Heaven without hope. We start with hope, and we ultimately end with power; but it is the power of the Holy Spirit within us that enables *(empowers)* us to be and do that which—before we "knew"—was not possible.[19]

The Centrality of Love (Agape)

One might use the word *cruciality* here instead of *centrality,* for the former is derived from the very Latin word *crucis,* which means "cross." The centrality or the *cruci*ality of love is symbolized by the position of the vertical bar of the crucifixion symbol. But it must first be remembered that before this instrument of ex*cruci*ating punishment, pain, and death is a salvation symbol, it is an unendingly lamentable tragedy in the history of humankind. Humankind must, therefore, always ask and reask itself just how the world could torture and kill a human being whose goodness was manifested so plainly for all to see![20] If goodness is not safe and cherished in any given world, it calls into question both the nature and the destiny of any given intelligent species—terrestrial or extraterrestrial! Hence stark, gruesome historical reality precedes the reflection upon the cross as a religious symbol of the human conquest of physical and moral disease, decay, and death.

Once, of course, the cross becomes a salvation symbol, then it becomes the ultimate answer to the tragedy of faithlessness and unfaithfulness, of hopelessness and despair. So it is the Creator's Eternal Love that binds together both the faith-to-wisdom and the hope-to-power dimensions of the Gnostic Cross. Love is the vital link between all these, forever joining the horizontal and the vertical dimensions of human experience, joining time and Eternity, earth and Heaven, body and Soul, mundane reality and Supramundane Reality.

Love and Gnosis

Love is, then, the *essence* of Gnosis, as Gnosis in its broadest spiritual meaning is the unified and sanctified field of the Christ Consciousness that potentially includes all the gifts (fruits) that the Holy Spirit nurtures in the human soul: "joy, peace, patience, kindness, generosity, faithfulness, gentleness, and self-control."[21] The entire attitude of distrust among theologians and clergy over the prospect that Gnosis may not be the enemy of authentic righteousness evolved because of the tendency in so many souls throughout history to claim Gnosis as their unique possession and/or to feign the possession of secret spiritual knowledge. But, more than this, such egoistic-gnostic beings often made such claims for the ulterior motive of exercising political-religious power. Whether in the form of a gnostic asceticism or a gnostic sensualism, this blight upon the prospect of a truly enlightening Gnostic Vision should not be allowed either to prevail or to close the heavens to those who are normally hungry for "solid food," not milk.[22]

The only decisive credentials which anyone who claims to be a true Gnostic can have is to possess, or to be possessed by, the Power of Love. Love, said Augustine, is the one virtue that encompasses all other virtues. However, because it is not a capacity initially full-blown or self-cultivated but a unique gift of Divine Grace, it has rarely been consistently seen in major numbers among world populations. As a gift of Divine Grace, "Love divine, all loves excelling"[23] is not really subject to any given theological or sacramental system of salvation. It resides originally and germinally in the deepest recesses of any human soul and tends to blossom with the advent of childlike humility, whether that soul be an Aborigine, or a Plato, a king, or a peasant. That Divine Grace is thus a Universal Grace and is not, therefore, mediated exclusively through a particular religion, although the Christ Consciousness that was in Jesus of Nazareth has become a worthy norm for billions—both inside and outside Christianity—by which to measure all other human incarnations of Grace.[24]

It is by the Spirit of the Creator, nonetheless, that the blossoming takes place. It is the Spirit that gives us growth.[25] Psychologist Eric Fromm was probably one of the earliest modern thinkers to become instrumental in decentralizing the idea of Divine Love (Agape) from its theological and sacramental confinement through his book, *The Art of Loving*. His final concern with love was humanistic and ethical in nature and was related to what he saw as the threat of the disintegration of the Western capitalistic system. His most despairing view was that "the disintegration of the love of God has reached the same proportions as the disintegration of the love of man."[26] Fromm confessed that he himself was not a believer in theism or the existence of a God. Nonetheless, he saw a very close connection between the quality of what the Christians call "Divine Love" or God's Agape and the (matriarchal over the patriarchal) quality of the love of mother for her child.

It may surprise some to discover that there are countless Christians who do not know of the existence of Christian love under the name of Agape. But, known or unknown, one should be less surprised to find out that the manifestation of such a quality of love (sometimes called "unconquerable good will" or "unconditional positive regard") has been so tragically absent in the behavior of so many who call themselves Christians. Yet Agape "knows" nothing of sexism, racism, or classism. Agape transcends all human boundaries and is so very magnificent and magnanimous that persons from the time of Jesus to the Quakers in our time regard Agape itself—without parapsychology—as the most exquisite "proof" that there is something truly immortal in human life (the *soul* with Agape) amid the Universe of Worlds. Concerning Jesus, then, hosts of persons have been willing to affirm with literal conviction against the bleakness of death that "it was impossible for him to be held in its power"![27]

It is finally what has been called the Christian "Hymn of Love," written by Paul of Tarsus,[28] that reveals a Realm, a Power, and a Glory so great that it is subject to challenge the followers of all the world's religions wherein or wherever there has ever been a call to care for other human beings. For example, Mahatma Gandhi was dramatically inspired by Jesus of Nazareth both because of Jesus' testimony to the Power of Truth[29] and Jesus' manifestation in the Gospels of a quality of Love upon which Paul's "Hymn" is based.

Love . . . bears all things
believes all things
hopes all things
endures all things
Love never ends . . .[30]

Love—and Forgiveness as Love's Unique Act

How often have you heard the saying "To err is human, to forgive, divine"? Though truly inspiring, the saying is only partially true. For contrary to those who say that angels possess no free will, both Scripture and tradition testify that divine beings, too, can err (e.g., the fall of Lucifer, the Adversary, Satan). And this erring on the part of beings, human[31] and divine, is due primarily to two very humbling realities: (1) that all beings, by necessity less than God, are subject to moral and spiritual error; and (2) the process of God-realization (or Christ Consciousness) entails perpetual interangelic or interpersonal relations. Such relations, therefore, involve fallible beings at various levels of being with characters bent toward either self-serving love or self-destructive hate.

There is, to be sure, something inevitably sad and glorious about both the fact and the feeling of forgiveness. Sad, in that we are so often in need of it (which may also apply to the giver of it); and glorious, because it has been given to us to exercise such a great and transforming power (which can be a unique form of release for the person forgiven).

> Who gains by being forgiven and by forgiving? The one that forgives is lord even of him that he forgives. Be ye, then, in that way of [being]—in principle and purpose—divine.[32]

What is forgiveness? Forgiveness is the act and ultimately the art of standing under, hovering over, going before, or passing beyond the effects of another's violation of one's human body, mind, or soul, through the power of Divine Love.

Here, then, "Divine" means more than transhuman; it refers to a *quality* of love that presupposes something originating in the heart of a person that ultimately originates in the heart of God. For God *is* Love.[33] Forgiveness is thus a heart-originating gesture of love on the part of an individual who tends to keep "no record [or score] of wrongs."[34] It is a gesture which can gradually, or suddenly, but certainly and finally, dissolve the sting or immense pain or hurt that a neighbor has brought upon us, intentionally or unintentionally. Of course, the latter is less difficult to forgive.

The essentially unique power of forgiveness lies in the fact that forgiveness is never really deserved. It is a loving gift, freely given by a forgiver for something that really cannot be repaid or undone; and that is why it is so very dismaying and, in the long run, redemptively disarming. When we forgive, therefore, we are performing an act contrary to all earthly reasoning and which in the end allows for no other response but acceptance or rejection. Neither denial nor bargaining can ever deal with the quality of Love's forgiveness. For this forgiveness is one of the purest imitations of the essence of God's character known to humankind—the Creator's Love. Imitation here, then, bears relation neither to metaphor nor to the value of "jewelry," but to the kind of understanding that the Christian mystic Thomas à Kempis reveals in his *Imitation of Christ:*

> He is truly great, who is great in the love of God. He is truly great, who is humble in mind, and regards earth's highest honours as nothing. He is truly wise who counts all earthly things as dung, in order that he may win Christ. And he is truly learned, who renounces his own will for the will of God.[35]

But many may still ask, "Why should I forgive?" There are some things quite seemingly unforgivable! Yet, not only should we forgive because we have already been forgiven (by family members, friends, co-workers, "significant others"—and God!), but it happens to be the universally startling nature of forgiveness that it is the only logical solution both to the forgivable and to what is sometimes called "the unforgivable." The very unforgivable nature of the thing to be forgiven is why forgiveness is its only ultimate solution. We do not fully understand the depth, the breadth, and the height of God's Divine Love[36] until we are empowered by it to love both the seemingly unlovable person and the loveless person who has committed the most unlovely act.

The irony is that without this unique act of Grace (whereby we become gracious), even a tiny hurt can increase in size, and an immense hurt can become utterly unbearable. When that happens, especially in the case of the latter, we want to deny the option of forgiveness as an act of Divine Creativity in us; and we are even subject to entertain the idea of committing acts of destruction against others; but ultimately such acts only turn out to be acts against ourselves. Irony thus becomes tragic irony when it becomes apparent that in our contemplation of destructive activity, we find ourselves employing the very same cosmic principle that creativity does, *in reverse*. We imagine that we can cancel out a hurt, a wrong, a grudge, by thoughts, words, or deeds through negative means; but that really only gives life over to more hurts, more wrongs, and more grudges in relation to those who we consider deserve to suffer.

But such a recourse only creates a vicious circle of mutual nonforgiveness, for which then, in turn, *we* need to be forgiven and em*power*ed to overcome within the deepest depths of our souls. For it is within our souls that our most sincere desire to overcome meets the All-Absorbing, Divine, Forgiving Love of the Creator.

Forgiveness is, in the final analysis, a translogical act which by its very nature has the power to negate-the-negative—the force of evil. Forgiveness has the power to create a new, positive reality with which evil cannot reckon and to which forgiveness remains a perpetual mystery.[37] For forgiveness is almost always baffling. It is baffling because it is the consummate contradiction of all the claims of human justice. Even Confucius could only say that we should "recompense kindness with kindness, and unkindness with justice." But Jesus of Nazareth fully baffles us with the words spoken during His crucifixion—a time of unforgivable violation of His body, mind, and spirit. He said, "Father, forgive them; for they *know* not what they do."[38] In these words plainly reside not only what *unknowing* (agnosis) can lead to, but also the incomparable compassion of the most Christ-conscious being who has ever appeared on the earth. In these words the vital link between Christ Consciousness, love, and forgiveness is summarized. It is Jesus' own demonstration of the ultimate capacity of a soul to forgive the unforgivable. When we reflect upon a moment like this in history, it is indeed hard to accept how anyone can doubt that we have in fact heard from Eternity. Earlier Jesus uttered other astonishing words which—in view of humankind's long hostile history—also seem to come from another dimension, another world in terms of their translogical power: " . . . I say unto you . . . resist not evil . . . "![39]

By encompassing these cosmic ethical gems, which presuppose the forgiving heart, forgiveness, therefore, covers the smallest to the largest misdemeanors known to the human race. Hence the words of Peter the Disciple: "Above all, maintain constant love for one another, for love covers a multitude of sins."[40] The idea of "covering" is associated with ancient Near Eastern ideas of atonement, but it carries with it the notion of "wiping clean" something that has been sullied or made impure. Forgiveness in the deepest spiritual sense is a gift of God, is finally an infusion of the Divine Love (Agape) into the human heart, so that it becomes a heart filled with the *Creator's* Divine Forgiving Love.

This author is convinced that Agape in its deepest and purest form requires a special anointment (or christening) by the Holy Spirit of Truth. Yet all beings are gifted with the potential for Agape by virtue of their creation in the image of God. The Fall of Adam and Eve, then, applies not to the entire human race but is a paradigm of what *can* happen, *has* happened, and *does* happen in connection with human beings who seek to become wise, or knowledgeable *(gnostike) without* the Wisdom of God.[41] Thus the Light of Agape is the same Light that "enlightens everyone."[42] That potential is intended to be nurtured in the nuclear family or through other social media of Grace (relatives, friends, cell-groups, congregations, associations). But if the Original Light is not nurtured early on because of psychologically and sociologically nuclear *explosions* in situations intended to enhance it, then the development of the inclination toward forgiveness as a divinely inspired act—and art—will fail. And where there is no forgiveness, there follows the most dramatic manifestations of an individual's potential for cumulative destructive power (evil).

In the end—in the face of evil—only forgiveness will do. The internationally renowned historian of religions, Mircea Eliade, speaking of "loving," said, "It is the only form of behavior that really enables one to cope with evil . . . "[43] Forgiveness, of course, may be temporarily rejected, but it cannot finally be forgotten. We often hear the saying, "I can forgive, but I can't forget." The truth about genuine forgiveness is that one need not forget at all. Genuine forgiveness is in the remembering *without* feeling the sting of the original act or cause of one's misgiving. Paul of Tarsus, by analogy, helps us here by asking death, "Where, O death, is your sting?"[44] Likewise, where is the sting of hurt, resentment, anger, or frustration when the heart has been saturated with the Divine Forgiving Love of the Creator? To err is both human and divine, to forgive is to become one of the peacemakers—one of the children of God.

Enshroud me with Thy Divine Protective Light;
Infuse me with Thy Holy Spirit of Truth;
Saturate me with Thy Divine Forgiving Love.

Endnotes

1. I Corinthians 13:13.

2. See Pagels, *The Gnostic Gospels,* p. 52. The reader should understand that, here and in other notes in this chapter, I am intuitively making choices among various "gnostic" options; and thereby suggesting what has for me (and may have for others) extraordinary meaning today.

3. Exoterically, respectfully, creation, revelation, redemption.

4. See Matthew 17:1-5, especially v. 4. The point is that God decided to bypass Peter's misguided material concern even "while he was still speaking," by allowing even the disciples to be "overshadowed" by "a bright cloud." Have the material Christians today yet gotten the point?

5. Ephesians 4:5.

6. Matthew 11:19.

7. Cited in Houston Smith, *The World's Religions: Our Great Wisdom Tradition* (New York, N.Y.: HarperSanFrancisco, 1991), p. 31.

8. In gnostic circles this is the paramount level of being a *pneumatic* or spirit-infilled soul; see chapter 6, p. 125 in this book.

9 . Jose Pieper, *Hope and History,* tr., Dr. David Kipp (San Francisco, California: Ignatius Press, 1994), pp. 30, 34. Italics added.

10. *Ibid.*, pp. 21, 28-30.

11. *Ibid.*, p. 24: a statement which, it appears, Marcel does not take far enough (*ibid.*, p. 28).

12. *Ibid.*, p. 112; see also I Corinthians 2:9.

13. For example, from interminable, perhaps painful, illness; although Pieper considers how one even in that situation can be partly victorious (*ibid.*, especially pp. 29-30).

14. Romans 13:7, 15:13. Commentators point out that in 15:13 it is the hope that comes *from* God, not that God is the One Who hopes.

15. I Corinthians 13:13.

16. Romans 5:5: " . . . and hope does not disappoint us . . . "; cf.; Isaiah 57:10 (RSV, NRSV).

17. Romans 5:5; in full (KJV).

18. See I John 3:3; Romans 8:24.

19. Mark 10:27.

20. See Acts 26:26: " . . . for this was not done in a corner." For a dirgeful lament on how the world could ever kill a good human being, see The Wis-

dom of Solomon 2:12-20. The reader will find it virtually impossible not to think of the exceptional character—but then the tragic *cruci*fixion—of Jesus of Nazareth.

21. Galatians 5:22.

22. See chapter 2, p. 21 and endnote #1 in this book.

23. The title of a hymn by Charles Wesley (1707-1788) and John Zundel (1815-1882); see especially verse 1.

24. For the relevance of "Jesus-with-Christ Consciousness" to other world religions, see Drummond, *A Life of Jesus the Christ,* p. 168ff.

25. I Corinthians 3:6.

26. Erich Fromm, *The Art of Loving* (New York, N.Y.: Harper & Row, Publishers, 1956), p. 87; see also pp. 54ff., 61-62; 68-69. He culminates his concern with a vision of "humanistic socialism" in his *To Have or to Be?* (New York, N.Y.: Bantam Books, 1982).

27. Acts 2:24.

28. I Corinthians 13:1-13.

29. Especially John 8:32.

30. I Corinthians 13:7-8.

31. The Adam and Eve story (especially Genesis 3) is, of course, the model of human sin/error for many.

32. Edgar Cayce reading 585-2.

33. I John 4:8. Biblical scholars sometimes worry that individuals will dangerously think that this means *Love* is God—and leave it at that! John, however also says, "Beloved, let us love one another, because love is *from* God" (4:7); cf. endnote #12 above.

34. I Corinthians 13:5 (New International Version).

35. Thomas à Kempis, *The Imitation of Christ,* tr., L. Sherley-Price (Harmondsworth, Middlesex, England: Penguin Books, Ltd., 1959), pp. 31-32.

36. Ephesians 3:14-19.

37. See John 1:5 (KJV).

38. Luke 23:34. Italics added.

39. Matthew 5:39.

40. I Peter 4:8.

41. Hence Adam and Eve's sin was not the mere desire to be *knowledgeable* as such, but to become so *without* surrender *(islam)* to the sovereignty of the Creator; cf. Qur'an 7:19-27.

42. John 1:9.

43. Mircea Eliade, *Ordeal by Labyrinth: Conversations with Claude-Henri Rocquet,* tr., Derek Coltman (Chicago, Illinois: University of Chicago Press, 1982), p. 170.

44. I Corinthians 15:55.

8

Faith, Healing, Community, and Holiness

T*he following is* not intended to be a fully detailed essay on the subject of healing. It is, instead, intended to highlight some very important concepts concerning the subject of healing as it relates to one's self-understanding within a framework of an authentic way of spirituality. The way of spirituality, as I understand it, knows no biological, geographic, political, or religious boundaries.[1] The Creator and the Creator's Universe operate only on the basis of cosmic law; and cosmic law, grounded in the Creator, knows only the inner realm of a human being's Divine Light. This is the Light that "enlightens" every one who comes into the world.[2]

The Heavens Are Open to Anyone's Need for Healing

No single religious system on the earth has a monopoly on mediating the occurrence of healing as a religious experience. For just as the oxygen we breathe as we are born is, and was, always there and used by all forms of life, human and nonhuman, the heavens have always been open to reveal the Glory of God to souls that are ready to receive it. My continual need for maintaining a radical sense of the universal interrelatedness of all humankind is symbolically reenlivened by recalling the words of a visiting country preacher who once came to my community church in Arlington, Virginia. He reminded the audience that "that moon out there is the same moon under which Abraham sat!" It was as if he were trying to tell us, to use a satellite analogy (the moon), that Abraham's upward gaze upon the moon was as a radio wave or beam of light streaking straight toward an intergenerational satellite. And that wave or beam of light, as it encountered the moon, was then transmitted downward to our present world as a spiritual signal to future generations of their sacred link to all their ancestors with whom we as a collective consciousness are linked to the Presence and the Glory of God.

Later on, I thought, it is also the same moon upon which the prehistoric being, Neanderthal, gazed during the Upper Paleolithic Age. One may, then, look back further thousands and thousands of years—even more—and encounter the shamans of various countries whom historian of religions, Mircea Eliade, called the "technicians of the sacred." And then, should one move on throughout all of human history, it would become plain that the Creator has not depended upon the missionaries of any particular religious movement to convince humankind that human illnesses can be cured through the Presence of the heavens opened.[3]

The primary function of the shamans and shamanesses was to heal. Moreover, they were known for practicing the art of out-of-body experiences. They could, therefore, travel into other dimensions to rescue souls of the sick believed to have been taken captive by demons. In summary, then, they served—and serve still—as symbols of the physical, psychical, and spiritual integrity of the community.[4] Under the influence of recent collaborations of shamans and modern physicians in Africa and elsewhere, we are now much less prone to laugh at one who, for years, was depicted by Hollywood as an eccentric and ludicrous witchdoctor. Yet it would pay for those who are still prone to laugh to seek out the very origins of the word *witch,* if they wish to "know."

It is the shaman who originally perceived the psychosomatic nature of much human illness,[5] the intimate relation between human diet and the prevention of disease, as well as the indispensable link of medicinal herbs and techniques of trance with transorganic reality—the realm of the supernatural or the realm of hidden natural potentiality. This phrase is used in remembrance of Leon E. Wright, my spiritual mentor, who had this to say about what was *really* happening when healing "miracles" have occurred:

> Cosmos admits no miracles . . . Cosmos does not violate its own integrity. In those situations where this spiritual overflow was effected, Jesus had ascended—or caused the patient to ascend—to those levels of spiritual resource commensurate with the healing involved . . . "Your faith has made you whole" [Jesus said] . . . healing . . . is contact with the deepest levels of one's own psychic outreach to higher levels of spiritual power . . . healing is . . . rigorously accomplished within the framework of cosmic law.[6]

Undoubtedly, Jesus of Nazareth represents the culmination of all the shamanic and the prophetic traditions of the tribal and the ancient Near Eastern worlds, respectively. He is even referred to in terms that remind us dramatically of the shamanic act of rescuing souls from other dimensions as a form of dramatic healing power.

> He was put to death in the flesh, but made alive in the spirit, in which also he went and made a proclamation to the spirits in prison . . . For this is the reason the gospel was proclaimed *even to the dead,* so that, though they had been judged in the flesh as everyone is judged, they might *live in the spirit as God does.*[7]

Whether, then, we begin with the tribals of the earth and pass on to the Egyptian medical genius Imhotep, the Greek god-physician Asclepios (and his temples), or to Hippocrates, and finally reach over into the Oriental systems of yogic meditation, the truth of the line from the immortal *Desiderata,* "You are a child of the universe," encompasses widespread sacred meaning.[8] For what Jesus did testifies to the great and unfathomable depth of the love the Creator has for all of us,[9] in that even death cannot separate us from God despite how unready we may be to reenter the Inner Realm of God's Eternal Light. It also remains a remarkable tribute to the shamans, past and present, that the World Health Organization has called for their medical representatives in the field to seek to collaborate with indigenous shamans in various countries to better serve those in need.[10]

It also explains why the testing of the principles of Transcendental Meditation and other mind-body interaction theory has occurred in scientific laboratories (e.g., Harvard Medical School and others)[11] with provocative positive results. Some might be disturbed at the implication that totalistic healing can occur outside or beyond what James Rush calls the "assumptive world-views" of various major religions.[12] But it is really not the idea of a Creative Cosmic Intelligence that disturbs so many, but the thought that they have to change their conception of God from that of a stern, provincial Patriarch to that of a Caring Presence ever ready to listen to any heart whose prayer echoes with humility.

No doubt it is physician Larry Dossey's research into unconventional medical territory, in relation to human and subhuman experience, that remains a germinal force in the formation of a new paradigm.[13] And it is his book *Healing Words* that is causing many to reconsider their attitudes toward the assumption of so many conventional religious persons that healing must occur only within an exclusively specific, often dogmatic religious framework. Dossey has taken by surprise, if not shocked many intellectuals by showing that there exist over 130 scientific studies on the subject of prayer; although there is no universal consensus as to the real and possible positive effects. Dossey shows us, nonetheless, how very much "the heavens are open" by contemplating that it is not simply a matter of praying, as such, but, more important, an attitude of prayerfulness that is a key to a deeper dimension of personal wellness and fulfillment.[14]

This means that there is obviously a vital link between the attitude of prayerfulness and the form of prayer earlier mentioned here as contemplative prayer. Prayer as formula is thus not necessarily prayer as *faith*. And prayer with open faith can turn the believing heart of one faith or religion toward the believing heart of another by virtue of the very presence of the prayerful attitude. Furthermore, the prayerful way of being in the world happens to increase the chances that one will eventually enter into a mode of living that has been called the contemplative life. Is this not what Jesus meant when He said, "Men ought always to pray";[15] or Paul of Tarsus, when he said, "Pray without ceasing"?[16] With keen insight, Thomas Merton, while insisting that prayerfulness is not contemplation per se, yet "a great good," puts the matter this way:

> I speak only of contemplation that springs from the love of God . . . Contemplation is the highest expression of . . . [the] intellectual and spiritual life. It is that life itself, fully awake, fully active, fully aware that it is alive. It is spiritual wonder. It is spontaneous awe at the sacredness of life, of being. It is a vivid realization of the fact that life and being in us proceed from an invisible, transcendent and infinitely abundant Source. Contemplation is, above all, awareness of the reality of that Source. It *knows* that Source . . . [17]

It may seem strange to some to hear that there is even an esoteric dimension to prayer. But there remains a mystery of God that lies hidden beneath the words of Jesus that "Your Father knows what you need *before* you ask him." (Matt. 6:8) And this is true, especially since that statement is inseparable from the affirmation that God loves us! This mystery of prayer is in part related to Merton's insistence on the fact that, with God, we are encountering "neither a 'what' nor a 'thing' but a pure '*Who*.'"[18] But it is also esoterically related to the fact that "individuals—if their *thought* (prayer, hope, wish, dream, fear) is amazingly strong—can, in and of themselves, produce such results . . . Many Masters have known this [e.g., Jesus]. Many know it now."[19] Prayer, then, to a God who already knows what your need is can only be *a ritual gesture* that the soul employs in its endeavor to reinforce its conviction that what is already true is most certainly true. But, of course, there *are* those who would seek to cajole God, to coerce God, to beg God, even—probably—to bore God!

Moreover, there are those who insist, for example, that if one does not end one's prayer with the words, "In the name of Jesus," nothing significant will come to pass. In fact a letter to the editor of a weekly national magazine some years ago, in response to the question, "Does God hear Jews?" said this: "God does not hear the prayers of any person who says Jesus Christ is not the Messiah. Nor does God listen to the needs of every person who calls on Him. It has nothing to do with racism, culture, or class." A respondent finally wrote: "If God cannot hear a Jew's prayers, how could He hear those of Jesus, a Jew?"[20] Even those of us who know better do not really know better if we do not compassionately realize that in our long reincarnational evolution, we, too, once prayed with a semblance of devotional bias, magical formulas, often with the ego and not the heart, with the mind but not with *gnosis*. Christ-conscious gnostic prayer, therefore, has strong kinship with the mystic attitude reflected in the words of the Sufi, Rabiah. Translated for many moderns, this means that I can feel free to ask God anything, but what God is asking of me is so important to the salvation of my soul that I should not have to have even what I want most in life to be at peace with God, myself, or my neighbors. For is not God what I want most?[21] Now, frankly, if you do not feel like this, be prepared to be "mad at God"!

That it is your destiny to participate in the mystery of prayer explains why in so many instances Jesus grew impatient with His disciples who would ask Him to take care of situations that He thought that they should have been able to handle.[22] But we must not forget that human beings, gnostics or not, tend to alternate between the exoteric and the esoteric in their process of spiritual development. Thus the relation between the Open Heavens (higher levels of spiritual consciousness) and healing is one that fully depends on how open one's Self is to receive the Glory of God; although it may require in any given case a persistent practice of the Presence of God not generally seen among humankind. "For the gate is narrow and the road is hard that leads to life, and there are few who find it."[23] Are you one of the blessed few?

Curing and Healing Are Not Always the Same

Curing is not always the same as healing! This penetrating insight, though it need not be seen as unique, is an essential part of the healing traditions of the Akan people of West Africa, according to author, Kofi Appiah-Kubi.[24] For the Akan, then, curing has the nature of fixing body parts, and it does not matter who does the fixing. Thus it is more the work of humans (physicians, surgeons, priest-healers).

> Healing, on the other hand, is a process entailing a long, complicated interaction of other human beings and of the *community*, and entailing, above all, the intervention of God. Thus, one can be cured of a disease but still remain unhealed. Healing implies the restoring of equilibrium in the otherwise strained relationship between a person, fellow human beings, the environment, and God. This process includes physical, emotional, social, and spiritual dimensions.[25]

Appiah-Kubi, of course, notes that the terms *curing* and *healing* "seem to be used interchangeably in modern medical discussion."[26] If that is allowed, one might say in the final analysis that curing is care's intimate goal, while healing is care's ultimate goal.

There is no more pathetic posture a religious being

can take, perhaps, than to become more concerned with being "cured" of a disease or other illness than with undertaking to reflect on the possible symbolic significance of that condition. You have, of course, heard the oft-made remark about the existence of God, that "there are no atheists in foxholes." There is much truth in that statement—though it is probably not universally true. But it is certainly near universally true that the first thing that comes to mind in times of sickness and disease is "How can I conquer or get over this thing?" Nothing, it seems, has the capacity to spur us on to reflect on the relation between what ails us and our total lifestyle (way of being religious in the world) than a health crisis. Sometimes all the money of the rich and their wherewithal to pay for the very best medical care cannot save them, physically, mentally, or spiritually.

Yet is that what illness is all about? While it cannot be said that every form of limitation placed upon us is due to the law of karma,[27] we are intended to use our moments of physical debilitation as opportunities for reflecting on our lives. Here are two things that I immediately assume when confronted by such a situation.

The *first* is an insight traditionally seen as an "Old Preacher's Greeting to a New Day." I found it on a two-and-a-half by three-and-a-half-inch religious thought-card (placed on my car dashboard) which reads: "Lord, help me to remember that nothing is going to happen to me today that You and I together can't handle." This simple affirmation contains more profound insight into the nature of faith and life—especially healing—than volumes of abstract theology.

It is Jesus of Nazareth who tells us something about the nature of illness and our response to it that should apply to persons of faith everywhere. He tells His disciples who have related to Him that Lazarus has taken ill that "This illness does not lead to death" (John 11:4). But later Jesus in fact tells them that "Lazarus is dead" (John 11:14). This curious combination of sayings in the Gospel of John gives us a very important spiritual insight. It shows us that there are indeed esoteric (hidden) meanings in many of the words of Jesus (see John 11:24-26). They also strongly suggest that one needs always to pray, to meditate, and to ponder the possibility that an illness may not always be due to sin, but (as Jesus said), it is "rather . . . for God's glory, so that the Son of God may be glorified though it" (John 11:4).

It is also in complete harmony with the deepest insights of the Sufi Muslim mystics, who make the same claim about their relation to Allah. For they think and act this way when they wish to affirm their faith in the Creator's greatness as being *so great* that it becomes a living paradox that resembles pure destiny. Thus they know that nothing, pleasant or unpleasant, can happen to them that the Creator cannot make the means by which the soul can be further "submissive" or attuned to the Creator Who Is Light (*Holy Qur'an,* sura 24:35).

The *second* is that, armed with the foregoing insights, you should be able to submit yourself to healing care, whether through home, hospital, or a hospice, with the understanding that you are still "on spiritual assignment." Your illness or disability, then, though it may medically persist, does not mean that you are being called into "spiritual retirement." You are, instead, being sent or placed where you are because it represents the fruits of all that you have been and/or what you are intended to become. But, in any case, this means that the persons (patients and/or nurses, doctors, etc.) you are to meet in your new situation are intended to be blessed by God through you—and you by them. But what is primarily important is that you are, then, the means through which God intends to effect a blessing upon others. Christ said it all when He declared: "The Son of

Man came not to be served but to serve . . . " (Matt. 20:28). Of course, this saying essentially refers not to the fruit on a hospital meal-tray but to the manifestation of the "fruit of the Spirit" (Gal. 5:22-23).

Sin and Illness and Healing

The physical-metaphysical link between sin and illness is firmly given in many esoteric religious traditions. But that connection, too, is certainly capable of being misconstrued and misapplied if it encourages negative, judgmental attitudes on the part of individuals, exoterically or esoterically inclined. Hence we are warned not to judge lest we judge falsely or inaccurately. In fact, we are not told not to judge merely in order to make us nicer persons. Rather, it is because only the Creator fully knows and understands the breathtakingly complex circumstances that surround the life of any one soul in suffering or in difficulty. Thus Jesus offers no particular reason that Lazarus or blind Bartimaeus had gotten ill. His only concern is that we come to realize that the Creator can use any manifestation of physical debilitation, mental fragmentation, or spiritual alienation as a means through which the Glory of God can be manifested, made present—ready to burst forth in winning resplendence. Have you glimpsed the resplendent Presence of God in a retarded child lately?

The phrase above, "that the Son of God may be glorified through it," (John 11:4) refers esoterically, therefore, to that fact that (1) even an "undeserved" or "unselfmade" handicap or any other disability may be intended to be cured to reveal God's glory, either through medicine and/or miracle (as in Lazarus's or Bartimaeus's cases); (2) cured or not, you are where you are at the moment because you are intended to develop a particular spiritual virtue or a nexus of spiritual virtues (e.g., patience, tolerance, wisdom). I once saw a mother blandly telling her hospitalized daughter in endless repetition that "faith in the Lord" was all she needed to be cured and let out of the hospital. But consider my former remark: that, perhaps, faith was not her primary problem. Suppose she was there to learn patience—or humility? This means that, contrary to the usual panicky enthusiasm persons tend to have about getting better or getting well, there is the probability that for a given individual it may not be faith for the sake of being "cured" that one really needs, but perhaps the need to learn how to *hope* or to *love*—to *be* loved. In this last case, Bob Trowbridge adds much wisdom here by saying, "One of the reasons for contracting a serious illness may be to find out that you're *loved* just because you exist, not for what you produce or accumulate."[28] What follows is an incident in my life—more precisely in my sister's life—which should vividly illustrate several of the foregoing insights.

It was another sad day for Paddie in that New York hospital. Upon our arrival she told us abruptly to pull the curtain around her bed. She did not want to see or be in the same room as those "weird" creatures with whom she had to share her presence. One of them was diminutive and hunch-backed. The other was "big and sloppy—a slob" and had the fate of passing gas recurrently for all to inhale. But one day, when Paddie was nearing her physical death, and after my mother, DeAnna, and I had, as usual, prayed beside her bed before leaving, she surprised us. As we were about to pull the curtain around her as before, she stopped us, and with words that dramatically illustrate what I just told you, she said, "Leave the curtain alone . . . I want to be able to see 'my friends'"! Truly the Son of God (the Christ Consciousness) was being born in the heart and mind and soul of Paddie. She was not being cured . . . *she was being healed!*

Pondering as Religious Experience

The earlier call to *ponder* is not intended to become a self-indulgence in guilt feelings, self-depreciation, or self-condemnation. It refers to the idea that, aside from cases of interminable pain,[29] there are moments when we find ourselves able to "catch our breath" during a discomforting sickness or illness. But what do so many persons do when that happens? Too many become so elated at the experience of being temporarily relieved that they go back to thinking, willing, and doing the same things they were doing before. And this refers to attitudes and emotions which may very well be connected with the onset of the discomforting condition in the first place.

At these times, however, what one might consider doing is to realize that one has just experienced the Grace of God in the form of that nonsuffering interlude. That is the moment when one should endeavor with all one's heart and mind and soul and strength to attune or reattune oneself to the Creator. This means with the heart, mind, soul, and strength as much as one has at the time, for one ounce of true inclination in this respect toward the Creator is worth a pound of unenlightened enthusiasm.

This may take the form of a grace-laden sigh all the way to creating a healing mantra for one's own personal use. If you are a person who suffers recurrent depression,[30] for example, what do you do when you are not depressed? For it is at those "auspicious moments"[31] when one experiences the grace-given interlude that one should seize the opportunity to prepare oneself, spiritually, for the oncoming of the next bout with depression. This grace-given interlude has been referred to as both "the auspicious moment" and (in Chinese Buddhism) looked upon as a transformative opportunity. It is a moment of truth when one must have faith that one's

"Healing Source"[32] has indeed pledged "to assist [you] not only to become healed, but to attain enlightenment in the process." But then, it is also true that, enlightenment or not, a prayerful, meditative pondering in the right sense could also heighten the prospect that the creation and re-creation of what we might call a spiritual mood-swing can directly relate to affecting the nature and intensity—even the future occurrence—of depression. For millions it has probably proved pretty hard, but not impossible, to have faith that though "with men it is impossible . . . with God *all* things are possible" (Mark 10:27; italics added).

In terms of practical creativity I have had the occasion to call to the attention of a number of audiences that there are literally anti-depression mantras (in the form of Psalms) already contained in the Hebrew Scriptures—in fact 150 of them! Psalm 42 is one of the best of them. This suggestion is not intended to play down or trivialize the utterly indescribable nature of the depression experience. I have lived with depressed persons and have been told in no uncertain terms that it is as if one were living in a psychological "black hole."[33] Yet one of the reasons that some people will not consider this form of self-help in paradoxical relation to the Power of God is that they do not realize that a mantra can become as a seed planted in the unconscious. For it not only helps to root out the weeds of willfulness and the garbage of guilt in the unconscious that block the upsurge of God's own creative action in one's behalf. It also acts very much like a modern time capsule to give off curative and healing energy in the event that one's replaying of VCR (Vicious Circle Responses) tapes in one's unconscious may re-induce depression, anxiety, panic attacks, or any other dreadful thing that the unconscious—or conscious—mind can muster.

The entrapping and liberating thing about the astrophysical metaphor of the black hole, however, is something more than its highly vivid analogy of all the light of one's joy-of-life being trapped in a blackness or darkness from which no psychological escape seems possible. It is indeed that fact that (1) it calls to mind the view of the cosmos held by dualistic gnostics regarding the Primeval Fall of souls from the Realm of the Fullness of God's Inner Light and their entrapment in this worldly astrodome of darkness; and (2) it calls to mind one of the major cosmic meanings and purposes of Jesus as Son of God (Christ Consciousness Incarnate). That is, it demonstrates to us that it is not beyond the Kingdom and the Power and the Glory of God to empower the light of the soul eventually to break out of the black hole and shine through the deepest darkness of the mind and the bleakest bondage of the soul.

It must be pointed out that all this does not exclude the vital role of the physician and the considerate use of medication-and-therapy as a coexisting form of treatment. To paraphrase Father MacNutt, a leading authority on spiritual healing in the Catholic Church, "While the physician is 'looking for the right diagnosis,' the theologian is looking for the right *discernment*." But this entails (through prayer and meditation) one's grasping and being grasped by one's own testimony of what is wrong, listening to God who has the power to enable one to see the larger (spiritual) diagnostic picture, and preparing oneself to be used as a channel of the Creator's unique healing power.[34] I take Father MacNutt's "discernment," therefore, to be assimilable not only to a process of discernment by a spiritual specialist, but also to the necessary process of self-discernment, of pondering the inner meaning of one's present situation.

Once faith in the possibility of discerning what-is and what-can-be comes into play, the body itself—which, of course, had already become a microcosm of that black hole—will in turn respond to the irresistible pull of "the Spirit witnessing to our spirit" that we are indeed "the Sons and Daughters of God." And this, in addition means that it cannot be ruled out that the body can be freed even at the psychological-neurological plane. It is literally now a case of "deep calling unto deep" in the form of "light beaming unto light," "Eternal Light calling unto the entrapped light of the soul." Is it any wonder that Paul of Tarsus could affirm that "in all these things we are more than conquerors through him [Christ] who loved us"?[35] Surely, this is the kind of triumphal thinking that inspired Jacob Needleman when he noticed how his authentic gnostic Catholic priest, Father Sylvan, went on to comment on the inner meaning of what even the "heretical" gnostics were trying in a biblical but misconstruing way to say to the early church.

The Need for an Interdimensional-Communal Healing Perspective

This profound mystical perspective makes it possible for wonderful things to happen both in medicine and through prayer-and-meditation which are all "miracles" in themselves. Our challenge, therefore, is to realize that we live in an incredibly vast and largely incomprehensible universe. But thanks be to the Creator that we have literally "heard from the universe"! Yet it is a universe that is multidimensional and kaleidoscopic in nature. In keeping with the spirit of Teilhard de Chardin, modern physicists by acknowledging a principle of nonlocality at the subatomic level of reality are paving the way for a greater complementarity of science and religion.[36] Thus the theme of the nonlocality of human consciousness propounded by Dossey is in harmony with the spiritual intentionality of a simple line uttered by actor Jeffrey Hunter as Jesus of Nazareth in the film *King of Kings*. After having declared to the Roman centurion guarding John the Baptist that He had come to free John, Jesus was smugly asked by the centurion, "And just how do you propose to break him free from his cell?" Jesus answered, "I come to free him *within* his cell"![37]

Likewise in relation to the discomfort—and even the terror—of sickness and disease, we are finally intended to become free of all the limitations and frustrations of the human situation while remaining fully amidst their furor. This accounts for the remarkable saying among those who appreciate the role of mysticism in any deep knowledge of spiritual things that "the true mystics are at home in the world." This means that "for the mystic daily life and moment-to-moment thought are linked intimately with spiritual issues."[38] How many times have you heard someone (even a religious person) say, while discussing money, "I am talking about economics, not religion!" That individual needs to be told that about one-sixth of the teachings of Jesus of Nazareth is concerned with the spiritual problems raised by one's attitude toward money!

So the element of the nonlocal existence of the human consciousness itself implies the interdimensional (or multidimensional) nature of the universe. Yet one needs to be super-cognizant of that fact in order to bypass the childishness that so often characterizes those who say that they have faith—yet during recurrent or prolonged illness continue to live on the edge of despair. One needs to answer three important questions: "For what purpose did I come into the world?" and "For what purpose did Jesus come into the world?" and "Is there not, after all, some vital connection between *His* purpose and *my* purpose?"[39]

Tradition tells us that Saint Bernadette was told by Mary, the mother of Jesus, that she could not promise Bernadette happiness in this world. Even the spirit of childlikeness, then, cannot allow itself the naiveté of thinking that pain, as Buddha taught us, is anything else but inevitable. But it is not pain per se that is the problem. It is the fact that we are so naturally undesirous of experiencing pain for *any* reason. Understandably we hate the pain inflicted upon us by others—and often we regret the pain that we inflict upon others—and ourselves. Yet, asked to experience pain in self-sacrificial love for the sake of witnessing to the truth of the Realm of God and not even as the natural and supernatural karmic result of our foolish hearts, we shrink back as if pain for the sake of spiritual growth or as a spiritual example for faint hearts is not worth it. It remains significant, then, that what was for Bernadette a genuine "practical mysticism" was also accompanied by excruciating bodily pain which she endured without complaint.

No doubt the world continues to suffer a lack of unswervingly loyal "role models" for the Realm of God. Ask the young people who have so sadly observed the broadcasting of scandal after scandal in the headlines involving souls who were supposed to know better. Though we cannot afford to adopt a self-righteous attitude toward such beings, what does it mean if, unlike many of them, we ourselves utterly refuse to be on our spiritual guard against repeating the tragic human past? But to be a true role model in terms of the experience of illness in life, we need to adopt a perspective like the one Jesus had regarding the threat of evildoers against our bodies. He said, "Do not fear them who can kill the body, but cannot kill the soul . . . "[40] Likewise, in the case of a serious illness, is it not more spiritually enlightened to think in the case of terminal cancer, for instance, that it is really the *cancer* that is terminal and *not* the patient?

The only sure way, then, to handle the plight of illness, in addition to the pondering mentioned earlier, is to develop a superconscious awareness of the truth of the reality of immortality. But with Jesus, Paul, and John, it is not merely a case of the immortality of the soul but also the truth of the reality of the inseparability of immortal life and eternal love. We have to remember that, even in a negative sense, the very biblical idea of being cast into outer darkness is consistent with the hope that we live on after the death of the body. So, although in a positive sense John calls it "Eternal Life," he means by it *something that far surpasses merely living on after death.* He is referring to a distinctive depth-dimension of a certain quality of ongoing Life. The modern new age enthusiasm for the mere fact of immortality is thus another, neo-Gnostic misconstruing of a biblical truth.

Eternal Life is thus inseparable from the Eternal Love emanating from the Creator; and it is the factor of Eternal Love that germinates in the heart of the sickest faithful individual a depth of spiritual strength "in quietness and in confidence" due to a single glorious fact (Isaiah 30:15 KJV).[41] And that is, that a man's, a woman's, or a child's intended transition from one plane of existence to another plane of resplendent spiritual reality is under the direct supervision of the Creator and the Angelic Hosts. But often the transition is assisted by loved ones and other compassionate discarnate beings. Not only have we heard of interdimensional (joint) emergency medical operations by physicians on both human and astral planes, we have also heard of the possibility of our "entertaining angels unawares" (KJV).

> Let mutual love continue. Do not neglect to show hospitality to strangers, for by doing that some have entertained angels without knowing it.[42]

So, it is now not only time to become increasingly receptive to entertaining angels "awares," it is also time to anticipate with the deepest possible intuitive, spiritual knowledge (gnosis) that (to rephrase John the Divine) there may indeed be both "a *sickness* that is not unto death," and "a sickness that is unto death."[43] Come death or not, the man or woman with Christ-conscious gnosis can only be one who has been empowered by the Holy Spirit of Truth to approach death at least with a certain spirit. Perhaps, some might suggest, with the spirit of William Cullen Bryant's poem, *Thanatopsis*, which bids one to "go not, like the quarry slave at night, scourged to his dungeon, but [rather, inclined to] lie . . . down to pleasant dreams."[44] Surpassing Bryant's "dreams," however, the individual with Christ-conscious gnosis must, therefore, be able to assume an already accomplished victory over death. He or she must go on beyond mere pleasant dreams to the reality of other sacred worlds and eventually reenter the Inner Realm of the Fullness of God's Eternal Light (the Pleroma).

The Healing Dimension of Transformative Community

There can be no question that a new spirit of radical individualism has gone hand in hand with the rise of the new age movement and its various "*gnos*eological" manifestations.[45] No doubt this movement has given millions the opportunity to experience what seems radical spiritual freedom as an intuitive way of life. But, at the same time, it has presented mainstream religious communities with an ironic development, apart from the mere gnostic elements reflected in new age cosmologies. That is, unfortunately, its tendency to encourage a diminishing sense of commitment to spiritual community.

The person who influenced me the most to realize or rediscover the ongoing role that community must play in the life of individuals, both in sickness and in health, is the late Dr. Harmon Hartzell Bro, author of a major biography of Edgar Cayce, *A Seer Out of Season.*[46] Though not true of all new agers, the element of individualism that has long been associated with the spirit of capitalism so easily creeps into the most well-intended quests for radical spiritual freedom. In a work entitled *Growing Through Personal Crisis,* authored with his spouse, Dr. June Bro, they call our attention to two kinds of individuals: those who adhere to what they call "the closed secret," if not, "the closed saving secret"; and others whose lives are centered on "the open secret."[47] The first is characteristic of those who may indeed have undergone a religious experience of transformative power, but who may also suffer the limitation of an exclusiveness of wisdom and without a consecration of the "unfortunate" or the ordinary life. This orientation, incidentally, has indeed been seen as a form of modern gnosticism, including all the dangers Paul of Tarsus found in the Corinthian church. The second, which also includes the element of transformative power, is more diversely outgoing in loving service to the world and may also include a "quiet growth in mystical companionship with the One."[48] The Bros, however, prefer what they call the "shared secret," which has more clearly to do with salvation—and community. The value of spiritual community—or communities—is brought home to us in this statement:

> Such communities can be small gatherings of companions of the way, who meet weekly to explore life's big issues in disciplined adventures; and larger congregations and institutions, which offer engagements across age levels and social classes, rich corporate worship, potent historic concepts, vital activities of social service and social change, and daring cooperation beyond the local level. Each type of effort, small and large, stretches and renews the other, moving together, in a modern pilgrimage

> that includes both communitas and structure, toward a world that can be—in Martin Buber's words—"*community all through.*"[49]

A highly moving example of the right kind of attitude toward illness and the transformative power of spiritual community is shared with us by Ken Wilbur and especially his spouse, Treya. For Treya, in 1984, discovered just ten days after marrying Ken that she had breast cancer. Treya and Ken give a penetrating response to those new agers and others who proclaim, literally, "You create your own reality," but who largely leave it at that. In an article entitled "Do We Make Ourselves Sick?" they contend that the new age notion that each of us creates his or her own reality is an oversimplication of a much more complicated human and cosmic situation.[50]

Furthermore, Treya has something quite different and more profound to tell us than do new agers in her accompanying piece in the same article entitled "When Bad Things Happen to Good People." She says, "I have come to see that life is too wonderfully complex and we are all too interconnected—both with each other and with our environment—for a simple statement like 'you create your own reality' to be literally true. In fact, a belief that I control or create my own reality actually attempts to rip me out of the rich, complex, mysterious, and supportive context of my life. It attempts, in the name of control, to deny the web of relationships that nurtures each of us daily."[51] She then concludes, "I try to stay open to the many moments of humor and joy in life, open to the many opportunities for psychological and spiritual healing all around me, open to the pain and suffering that call for our compassion."[52]

No doubt in many instances individuals have been seeking to escape from what seems the sterile and dogmatic orthodoxy of institutional religion. Yet consider, if you will, a persistent irony: that within those very so-called sterile and dogmatic orthodoxies there have always resided potentially liberating, gnostic elements.[53] Yet if the clergy, rabbis, or other leaders of such orthodoxies had dared to enter into the contemplation of the mysteries that lie hidden (esoterically) even in the doctrinal, liturgical, and sacramental mysteries of often petrified traditions, two contrary but positive developments might have occurred instead. One is that souls hungry for a deeper experience and understanding of their particular faiths might have found it unnecessary to leave their spiritual homes or familiar fellowships; and, two, those who yet felt that they needed to explore other forms of spiritual experience might have remained inclined both to face their need and to trust in the power of (their own) spiritual communities to give them direction. Spiritual community, to be sure, is certainly not to be confined to the word church, or temple, or any other rigid institutional form. In a number of readings that "refuse to give any *ultimate* spiritual significance or authority to ecclesiastical organizations, structures, or personages," the seer, Edgar Cayce, did *not* set aside the traditional church as such; for, as he says, it "centers the mind." (3350-1) Nevertheless, he stressed instead not institutional forms but the element of service as the key to involvement with groups committed to the truth and spreading goodness: "Are there not trees of oak, of ash, of pine? . . . Find not fault with *any* ["whatever its name" (3342-1)], but rather show forth as to just how good a pine, or ash, or oak, or *vine* thou art!"[54]

There are basically two words for what tradition calls church. Early Christianity, to be sure, started out as an "ekklesia" (a called or summoned assembly of believers) *before* it became associated with a "kuriakon" (the Lord's house). But subsequent history saw the merger of ekklesia and kuriakon in a way that would later become spiritually problematic. The faithful were rigidly and threateningly led to believe that the ekklesia was invariably intended by God to gather *in* the kuriakon. Jesus, however, used the word *church,* as it were, only twice in all His teachings,[55] and it is ekklesia that He used. It is thus essentially only the church as a highly dynamic, transportable (i.e., local and *trans*-local) charismatic community that can take on the world and prevail even against the gates of hell—*not* the institutional church as such. More than a few theologians have dared to contemplate that the church, as we know it, may eventually go out of existence. How can one be dogmatically charged to go to church, when one understands oneself to *be* the church, or, at least, a cell in the Mystical Body of Christ, or what is ultimately an interdimensional cosmic, creative, spiritual community?[56]

Just as, therefore, in many traditional societies, illness is not conceived as a solitary spiritual adventure, human beings in the modern era need to develop a sense of the transformative power of the communal-caring consciousness; and this applies even to those who profess to have gone beyond the worship of doctrinal forms and ritual formulas.[57] Thus we learn that the previously mentioned Akan of Africa hold that "when one person is ill, the entire society is ill";[58] and, on a larger scale, there is "the World Health Organization's campaign of 'health for all by the year 2000' . . . incorporating the WHO's concept of health as not merely the absence of disease but the 'well-being of body, mind, and society.'"[59] There are those, of course, who have still not grasped the ethical-spiritual meaning of John Donne's words, "Any man's death diminishes me . . . " (*Devotions upon Emergent Occasions,* Meditation XVII, 1624)

A vision of community is not complete, however, until one realizes that it must be an ecumenical spiritual vision that transcends all the boundaries of our former entrapment in denominational theologies' worldviews. Both those who are concerned and not so concerned about the New Gnosticism they see emerging in American Protestantism (and other religious circles, Jewish and Catholic) have opinions that go in two different directions. One direction is a further entrapment in the spirit of individualism; and the other goes in the direction of calling for more community against that individualism.[60] What in fact we need is a new sense of the individual-in-community, through which one may choose to remain in a given spiritual community and yet feel free to explore the mysteries of the Realm of God in response to a call from within. This appears to be the spirit of Harold Bloom's allusion to the mysticism of Walt Whitman, who "sings two selves at once."[61]

This idea, then, envisions a positive gnostic freedom to move, as Jesus said of "everyone who is born of the Spirit,"[62] wherever one is driven by it to go in search of the truth; and it envisions a perspective of community that cuts across all the barriers of religion, doctrine, custom, and whatever else that may stand in the way of the advancement of the Realm of God into the life of an individual, a group, and/or the earth itself. I have been inclined to refer to this vital discernment by calling for a new attitude toward receiving religious experience beyond belief boundaries, and a bold receptivity toward interrelating beyond customary limits of closeness and cooperation.[63]

The Relation of Health and Spirituality

Under the influence of the new age movement, in a positive sense, it has become increasingly imperative to distinguish the term *spirituality* from that of *religion. Religion* (sometimes religiosity) is an extremely broad term. And though it has been traditionally associated with the supernatural, it is fraught with variety in thought, in form, and in practice, thus allowing for almost anything to be done in its name, good or bad. *Spirituality,* however—not spiritualism—tends to point immediately—and only—to a positive quality of existence in the world. It bears an essential meaning in the world, as a vision and a way that do not make it easy to be other than what one seems to be. No doubt, as so many experimenters with truth have avowed, it is because of the elements of humility, devotion, and consistency that any spirituality was/is ever attained or maintained. This remains true whether a particular vision and way of spirituality was/is conceived in terms of prayer or meditation, self-effort or grace, a karma of merit or an act of divine predestination.

Spirituality in its broadest sense, then, encompasses physical health, personal immortality, and paradisiacal salvation as vital aspects of human nature and human destiny. Yet the word *health* deserves to be used in a holistic sense, since it is originally related to the word *heal,* and the word *heal* is inseparable from the concept of *salvation.*[64] As both a vision and a way of being in the world, spirituality thus encompasses (1) health as a style of life, (2) health as a quality of life, and (3) health as a continuity of life.

Health as a style of life begins with the recognition and acceptance of two important facts. One is that we ourselves are units of nature-at-large; and the other is that the ecological balance that we see in nature's own is meant to be our own in microcosm. Hence a balance of the psychological and physiological functions and forces in ourselves is key to the manifestation of the kind of wholeness of the universe that is symbolized so very much in the natural world around us. The absence of balance usually shows itself in our inordinate physical appetites, economic ambitions, and our sociopolitical conventions. It has proved very hard to convince millions of individuals worldwide that they should not eat too much and to eat the right kinds of foods. But even more difficult is to impart the conviction to dieters themselves that dieting, as such, can be an integral part of one's own spirituality; that we should not be seeking merely "the body beautiful" or trying to avoid illness—or even fighting off the aging process—as ends in themselves. As the adage goes, "Beauty *is* as beauty *does*"!

An advertised ecological statement once published in the *New York Times,* apparently reflecting a sensitivity to what many call the "rape of nature," contained a line that says it all: "Pollution is a state of mind." Physicists call it *entropy* when systems, organisms, and other things tend irretrievably to lose their energy and integrity, to run down and become chaotic.[65] But we know, upon further reflection, that human beings, prematurely, can indeed hasten disease, decay, and death through uncreative, unbalanced, unwholesome lifestyles. A suicide, therefore, can be a highly dramatic instance of this lack of health as a style of life. We should, instead, be seeking wholeness, balance, integrity—not in the sense of the oversimplified meaning of moral honesty—but integrity as the integration of all aspects of our style of life.

Health as a quality of life begins with the recognition and acceptance of the intended psychosomatic integrity of human life. It involves, moreover, the necessary conviction that mind is the maker, or as Edgar Cayce often said, "Mind is the builder"; so that though mind and body do work together, the thoughts that the mind entertains are "things" or can become things or forces on the borderline between spirit and matter; and, thus, they can influence directly the possibilities and the limitations of our sense of well-being, or what many called happiness or contentment, or "easiness" in life.[66] And so, mind is where our value systems and our nervous systems are decisively coordinated. One must, therefore, ask oneself and answer for oneself at least two fundamental questions before the years pass one by, if one is to achieve meaningful health as a quality of life in the spiritual sense. What is my frame of reference? And where is my center of gravity? The first concerns what you conceive to be your ultimate place in the universe as you perceive it; and the second concerns what the one thing in your life is without which the entire meaning of your existence would disintegrate.

Health as a continuity of life is encompassed by contemplating the following momentous questions: If there is not something on earth greater and more important than physical and mental health as such, how can one meaningfully encounter the prospect and/or the inevitability of death in a spiritually meaningful way? What kind of perspective allows for both the human striving for continued health (and thus, apparently, longer life) and for what seems no ultimate victory but rather an absolute ending to all deeply cherished human values? Does not a truly holistic healing perspective, therefore, require a perspective of religion, faith, and healing that transcends even the bounds of earthly life itself in terms of the broadest and deepest holistic concept of wellness?

Healing, Holism, and Holiness

In a word, healing is the process of attaining, maintaining, or recovering a state of physical, mental, and spiritual wholeness, equilibrium, even holiness, within a cosmic framework of meaning that encompasses various modes of understanding the universe. To cite Ken Wilbur, author of *The Eye of Spirit*, who attempts to comprehend and integrate a host of understandings about the nature of things, " . . . there is more room in the Kosmos than you might have suspected."[67] It is the discovery—indeed, the rediscovery—of the vital link between healing and holism[68] during the last two decades that has helped to bridge what seemed before a great gulf between medicine and religion.[69] The word *holism* comes from the Greek *holos* (whole, complete). Holism has meaning for both the social and natural sciences in that it emphasizes wholes more than parts. In religion, however, it has now reached a point that suggests we are on the verge of a quantum leap in our understanding of the convergence of the physical, psychical, and spiritual dimensions of the human being.[70] A point of continuing controversy, however, is whether this means that "wholes are more important than the sum of their parts" or that "wholes are merely the sum of their parts." Medical science under the form of "holistic medicine" has certainly touched on an understanding of this physical-metaphysical mystery by offering the following four general principles regarding optimal personal health:

1. Your mind and body are inseparable . . .
2. You have the power to heal yourself . . .
3. [You need to have] a positive, supportive relationship between you and your doctor . . .
4. [You should emphasize] preventive medicine . . . [71]

Nonetheless, in relation to holism and the spiritual reality of holiness, healing is an experiential-faith reality, but it remains by and large an ongoing mystery. In Christianity, for example, the reality of a holistic vision of faith in Christ takes the form of the concept of the (Mystical) Body of Christ, in which "the sum of" and "the greater than the sum of" perspectives are united in an experiential physical-metaphysical mystery.[72] Complete healing, then, under the light of Eternity, is an experience in communal holiness.

The truth is, therefore, that with all medical science has to offer, it is ultimately necessary for all of us to realize that it is, again, "not by might, nor by power, but by my spirit, says the Lord of hosts."[73] Thus the ultimate aim of all manifestations of caring and curing and healing is not health per se but the cultivation of the art of holiness.

Yet it is simply false to assume that *all* sickness is the result of sin, or that all human beings are intended to postpone physical death indefinitely, or that sickness itself cannot be a gift of God's universe in order to make one holistically well—but, certainly, spiritually well! For there is in the ultimate scheme of things an inseparable connection among healing, holism, and holiness. This priority of holiness is so important that in his little book, *The Greatest Thing in the World*, Henry Drummond tells us that there is only one thing in this world greater than happiness—and that is holiness!

What is holiness? Holiness is that aspect of human experience which is distinctively of transhuman origin. Holiness, ultimately, originates in the Inner Realm of the Fullness of God's Eternal Light. In human spiritual experience, holiness is superawareness in one's being of a Divine "Presence"[74] that by its very nature seems to separate one from every other thing that is not holy (the profane).[75] Though scholars of the Bible have tended to emphasize this element of separateness, there is some justification for tracing the idea of holiness back to an ancient Near Eastern connection with the phenomenon of light. This vital link among separateness, light, and Presence is strongly evident in the Hebrew Scriptures. And Jesus of Nazareth calls us to be incarnations of the Eternal Light of God to the world.[76] The Light of holiness, though it is the most exquisite religious symbol in the entire history of religious experience, is more than just a tremendous and fascinating mystery that makes us conscious of our separation from the darkness of spiritual ignorance and sin. It is, finally, that which, like the commonplace light of the sun itself, shines on everything.

The Light of holiness is, then, that which unites beyond separation. Ultimately, it unites the sacred and the profane by showing us how to live in the power of the sacred in the profane or the ordinary life. To reiterate the words of Raynor Johnson, author of the pathmaking book, *The Imprisoned Splendour:*

> To find the presence of God in the Beyond is good, but to find it on Earth is a greater achievement.[77]

Thus holiness is inseparately related to a form of ethical spirituality which both the prophets of Israel and Jesus of Nazareth had in common. To reiterate the familiar truism on beauty, "Holiness *is* as holiness *does*"! Holiness does not require that one be in a state of perfect physical, mental, or spiritual health. Larry Dossey practically jolts us in the right direction when he mentions several of the great minds in human spirituality who have died of painful diseases. They include, for example, Krishnamurti, Suzuki, Maharishi, Saint Bernadette, and others.[78] Recall, too, if you will, an occasional incident wherein a nationally prominent "wellness" proponent, either through his or her books and/or TV, has either succumbed to disease or suddenly expired. In fact, Dossey begins his chapter on "Saints and Sinners, Health and Illness" by referring to Buddha, who "died from food poisoning, having been fed tainted meat in what proved to be his final meal."[79]

The lessons of the lives and teachings of those who have given us the richest heritage of what it is to be holy thus tend to teach us some very important things. One is that to live on earth as such is to face suffering as an inevitability in one's life. Another is that, in any given case, there may not be any absolute connection between unholiness and the experience of suffering. Another is that, in any case, the reality of the holy life (being and doing good) does not guarantee that one will *not* suffer, either due to an accident of nature or at the hands of beings who have come to despise the good. And another is that suffering, though not to be desired but rather to be prevented or overcome, can be used as an initiation into a deeper experience of ego-denial that allows for a greater infusion of Divine Grace—that is, the Divine Grace that leads to ego-transcendence, ego-transformation, ego-assimilation to the Pattern of the Christ Consciousness. Finally, no redemptive suffering (i.e., for the sake of others) is ever in vain or the ultimate effects of it lost to whom it is intended to bless. The truth is that in the matter of the relation among faith, healing, community, and holiness, the words of two brothers born of the blood and the Spirit can be completely trusted: "that the testing of your faith produces endurance" (James); and that "the one who endures to the end will be saved," for "by your endurance you will gain your souls" (Jesus).[80]

I should like to close this chapter with the following series of mantras that were born out of my prayers and meditations over time. You may or may not be already familiar with mantras; in any case it pays to know that, whether contemplated, uttered, or written, their repetition can become a source of God's Sacred Healing Power; and this is especially true if you should internalize any mantra with a sense of having prostrated the ego before the Source of "the Kingdom, the Power, and the Glory." Whatever your situation, mantras are intended to be at first memorized, then internalized, and further on realized.

Memorized to the extent that their utterance—if more, their contemplation (in silence)—means the words are no longer being said with self-conscious recitation; internalized to the extent that their spiritual intention (their spiritual aim) has become a spontaneous, intuitive, and compassionate part of your inner being; realized to the extent that you are becoming superconsciously aware of being empowered (spirit-infilled) as a channel for both self-healing and the healing of others. This last phase may include and go beyond curing as it has been discussed above. It is, finally, about becoming not only holistically healthy—but finally—holy.

Seed-Mantras for Encountering Sickness with Yearning for Deliverance (Curing) and Yielding to God for Salvation (Healing)

A Mantra of Yearning and Yielding

This is the body that Thou hast created.
This is the mind that Thou hast illuminated.
This is the soul that Thou hast emanated.
Transubstantiate this body into an instrument of Thine everlasting peace.
Transform this mind into a medium of Thy sacred healing power.
Transpierce this soul and make it a channel of Thy redemptive love.

A Mantra of Healing or Maintaining Holistic Health

There is only *Life* in this body;
There is only *Light* in this Life;
There is only *Spirit* in this Light;
There is only *Love* in this Spirit.

A Mantra of Yearning/Yielding and Healing Blended

This is the body that Thou hast created.
Let there be only *Life* [and Health] in this body.
This is the mind that Thou hast illuminated.
Let there be only *Light* in this Life.
This is the soul that Thou hast emanated.
Let there be only *Spirit* in this Light.

Transubstantiate this body into an instrument of Thine everlasting peace.
Transform this mind into a medium of Thy sacred healing power.
Transpierce this soul and make it a channel of Thy redemptive love.

The Healing Mantra Devolved

Let there be [or "There is"] only Life [and/or Health] in this body.
May every gene, chromosome, and cell in this body be filled with Life,
Light, Spirit, and Love.
Let there be only Light in this Life.
May my every thought, word, and deed be permeated with the Good, the True, and the Beautiful.
Let there be only Spirit in this Light.
May the Holy Spirit of Truth empower me always to overcome "the world, the flesh, and the devil."
Let there be only Love in this Spirit.
May Thy Life, Thy Light, Thy Spirit, and Thy Love saturate my body, mind, and soul with humility, strength, kindness, patience, and courage.

A Daily Mantra for Holistic Abundance

O Thou Who art the God of Eternal Mind!
Make me an instrument of Thine Everlasting Peace,
A medium of Thy Sacred Healing Power,
A channel of Thine Everlasting Love,
A vehicle of Thine Enlightening Truth.

Endnotes

1. See John 1:12-13.
2. John 1:9 (NRSV). In this context, the Creator's Light is referred to as "Eternal Light." While it is the same Light, its manifestation in human beings is referred to in this book as "Divine Light." This is done to emphasize that the Creator is the Source of the "Divine Light" in us.
3. See James E. Rush, *Toward a General Theory of Healing* (Washington, D.C.: University Press of America, Inc., 1981, Table I, pp. 168-176), which summarizes religious orientations toward healing from 10,000 B.C. onward. Acknowledging healing to be "a very complex phenomenon" and using "general system principles," this author introduces the "root metaphor" of attunement as a significant universal key to a variety of healing systems.
4. Echoing Mircea Eliade, cited in W. C. Beane, "Occult Aspects of World Religions," *The Journal of Religious Thought* (Autumn-Winter, 1977), p. 13f.
5. According to Robert C. Fuller, *Alternative Medicine and American Religious Life* (New York, N.Y.: Oxford University Press, 1989, p. 127), "*studies reveal that up to eighty percent of all illnesses are psychosomatic.*" Italics added.
6. Leon E. Wright, *From Cult to Cosmos: Can Jesus Be Saved?* (Petaluma, California: Crystal Press, 1978), pp. 78-79.
7. I Peter 3:18-19, 4:6. Italics added.
8. For a survey of healing systems of many sacred traditions, see Lawrence E. Sullivan, *Healing and Restoring: Health and Medicine in the World's Religious Traditions* (New York, N.Y.: Macmillan Publishing Company, 1989).
9. See Ephesians 3:14-19.
10. This could also apply to medical missionaries and Peace Corps volunteers. Such collaborations are already occurring between modern medically educated tribal sons and daughters and their shamanically initiated fathers and mothers whose traditional (e.g., African) medical practice those children defend.
11. Dossey, *Healing Words: The Power of Prayer and the Practice of Medicine* (New York, N.Y.: HarperSanFrancisco, 1993), pp. 91-92; note the participants' use of key lines of Catholic and Protestant prayers as mantras as such (Ave Maria, the Lord's Prayer, and the 23rd Psalm, etc.).
12. Rush, *Toward a General Theory of Healing, op. cit.*, p. 19 *et passim.*
13. Dossey does this in his pathmaking book, *Space, Time, and Medicine* (Boston, Mass.: Shambhala Publications, Inc., 1982).
14. See Larry Dossey, *Healing Words, op. cit.*, pp. 24-28. Dossey, *Space, Time, and Medicine, ibid.*, p. 215, has this insight for everyday living: "A reverential attitude that bespeaks a oneness with the universe can transform the commonest act."
15. Luke 18:1.
16. I Thessalonians 5:17.
17. Thomas Merton, *New Seeds of Contemplation* (New York, N.Y.: New Directions Publishing Corporation, 1972), p. 1.
18. *Ibid.*, p. 13.
19. Walsch, *Conversations with God*, p. 55.
20. *Time*, September 29, 1988, p. 5.
21. See the "yes, yes/no, no/yes and no/yes" phenomenon of Paul of Tarsus, II Corinthians 1:17-22.
22. See, e.g., Matthew 8:22-25.

23. Matthew 7:14.

24. Kofi Appiah-Kubi, "Religion and Healing in an African Community: The Akan of Ghana," in Sullivan, *op. cit.*, p. 216.

25. *Ibid.*, 216. Italics added.

26. *Loc. cit.*

27. See John 9:1-3.

28. Bob Trowbridge, "Will the Millennium Bring Enlightenment?" *Venture Inward* (January/February 1998), p. 25.

29. I intend to deal with this specific issue in another work to follow.

30. For a convenient summary of its nature, psychogenetic links, and medical prospects, see the lead article, "Depression," in *Newsweek* (May 4, 1987), pp. 48-54, 57.

31. The "auspicious moment" is mentioned especially in connection with the role of "anticipation" in ancient Greek healing tradition, in Rush, *Toward a General Theory of Healing, op. cit.*, p. 32, note #40. See also transformative opportunity, pp. 206-207 in this book.

32. Raoul Birnbaum, "Chinese Buddhist Traditions of Healing and the Life Cycle," in Sullivan, *op. cit.*, p. 47. I have used "Healing Source" here instead of Birnbaum's "Master of Healing" for ecumenical purposes.

33. Considering the demoralizing descriptions of depression by those who have lived it, it remains truly one of the miracles of life that statistics show that only about 15 percent of chronically depressed individuals take their own lives.

34. See Francis MacNutt, *Healing* (Notre Dame, Indiana: Ave Maria Press, 1974), p. 195.

35. Romans 8:37; see also v. 38-39.

36. Dossey, *Healing Words, op. cit.*, p. 84ff.; cf. pp. 38, 41, 43-53. As he indicates, the subject of nonlocality is (stunningly) explored in his *Recovering the Soul: A Scientific and Spiritual Search* (New York, N.Y.: Bantam Books, 1989).

37. Screenplay by Philip Yordan; a Samuel Bronston production.

38. Marsha Sinetar, *Ordinary People as Monks and Mystics: Lifestyles for Self-Discovery* (Mahwah, New Jersey: Paulist Press, 1986), p. 75.

39. See pp. 210-211 in this book.

40. Matthew 10:28a.

41. Isaiah 32:17 says again, "And the work of righteousness shall be peace; and the effect of righteousness quietness and assurance for ever" (KJV).

42. Hebrews 13:1-2 (NRSV).

43. I John 5:16, 17 (KJV). What John says of sin may also be true of sickness.

44. Tremaine McDowell, *William Cullen Bryant* (New York, N.Y.: American Book Company, 1935), p. 5.

45. A term sometimes used in intellectual circles; for instance, Francisco G. Bazan, in his article, "Matter in Plotinus and Sankara," in R. Baine Harris, *Neoplatonism and Indian Thought* (Norfolk, Virginia: International Society for Neoplatonic Studies, 1982), p. 186.

46. Subtitled, *The Life of Edgar Cayce* (New York, N.Y.: New American Library, 1989).

47. Harmon Hartzell Bro (with June Avis Bro), *Growing Through Personal Crisis*, gen. ed., Charles Thomas Cayce (San Francisco, California: Harper & Row, Publishers, 1988), p. 145.

48. *Ibid. Loc. cit.*

49. *Ibid.*, pp. 144-147, 148-149. Italics added.

50. Ken and Treya Wilber, "Do We Make Ourselves Sick?" *New Age Journal* (September/October 1988), pp. 50-54, 85-91, especially p. 50. Though he sees illness as related to karma, Ken says, for instance, that "Illness doesn't generate new karma or more karma, but—and this is very important—your *attitude* to illness can generate new karma" (p. 87).

51. *Ibid.*, p. 90.

52. *Ibid.*, p. 91.

53. See Matthew 5:26; cf. Luke 16:26; I Peter 4:6.

54. Reading 254-87; see Drummond, *A Life of Jesus the Christ*, p. 189. Italics added. For an indication of the receptivity of church members to the Cayce legacy, see James K. Brown, "Integrating Church and Cayce," *Venture Inward* (January/February 1992), Vol. 8, No. 1, pp. 18-22, 43.

55. See Matthew 16:18 and 18:17.

56. See I Corinthians 12:27 and Hebrews 12:1: " . . . we are surrounded by so great a cloud of witnesses." Many say these witnesses refer both to the local, the trans-local church, and even the church as an interdimensional cosmic community, which may include martyrs and other Christ-conscious angelic beings.

57. In fact, few such persons probably realize the very positive role of sacramental liturgy in the healing process. See, e.g., among Protestant and Catholic communions, statements by the International Order of Saint Luke the Physician, as well as by the Catholic Church, following Vatican II, in Rush, *Toward a General Theory of Healing, op. cit.*, pp. 154-160.

58. Sullivan, *op. cit.*, p. 215.

59. *Ibid.*, p. 231.

60. See Harold Bloom, *The American Religion: The Emergence of the Post-Christian Nation* (New York, N.Y.: Simon and Schuster, 1992), pp. 26-27, in response to Robert Bellah and Philip Lee. Cf. p. 219; cf. Wouter J. Hanegraaf, *New Age Religion and Western Thought* (New York, N.Y.: State University of New York Press, 1998), pp. 523-524. This admirably comprehensive and exceptional treatment of the subject requires recurrent and reflective reading.

61. Bloom, *ibid.*, p. 26.

62. John 3:8.

63. These gnostic freedoms will be explored in detail in my next volume.

64. *Salvation* is from the Latin *salus*, which derives from the Sanskrit *sarva* (i.e., "whole" or "all"), although *salvation* may also be derived from a more ancient Indo-European root, *sal*, "to rise." Nonetheless, the Latin word *salus* has influenced both the words *salvific* and *salutary:* the former, making for the saving of one's soul; the latter, making for the improvement of one's bodily health.

65. For a 1977 Nobel Prize-winning contribution by "a Belgian physical chemist, Ilya Prigogine," regarding how this degenerative process can be viewed differently when it concerns *people*, see the subsection, "The Science of Transformation," in Ferguson, *The Aquarian Conspiracy*, pp. 162-167; cf. pp. 167-176.

66. Compare the idea of ease and easiness with dis-ease or dis-easiness. To be called an "easy-going" individual can imply much about one's state of health spiritually.

67. Cited in Jack Crittenden's foreword to Ken Wilbur, *The Eye of Spirit: An Integral Vision for a World Gone Slightly Mad* (Boston, Massachusetts: Shambhala Publications, Inc., 1997), p. xi. This is certainly one of the most

brilliant and stirring recent books published.

68. As a philosopher-physician with a vision of human wholeness, which even included an emphasis on diet, environment, and one's lifestyle, Hippocrates was truly a forerunner of modern holistic medical practitioners; see Rush, *Toward a General Theory of Healing, op. cit.;* and a major work by Oswei Temkin, *Hippocrates in a World of Pagans and Christians* (Baltimore, Maryland: John Hopkins Press, 1991).

69. For how far we have come regarding models of understanding in the relation between medicine and health, see Fritjof Capra, *The Turning Point* (New York, N.Y.: Bantam Books, 1983), especially Part IV, chapter 10, "Wholeness and Health." See his definition of holistic, p. 38 (note).

70. For one of the best brief surveys of modern holistic thinking, see chapter 5 (in Fuller, *Alternative Medicine and American Religious Life*) entitled "The Contemporary Scene: Images of the 'High Self' in Holistic and Psychic Healing Movements." For an overview of the controversy over alternative medicine and "five M.D.s who took an alternative route," see, respectively, Sharon Begley, "Alternative Medicine: A Cure for What Ails Us?" and Nancy Wartik, "The Best of Both Worlds?" in *American Health* (April 1992), pp. 39-40; 44, 46; 50, 52, 54, 56; see also pp. 41-43, 45, 47-48. According to *Life* (September 1996, pp. 42, 46), "In 1992 the National Institutes of Health opened an Office of Alternative Medicine, which has awarded modest, but symbolically groundbreaking, grants to study 26 therapies . . . "; for exemplary clinics and outcries over motivations: "two strands—spiritual and economic—" see p. 39ff. A positively exemplary clinic with a primarily medical-spiritual orientation is the A.R.E. Clinic in Phoenix, Arizona, influenced by the medical readings of the seer, Edgar Cayce. See William A. McGarey, *Healing Miracles: Using Your Body Energies* (San Francisco, California: Harper & Row, Publishers, 1988).

71. Panati, *Breakthroughs: Astonishing Advances*, p. 3. See amazing mind-body links, pp. 4-11.

72. See I Corinthians 12:27; II Corinthians 3:17; John 17:21-23.

73. Zechariah 4:6.

74. "Presence" here is the *Shekhinah* (of Hebrew Torah and Kabbalistic mysticism).

75. See Leviticus 19:2, 20:26, 22:2.

76. See John 8:12—and then Matthew 5:14.

77. See p. 210 in this book.

78. Dossey, *Healing Words, op. cit.*, pp. 13-14. As I recall, this also applies to the sage Ramakrishna; see also the response of Sri Aurobindo, p. 14.

79. *Ibid.*, p. 13.

80. James 1:3; Matthew 10:22; Luke 21:19.

9

Faith, Gnosis, and the Christ Consciousness

Christian Gnosis and the Christ Consciousness

It was Dostoyevsky who wrote in his probing and disturbing masterpiece, *The Brothers Karamazov,* that there are three things human beings cannot live without: miracle, mystery, and authority. Starting with the last idea, we can certainly say that countless numbers of adherents to the world's religions have indeed given themselves completely over to ecclesiastical, if not, some form of religious, authority. But then, it is also safe to say that there are other souls in the world for whom the value of autonomy or self-reliance in religious matters has priority in their lives. As to the matter of mystery, the universe is most certainly the major ongoing mystery in the life of humankind; and the idea of God is becoming increasingly understood as inseparable from it. This notion has been called ecotheology,[1] although it was imagined by the ancients and now by moderns fascinated with the idea of process in the universe. But whether the universe be viewed as God, or a manifestation of God, or something more or less than God, it is undoubtedly a universe that is not only a physical but also a metaphysical mystery. As to miracle, we can boldly say, just as Shakespeare said that all the world loves a lover, that practically every believer loves a miracle!—especially if it is interpreted as a truly supernatural event. But then again the question arises, as it did before, whether human souls can long live on the impact that miracles can have in the humdrum of everyday existence. Yet whether we are speaking of miracle, mystery, or authority, the haunting question remains about just how feasible it is for humankind to save itself from self-destruction (that is, to be good *and* to do good) without some sort of Cosmic Support.

The Exoteric and the Esoteric Revisited

Though the universe continues to be a mystery in itself, it is in its metaphysical aspect filled with spiritual mysteries whose penetration requires keys to understanding the relation among God, humankind, and the universe itself. Yet none of these mysteries can become a matter of religious experience or gnostic awareness without our understanding that there are both exoteric and esoteric manifestations of the spiritual realities of the universe seen in the earth plane of everyday existence. The exoteric, as stated before, refers to the overt, ordinary, everyday, commonplace dimension of religious learning and experience; and the esoteric refers to the covert, concealed, hidden, or secret dimension of religious learning and experience. Authoritative (hierarchical) religious institutions have historically been terrified by the mere thought of having to confront the esoteric; lovers of miracle have historically been rather fainthearted to believe that the esoteric dimension is something that God or the gods intended us to ponder, if more, to understand. Those who profess to understand the mystery of human existence have themselves oftentimes been quick to divorce the content of esoteric tradition from the ethical-spiritual challenges that both perceiving and participating in those mysteries entails.

In the exoteric sense, then, Jesus of Nazareth came to reveal the truth of the immediacy and accessibility of God to the masses through the manifestation of a radical spiritual communion with God as a Heavenly Father. The exoteric manifestations of the Realm of God tend to be expressed through our concern with such things as creeds, dogmas, and denominations and their rituals. The esoteric manifestations of the Realm of God are expressed through our concern with things greater than creeds, dogmas, and denominations and their rituals; that is, the mysteries, the metaphysics, the principles and, as it should be, the practice of universal ethics. Of course, both of these types of manifestations should include a concern for the well-being of other human beings. For both perspectives, then, the exoteric and the esoteric, it was intended from the earliest times to be a matter of consciousness, conviction, and concern. It is just that, due either to ignorance or pride, there remains so much doublemindedness—if not, hypocrisy—even in the hearts of so many of those who profess to believe or to understand.

Yet the line between the exoteric and the esoteric is not rigid, for the secrets of the esoteric are often hidden in the leaven of the exoteric; and the exoteric has a way of enriching the esoteric because the beliefs of esoterics tend to be more conducive to the adoption of a pride of knowledge, or what is really a type of religious elitism. Hence, the provocative words of Jesus of Nazareth: "I thank you, Father, Lord of heaven and earth, because you have hidden these things from the wise and intelligent and have revealed them to infants."[2] The problem of our time, however, is not simply that the mysteries of the Realm of God have been kept from the masses, as if they were the forbidden fruit of old, but that with the advent of the so-called new age and the onslaught of a number of psychical phenomena and weird occult manifestations, it has become extremely necessary to clarify what is important amidst a sometimes confusing variety of religious experiences and a cumulative chaos of values.

But there is a sense in which Jesus also came into the world in order to reveal to us the esoteric or inner meanings of then and now existing credal, dogmatic, and denominational symbolic forms. He came to tell us and to demonstrate to us what the essence is of all these symbolic forms and what they point to in ultimate terms. In ultimate terms, then, all credal, dogmatic, and denominational forms are symbols of cosmic realities. They are symbols of things that are, therefore, true regardless of what forms those realities have taken in human consciousness and imagination and expression.[3]

So in the esoteric sense, Jesus of Nazareth also came to reveal to us what He called "the mysteries of the Kingdom of God." Those mysteries are fundamentally metaphysical in nature and are, therefore, to be appreciated and internalized. Now for them to be externalized as practical good will requires the presence of a mind that has set itself upon heavenly things.

Three Great Metaphysical Mysteries

Three great metaphysical mysteries that have remained with us for millennia are: the metaphysical mystery of the existence of the soul (which has to do with the essence-and-existence of God as the Supreme Cosmic Creative Intelligence); the metaphysical mystery of the freedom of the soul (which has to do with the potential and actual power for thinking, willing, and acting in harmony with the Creator); and the metaphysical mystery of the redemption of the soul (which, here, has to do with the quest-and-attainment of the Christ Consciousness). I intend to devote a major portion of my next book to these mysteries in light of the need to ponder their application to the concrete problems of everyday life.

These metaphysical mysteries tend to encompass all the other mysteries that are a part of the cumulative religious experience of humankind. They have otherwise been expressed in the form of three awesome questions, which I like to call the "three great questions of human existence." Those three great questions are: (1) what is the nature of reality? (2) what is the nature of human nature? and (3) what is the nature of human destiny? The thing that is "great" about these questions is that they do not only have to be answered by practitioners of religion, they also have to be answered in some way by natural scientists, be they biologists, chemists, or astrophysicists.

For instance, if any one in the latter three fields is concerned about the prospect of chemical warfare, it is because such an individual has implicitly made a value judgment about the nature of human nature. Likewise any woman who decides to have an abortion must deal with all three questions. For most of the time, when one ponders the answer to one of those questions, one tends to find oneself trying to answer them all—because they are so interlinked. The reader should by now have either guessed or foreknown that I am neither the originator nor the formulator of such questions. For they were originally asked in the furthest antiquity and began to be asked, and creatively "answered," among the philosophers of Ionia and later by their successors in Athens and Alexandria. And they were joined by the founders of the great world religions in the Near, Middle, and Far East (especially in India), and later still by the philosophers of Europe and America.

In the broadest sense, then, the metaphysical mystery of the soul is intertwined with the question of the nature of reality. This is the case because, insofar as we have been created and/or emanated in the image of God, we are the ones who have contemplated the Creator's existence and the meaning of our own in terms of a metaphysical kinship with the Creator; and this includes the conviction that whatever God is, we are potentially, if not actually, whatever God is. Again, the mystery of the metaphysical freedom of the soul is intertwined with the question of the nature of human nature. This is so because, though we cannot say with absolute certainty that all nonhuman organisms are unaware of the Presence of God as God-Force at some level of spirit, we seem surely to have been given the gift of freely manifesting the Glory of the Divine Presence in the form of spiritual values in the universe (as presently understood). Finally, the metaphysical mystery of the redemption of the soul is intertwined with the nature of human destiny. This, too, is so because, though it has been conceived in various ways, at sundry times, and among different peoples of the earth, there is an almost universal sense that humankind is caught in an ethical and spiritual predicament.[4]

Those who have dared to entertain the possibility that there are answers to such great questions and who are convinced that all the great teachers of humankind intended that we come to believe, know, and understand (transcendentally experience) those mysteries are usually called *mystics.* They may otherwise be called by a host of other names ranging from Gnostics to Theosophists to New Agers. The simplest definition of mysticism I have ever read is by Evelyn Underhill, who once wrote that "Mysticism is the art of union with Reality."[5] But one must be careful to acknowledge the existence of both popular (exoteric) mysticism[6] and philosophical (esoteric) mysticism.

But the distinctive characteristic of philosophical (esoteric) mysticism is twofold. First, it is inseparable from the experience of gnosis as a way of perceiving the relation of the formerly mentioned cosmic principles (see "What Do Gnostics 'Know'?" in chapter 6); and second, it is inseparable from the experience of gnosis as a way of understanding the dynamics of the application of those principles to the concrete, everyday problems and challenges of individuals and communities.

Christ Consciousness and Gnostic Mysticism

I would now like to share with you four very important things about an authentic gnostic esoteric mysticism to which the idea of the Christ Consciousness is essential. The first thing is that, in such a mysticism, the Christ Consciousness transcends both the individual (denominational) consciousness of Christ and the historical movement of Christianity as an institutional religious establishment. Even the church cannot be said to be equivalent to the Kingdom (or Realm) of God on earth, although that should be its greatest spiritual challenge as it dwells amidst the world. The Christ Consciousness is, fundamentally, a radical spiritual consciousness of the Reality, the Presence, and the Power of God.[7] The Christ Consciousness is, nonetheless, the consciousness which Jesus of Nazareth had of the ultimacy, the intimacy, and the efficacy of the Power of the Living God in our midst.

But it is not only Jesus of Nazareth who has appeared on earth that we might have faith in the existence of and knowledge of the truth of the former metaphysical mysteries. For the Christ Consciousness has appeared in and among all the great spiritual teachers of history. And it is a thing of such great wonder that men and women everywhere have remained in awe and are still being overcome by its wondrously creative and magnetic power. Merely consider, if you will, what happened, for example, in the case of Confucius, Laotzu, Buddha, and others—but certainly in the case of Jesus of Nazareth. Many of them were all later considered to be "God" or "gods" due to the super-charismatic nature of their witness to Something and/or Someone greater than themselves, whether it was the Dharma (Hinduism's cosmic law), Nirvana, the Tao, Heaven, or Paradise, or "the Father" in Jesus' case.[8]

Yet none of these spiritual beings ever intended that he was to be worshiped as the Ultimate Source of being, consciousness, and bliss; and I personally hold that the Eternal Divine, the Eternal Mind, foreknew and understands why such things would happen. But I also think that subsequent sages, priests, and teachers[9] should have made it their aim to educate or nurture the masses into the art of looking beyond the (above "super-charismatic") human symbolic forms to see the Eternal Formless Reality.[10]

Thus the title "Jesus Christ" is more than the Man, Jesus; but it also means that the Christ Consciousness became radically one with Jesus the Man—hence the name, Jesus Christ. Of course, *Christ* does not mean Savior as many think. It is the Greek correlate of the Hebrew word, *Messiah*. They both mean "Anointed One," to which I shall shortly return. Jesus, therefore, had an unexcelled consciousness of God, a conviction about our unlimited metaphysical possibilities, and an ultimate concern for souls. But He always points us toward the Source of His own reality, presence, and power.[11]

That Source has been known variously in the earth as The One, The Eternal One, The Eternal Light, the Boundless, the Tao, the Great Mystery, Brahman, Mahadevi (the Great Goddess), the Almighty, Heaven, Father, etc. Thus Jesus could, on the one hand, say, "My Father and I are one," and on the other, "My Father is greater than I." Again, He says, "He that believeth on me, believeth not on me, but on Him who sent me." In one of His most amazing manifestations of spiritual humility, He said, "I can do nothing on my own"; and then He said, "If I testify about myself, my testimony is not true."[12] It is, indeed, a mystery, but more, a matter of supreme spiritual encouragement that a being of such transcendent power could have possessed and retained such a depth of spiritual humility!

It is the emphasis of Jesus on the Spirit-over-the-flesh, however, and perhaps the call to be "born again" ("from above") which led Maurice Bucke to give Whitman an edge even over Jesus regarding the matter of the Cosmic Sense (see endnote #35). Yet that is probably because Whitman had not himself drawn out the very furthest implications of the traditional doctrine of the Incarnation. For that doctrine fully intends to affirm the holy wedlock of the long-held separation of the sacred and the profane. When, for instance, Jesus likened the Kingdom of God to "leaven" (which itself implies pregnancy symbolism), this signals that what Bucke calls the "old self" and the "new" are to be finally seen as co-extensive and, indeed—to use his term—"co-workers."[13] Hence Jesus could say, "My *Father* is still working, and *I* also am working" (John 5:17); and while Whitman could have his "leaves of grass," Jesus in the esoteric sense could have what I call His "stones of spirit" (Luke 19:40).

Christ Consciousness and the "Witnessing Consciousness"

Before going further, here is a word on the Oriental idea of the "Witnessing Consciousness." This concept has been brought to the attention of many Westerners by one of the greatest authorities on Indian spirituality, Mircea Eliade, in his book: *Yoga: Immortality and Freedom.* Eliade refers to four critical states of being or levels of *samadhi* consciousness that mark the ultimate conquest of egoism and materialism.[14] Three have been designated as Savicara, Nirvicara, and Nirvikalpa. Though these terms vary, they might be called, respectively, (1) Access Concentration, (2) Recess Concentration, and (3) Excess Concentration. These states are associated with both the Hindu Path of Yoga of Patanjali (the *Yoga Sutras*) and with the Buddhist Path of Purification *(Vishuddhimarga).* Yet it is the Nirvikalpa which brings us to the threshold of another (fourth) state of samadhi-consciousness, which is called Jivan-Mukti or Jivan Mukti Samadhi.[15]

It is at this level—Jivan-Mukti (a state of being spiritually liberated while incarnate)—that we encounter the concept of "Witnessing Consciousness." It is truly the most remarkable form of *samadhi,* for it is indeed the most exquisite state of spiritual equilibrium in which all previous states culminate and in which there is no time factor as to how long it can last. It is the power not only to remain in an excellent state of spirituality for longer than usual periods of time, but also in the waking state to live as if in *an eternal present.* It involves the paradoxical ability to remain personally involved with life and yet to stand dispassionately above it all in a state of "Witnessing Consciousness." Think of what a challenge this would mean for an individual working amidst the chaos of Wall Street! Nonetheless, to be both "with" and "above it all" means that one has the power to incarnate universal spiritual virtues in the most distracting and tempting human situations.[16]

This is where Jesus of Nazareth was "coming from" when He said, "Do not worry about your life, what you will eat or what you will drink, or about your body, what you will wear. Is not life more than food, and body more than clothing . . . So do not worry about tomorrow, for tomorrow will bring worries of its own . . . " (Matt. 6:25, 34) "I have said this to you, so that in me you may have peace. In the world you face tribulation. But take courage; I have conquered the world!"[17] But whether we are speaking of the quest and attainment of what has been called a "Witnessing Consciousness" or of a "consciousness witnessing" to the world in conventional evangelistic terms, Jesus shows us a form of Christ-conscious mysticism that both engulfs and surpasses the vision of the Christian religion as an ecclesiastical institutional form.

It is a duty of love for those of us who are experimenting with this level to encourage others mainly through personal example[18] to believe in this "witnessing consciousness," and to regard it as at least—to use a phrase of Ann Wilson Schaef—"a sacred possibility." Indeed we should take to heart words from her little book entitled *Meditations for People Who (May) Worry Too Much*: "Life exists on many levels. Just because someone is not on my level does not mean that one of us is wrong." But whether you intuit yourself to be in higher or lower levels of consciousness, beware of looking for formulas for the sake of experiencing miracles! Don't ask for Mt. Everest to move!—if it is not a moment of truth. God forbid that you should be allowed a positive answer to a prayer that gives rise to a tidal wave that might hit the Middle East while you are merely testing to see whether you can get Everest to be uprooted and cast itself into the Indian Ocean! Esoterically, the proverbial "mustard seed of faith" presupposes a sacred context (a moment of truth) that is beneficial to the bringing of the Realm of God closer to earth than a pietistic formula bound to make wonders happen.

The second item regarding Christ Consciousness is that the basic, fundamental, underlying key to the Christ Consciousness, then, was, is, and will always be the virtue of *childlikeness*. This is a state of mind, a quality of spiritual consciousness, a pristine attitude of soul, so simple that it is something that can even elude popes, monks, nuns, and many of the most pious clergy and laypersons or believers in God among the various branches of Christianity from the earliest times.[19]

In response to those who insist on knowing what one must do in order to achieve Christ Consciousness, as if it were a method,[20] I must say that with the achievement of childlikeness I have found the following to be true: (1) one will be spontaneously moved from within by the Eternal One to adopt a mode of being (or a certain lifestyle) in the world;[21] (2) urgently motivated to strive to internalize certain spiritual ideals[22] intended for one at this particular stage of one's development (e.g., in my case, love, wisdom, patience); and (3) surely guided into "the straight path" or led "into the path of righteousness," especially in times of storm and stress regarding life's most perplexing problem situations.[23] To be sure, the invitation to "seek," "ask," and "knock" all presuppose the spirit of childlikeness in the one doing the same.[24]

To be sure, to imitate Shakespeare, "all the world loves a method" when it comes to becoming outstanding in anything! And the quest for salvation itself has indeed spawned many a system of Evangelism, "New Thought," or Yoga, under a new name. But the childlikeness—and (only) its directive consequences of which I speak—were better understood if, in the spirit of Zen Buddhism, one were to not seek a method as much as a "spiritual receptivity," a "let go and let God" disposition, a totally noncapitalistic mode of being in the face of the Infinite. This is one of the most tragic and pathetic things overlooked especially in modern history—despite all our religious strivings—*We are still standing before the Infinite!* If, then, you listen to Psalm 46:10, perhaps you will receive the grace of Psalm 23:3.

But that childlikeness is not something known only to Christianity; it was perceived by Buddha of ancient India, Laotzu of ancient China, and others hundreds of years before Christianity as a movement began to gain momentum in the ancient Near Eastern world. The reason for the extreme difficulty of achieving childlikeness in its most pristine form, of having it and sustaining it, is that it is a practical and delicate balance in everyday life of self-reliance and God-reliance—majesty/dignity and faith/humility. This is something that the illustrious Rabbi Soloveitchik recognizes as a creative tension between "majestic man" and the "man of faith." Soloveitchik envisions their alternation as "willed and sanctioned by God." Yet, in a broader sense, he also envisions the futuristic harmony of both "the majestic natural community" and the "covenantal faith community," i.e., "the uniting of the two communities into one community where man is both the creative, free agent, and the obedient servant of God."[25]

But within the perspective of the Christ Consciousness, when the virtue of childlikeness: submission or surrender; dependence or reliance; sincerity, simplicity, or singlemindedness, vulnerability, grows in us, what for millions becomes a dialectical crisis can increasingly become a living paradox and an immediately redemptive reality; so that, again, like Jesus, one can say, "My Father is still working, *and* I also am working"; or Paul of

Tarsus could say, "It is no longer I who live, but it is Christ who lives in me."[26]

The third item is something that I regard as a momentous issue, in light of those who have already gotten carried away by "altered states of consciousness" that are so often without ethical-spiritual content. It is that the Christ Consciousness is not identical with cosmic consciousness, as some have taken it to be. I regard the Christ Consciousness as the ultimate aim of all mysticism, and any form of mysticism[27] that stops short of the Christ Consciousness is, as New Testamental theologian, Leon Wright, would say, merely a psychical experience. Although I hold that cosmic consciousness itself is included in any advanced state of Christ Consciousness, the distinction between cosmic consciousness per se and the Christ Consciousness remains crucial.[28] Cosmic consciousness refers to the magnification and the transformation of self-consciousness into super-consciousness; that is, an extraordinary awareness of the order, unity, and interrelatedness of all persons and things, including the existence of other worlds and dimensions.[29] It is definitely a larger way of perceiving and appreciating Reality and all forms of life, even extraterrestrial life.[30]

The Christ Consciousness refers to the magnification, the transformation, and the *sanctification* of self-consciousness to the extent that, by Divine Grace,[31] one has been anointed with the Holy Spirit of Truth, with the same Power that was in Jesus Christ; and to the extent that one is willing and inclined to live a life of consistent self-denial, self-giving, and self-sacrifice. But sanctification is inseparable from *purification!* It is indeed the element of purification that has so repeatedly eluded millions of believers and would-be Christ-conscious esoterics who have tragically deluded themselves while going on with attitudes of elitism, exclusivism, class-consciousness, racism, sexism, and the like; or with the façade of being "nice people"—hence "nice" Christians.[32]

In saying, therefore, that the Christ Consciousness includes and goes beyond cosmic consciousness per se, it is important not to overlook the fact that India has given us, perhaps, the most outstanding and enduring manifestation of cosmic consciousness that we, on the earth plane, have come to know. Let there be no mistake about it, the Hindu Brahmans and other Yogis have been the acknowledged masters of the art of cultivating and achieving cosmic consciousness. They have specialized in a form of experiencing the World-Soul, otherwise known as *Brahman.*[33] The Brahmans of India *knew*, through the art of *Jnana-Yoga*, how to enter into a state of oneness with the Cosmos.

According to Maurice Bucke, in his pathmaking book, *Cosmic Consciousness*, "the marks of the Cosmic Sense . . . are: (a) the subjective light, (b) the moral elevation, (c) the intellectual illumination, (d) the sense of immortality, (e) the loss of the fear of death, (f) the loss of the sense of sin,[34] (g) the suddenness, instantaneousness, of the awakening, (h) the previous character of the man—intellectual, moral, and physical, (i) the age of illumination, (j) the added charm to the personality so that men and women are always [?] strongly attracted to the person, and (k) the transfiguration of the subject of the change as seen by others when the cosmic sense is actually present."[35]

An account of Bucke's own "awakening" experience confirms the Oriental (Hindu) heritage in this manner:

> Into his brain streamed one momentary lightning-flash of the Brahmanic Splendor . . . Upon his heart fell one drop of the Brahmic Bliss, leaving thenceforward for always an aftertaste of Heaven.[36]

But this is something that can be attained, especially

should we grant the element of reincarnation, by human effort and without a conscious affirmation or focus on what has been called by some modern Hindu mystical monotheists, "the Supreme Personality of Godhead." I say by human effort because, though it would naturally seem to follow from our metaphysical kinship with the Divine Source, the path to cosmic consciousness is largely one of Self-Realization or Atman-Realization (as in Hinduism), if not one of awakening (as in certain sectors of nontheistic Buddhism). And these can be begun and enhanced through long-tested techniques of concentration and meditation.

It is thus of critical importance that an Indian Christian, J. Christie Kumar, has given a distinctive and creative Christian response to the traditional Hindu forms of mysticism. This thinker says that India needs the concept and the experience of the Holy Spirit, which "is the *new cosmic energy*, the Kingdom of God, the new order, the children of God, the new type that Christ has inaugurated."[37] Gandhi could not have dared to call India's long-forgotten "untouchables," the new name of "Harijans" (or "Children of Hari," God) without this new quality of consciousness—notwithstanding those who still wonder just how he got Christianly "baptized" without a sacramental rite. Yet it is this Something More than mere immersion in a cosmic world-soul (Brahman) or sacramental baptismal waters that was and is always needed in human life to move on to the plane of ethical-spiritual transformation. The human spirit thus continues to need Something/Someone More That/Who can not only transform human character but also add an abiding divine, forgiving love even to that traditional experience of being in Oneness with the Eternal Divine.[38]

Thus the Hindu philosophers gave us to know of the reality of cosmic consciousness under the form of a radical sense of the Oneness of all Being and the Unity of all

Things. But even this vision of the Cosmos at large, however, did not prevent the caste system from emerging in India. The notable Henry Nelson Wieman rejected the use of the term *cosmic consciousness* in theology or the philosophy of religion. Although this was not done in direct response to the more complex conception of it held by India's Brahmans, there is much to ponder about his statement that cosmic consciousness "cannot command the religious commitment of our lives, and, therefore, has not the value attributed to it by giving it the name of 'God.'"[39] But the case for a deeper spiritual understanding and a transformation of attitudes is only made more crucial when we consider that the Judaic and Christian theologians did in fact give us a vision of the Fatherhood of God that was meant to be understood as inseparable from the Brotherhood and Sisterhood of Humankind. Yet it still did not prevent the emergence of a rationalized "Manifest Destiny," class consciousness, slavery, child labor, or sexism, etc.[40]

The fourth item, therefore, is that it is the element of a practical-spiritual translation of cosmic metaphysical realities into ways of being religious that affect the ordinary life that has recurrently presented so much metaphysical, psychical, and occult speculation with a challenge it has seldom met. There has been throughout much of classical religious history a grave but inevitable tension between the psychical and the spiritual,[41] and the prophetic and the mystical.[42] Thus the formerly cited words of mathematician Raynor Johnson (who wrote the unforgettable work, *The Imprisoned Splendour*) continue a challenging echo: "To find the presence of God in the beyond is good, but to find it on Earth is a greater achievement."[43]

So if you want to know whether any acclaimed avatar, guru, swami, adept, or any other personage, either self-proclaimed, if not institutionally ordained, has really attained some level of "Christ Consciousness," consider whether that being can manifest the power to "love [his/her] enemies," "do good to those who hate," "bless them that curse," "pray for those who persecute and speak evilly," to "resist not evil" but with good.[44] See whether both wisdom and compassion are present in such persons and, indeed, whether such virtues have tended to prevail in such persons, especially compassion. See whether they have been willing to "see that justice is done, help those who are oppressed, give orphans their rights, and defend widows."[45]

Thus it is regarded as one of the most perceptive and crucial deeds of Paul of Tarsus that he placed even *gnosis* as mere gnosis below the glory of *agape* or spiritual love. He says that "if I understand all mysteries and have all knowledge [or gnosis] and have not love, I am nothing" (KJV), saying finally that there are only three things that endure in the Universe: faith, hope, and love.[46] Though earlier, then, for developmental purposes I made known my adoption of the formula "agape + sophia = gnosis," there yet lies potential in the deepest dimension and the widest manifestation of agape in the world, a free-flowing wisdom (sophia) that passes all human understanding. But agape, as love from God and as our love for God, does not require understanding; and there are no limits on how much of this love the heart can hold. Remember, Solomon had wisdom, but he also had seven hundred wives and three hundred concubines! Yet Solomon's wisdom, though it reflected, was later *deflected* from, the wisdom of God. In the light of what precedes, then, one can say that, while agape is the essence of gnosis, wisdom is the quintessence of gnosis.[47]

Christ Consciousness Encompasses East and West

It, therefore, took another form of esoteric Indian

mysticism, that of Mahayana Buddhist mysticism, to call attention to what the Brahmanic cosmic consciousness was intended to become. The Buddhists, then, have given us to know that same cosmic consciousness under the form of a radical sense of the interrelatedness of all things and the interdependence of all beings, but with the added dimension of compassion as the other side of metaphysical wisdom. Buddhist gnosis is thus composed of wisdom and compassion—hence Buddhism was, and is, fundamentally anti-caste. Furthermore, Buddhism's gnosis has radically positive implications both for ongoing political conflicts and for the environmentalist movement the world over.[48]

Right now, as you ponder the larger issues of your life against the background of what amounts to the possession of a "questing consciousness," you will need to consider something quite ecumenical in order to succeed in your quest. For you may find that you need to combine insights from both Eastern and Western mysticism.[49] You may need both the monism of Shankara (India's outstanding monist), wherein the World-Soul and the human soul are one in essence; and you may need the Christocentric mysticism of Meister Eckhart (where the Spirit of the Son of God as love [agape] is born into the human soul by the Living Word); you may need both the self-negating mystical monotheistic devotion of Islam's Rabiah (who turned away all her wooers or potential husbands because Allah was her only true, Eternal Lover); and you may need the paradoxical mysticism of Divine Grace and soulful "prayerfulness" of St. Teresa, who preferred to enter into the inner recesses of the Interior Castle, than to be taken captive by the world; and you may need the wisdom and compassion of the Buddha, who conquered all extremes and could walk a "Middle Way" narrower than a "razor's edge"; and you may need the agape and sophia revealed in the soul of

Jesus of Nazareth, who endured the contradiction of being supremely righteous and loving yet was condemned as a dangerous criminal; and you may need the experience of the Kabbalistic Shekhinah that is the Divine Presence of the One Holy Lord; and you may need the Lakota Sioux's primal awareness of Wakonda, or Wakan Tanka, "the Great Mystery."

Three Indispensable Spiritual Truths

Ultimately, it takes the Christ Consciousness as revealed, consummated, and demonstrated in the life of Jesus of Nazareth to hold before us a new dimension of cosmic power that even goes beyond a field of consciousness that is a radical awareness of the All, as pure being, pure consciousness, and pure bliss (cosmic consciousness). For that new dimension (the Christ Consciousness) includes a cosmic power that also transforms the human consciousness in terms of the quality of its ethical-spiritual character. This ethical-spiritual character brings together the psychical and the sacred, the material and the spiritual, the prophetic and the mystical, the Power of God in this world and the Glory of God in the next. The Christ Consciousness is thus the *fulfillment* of the Oriental "witnessing consciousness," insofar as it encompasses the prospect of experiencing both the deepest dimension of awareness of the Holy, an awareness that enables one to be in a state of what Merrill-Wolf, author of *Pathways Through to Space*, called "High Indifference," and the highest awareness of the need to be "conscious of witnessing" through love and compassion to a world that has serious doubts about the radical spiritual potential of human nature. Recall that I said that the Christ Consciousness refers to a process of consciousness magnification, transformation, *and sanctification*, which is essentially a state of *holiness.* Let me add, however, that the Christ Consciousness is ultimately a *God Consciousness.* But it needs to be referred to as the Christ Consciousness because it tends to keep us aware of three indispensable spiritual truths: our perpetual need for utter humility in order to become infused with God's Divine Grace; our need for the purity of heart in order to continue the process of sanctification; and our need for universal love. This last is still the final criterion for measuring the nobility of any outstanding moral character and the quality of any extraordinary spirituality.

The Dynamics of the Awakening of the Christ Consciousness in the Human Consciousness

Remember that there is an esoteric difference between what it is to be conscious *of* Christ (the consciousness of Christ, or to focus on Christ as a Savior-God) and the Christ Consciousness. The former corresponds to the state of those whom gnostics of old called "mental Christians," whose primary medium of focus is rooted in faith alone. Christ Consciousness, however, applies to those who were called "spiritual (or *pneumatic*) Christians." They are those who have been specially anointed by the Spirit, are true gnostics, and have entered into the mysteries of the Kingdom of Heaven. The Christ Consciousness encompasses both agape (love) and sophia (wisdom), even though, as Clement of Alexandria said, those who are not pneumatics can still enter into the Kingdom of Heaven. For me, all souls are at least *intended* to enter into the mysteries.

1. It all begins with your consciousness of (the Being of) Christ as the Pattern to be imitated by the searching soul. This must involve "conversion" (or, esoterically, "transformation"), whether a gradual process or a

sudden happening, from the tendency toward evil—a new spiritual disposition. In any given case, there may be a need for repentance, renunciation, forgiveness, but in every case the acceptance of and gratitude[50] for what Super-charismatic Beings (e.g., Buddha, Jesus, Muhammad) have done for humankind—in behalf of the soul's salvation.

2. The transformation process continues, with swellings and dippings, dippings and swellings in the process of prayer, meditation, and service until the Spirit within your soul, like a plumb line, reaches beyond the unconscious to your spiritual center of gravity, wherein the love of God penetrates the core of your being—where the Spirit of God encounters the soul directly.

3. Once at the core, your level of receptivity to the love of God, which in turn is influenced by the quality of your cumulative spiritual biography (present existence and past existence) determines the coming and the quality of an anointment (or recurrent anointments) by the Holy Spirit of Truth. It awakens the superconscious to the reality of the unity of all things and the interdependence of all beings (i.e., cosmic consciousness). This is one of the mysteries of the Kingdom of God.

4. This "cosmicization" of the consciousness of Christ leads ultimately, by a special act of Divine Grace, to the radical sanctification of the soul, whereby love becomes the atmosphere of your entire being, physically, mentally, and spiritually; and whereby Divine Love is fully realized to be the essence of gnosis and Divine Wisdom the quintessence of gnosis. This is the Christ Consciousness, and it provides vastly expand-

ing dimensions of interpersonal and mystical experience for you, incarnate, and limitless levels of metaphysical and pneumatic experience for you, discarnate.

5. The radical sanctification of the soul by a special act of Divine Grace further empowers your whole person to become a bearer of the Life, the Spirit, and the Love that emanate from the Fullness of the Inner Realm of God's Eternal Light (transfiguration). It is all One Realm, One Power, One Glory—the Pleroma.

6. The manifestation in the world of that empowerment takes the form of an inner childlikeness which signals, by its exquisite quality of vulnerability to God, the Presence of God (the Shekhinah) in you and a spontaneity of expression, intuitive response, and compassionate regard toward others in need, through your loving self-denial, self-giving, and self-sacrifice. Love has now become both the life of your soul and the basis of your co-creatorship with the God-Force in contributing to the total harmony of the universe.

7. The outer reaches of an ever-deepening life of Christ Conscious gnosis means a life of ever-increasing mystic enlightenment characterized by both an aura of holiness and a radical spiritual freedom whereby, being governed by the Spirit, you are no longer under the Law; for love has now become the fulfilling of the Law. The moment of your bodily death, translation, or ascension is now fully determined by the Creator.

Endnotes

1. See Mary Long, "Visions of a New Faith," pp. 39-41; cf. chapter 6, endnote #85 in this book.
2. Matthew 11:25; cf. Psalm 8:2.
3. For example, Trinities in various religions (Father, Son, Holy Spirit;

Brahma, Vishnu, Shiva in Hinduism, etc.) and the esoteric gnostic invitation to us to (re-)enter into the Godhead (or the Pleroma) symbolized (not theologized) by John 10:30, 17:21-23, 14:12; cf. Revelation 3:12.

4. See chapter 3, pp. 70-75 in this book.

5. Margaret Smith, *Studies in Early Mysticism in the Near and Middle East* (Oxford, England: Oneworld Publications, 1995, pp. 4-6), notes at least four elements which I believe have stood out (with variations) in all the definitions of mysticism given throughout the cumulative spiritual experience of humankind. Partially paraphrased they are (1) the soul can see and perceive by a unique spiritual sense or mode of perception; (2) the soul must be itself a partaker of the divine nature in order to come to the knowledge of God; (3) the soul cannot attain to a direct, intuitive knowledge or immediate perception of God without purification *(catharsis);* (4) the soul can only ascend to God through the guidance and inspiration of Love.

6. Via Pentecostal, Evangelical, and Fundamentalist adherents among whom, for some, Jesus is a Living "Mystical" Presence and for some of whom the very utterance of the name, "Jesus," tends to have the power of a mantra—a Christian mantra; cf. the Ave Maria, the Lord's Prayer, and the Twenty-Third Psalm, etc.

7. It was a renowned theologian, H. Richard Niebuhr, who once said that, for the believer, it cannot be solely a question of the existence of God, but more so the experience of the *presence* of God.

8. Both Muhammad and Jesus of Nazareth are exceptions (despite the Trinitarian view of multimillions of Christian believers). The priority of "the Father," due to Jesus' radical Christ Consciousness is confirmed by His words, "He that believes in me, does not believe in me but in him who sent me" (John 12:44); as well as "my father is greater than I" (John 14:28); although in John's Gospel Jesus' relation to God is presented as a living paradox, as in John 10:30 and 14:28.

9. This does not apply to prophets, for they are literally ones who speak for Another! Muhammad is, therefore, an excellent example of one who made all this plain by way of a warning (Qur'an 33:40, 45).

10. See in this connection a very important answer given to the question, "How does one directly contact the Divine and transform oneself without a mediator?" by Andrew Harvey, *The Return of the Mother* (Berkeley, California: Frog, Ltd., 1995), pp. 460-461; although I would not, as Harvey does, say that all the gurus are self-serving.

11. See John 6:57.

12. John 10:30, 14:28, 12:44 (KJV), 5:30-31 (NRSV).

13. See Bucke's statement on Whitman and Jesus, p. 232; cf. endnote #35.

14. The meaning of *samadhi,* like all advanced states of consciousness, tends to be intellectually elusive, since it is meant to be directly experienced, not figured out. Eliade understands it as "conjunction" (*Yoga,* p. 39). It refers to "the eighth and highest state of yogic *concentration,*" another meaning given to the term; see Edward Rice, *Eastern Definitions* (New York, N.Y.: Anchor Books, 1980), p. 310 (italics added); although it has also been referred to as "'equilibrium,' 'uniformity,' or 'equanimity'; or 'a state of tranquillity.'" See D.T. Suzuki, Erich Fromm, and Richard De Martino, *Zen Buddhism and Psychoanalysis* (New York, N.Y.: Grove Press, Inc., 1960), p. 46.

15. See Eliade, *Yoga: Immortality and Freedom* (New York, N.Y.: Pantheon Books, 1958), pp. 80-83; and Daniel Goleman, *The Varieties of the Meditative Experience* (New York, N.Y.: Irving Publishers, Inc., 1977), pp. 77-79.

16. See Philippians 4:8; Galatians 5:1.
17. John 16:33.
18. See Philippians 4:9.
19. This is certainly not to imply that it is so in all cases.
20. In this regard, see the specific reaction of the philosopher-mystic, Plotinus, to the gnostic in Pagels's *The Gnostic Gospels*, p. 135. I perceive that Jesus intended childlikeness to be a virtue common to exoterics and esoterics—hence Matthew 11:25; Luke 10:21.
21. Matthew 6:25-34 is not, then, a call to forget about certain normal life concerns, but rather not to allow oneself to worry about or become preoccupied with them, as if they had priority in one's life; only then will all things work toward one's fulfillment. Moreover, if needed, one could even be led to assume a certain form of worship or study, according to the Creator's knowledge of one's spiritual temperament.
22. See p. 254, no. 6, in this book.
23. See Proverbs 3:5-8; Isaiah 30:20-21; John 16:13, 13:26-28.
24. See Matthew 7:7.
25. Soloveitchik, *The Lonely Man of Faith*, pp. 9-27, 80, 84, *et passim*; cf. pp. 86-87.
26. John 5:17; Gal. 2:20. Italics added.
27. I say "mysticism" here because using the phrase "psychical experience" does not necessarily apply to an exoteric but true devotion to the Eternal Divine, for wherever there is a pure devotional spirituality, there is a consciousness of Christ; and wherever there is a consciousness of Christ, there is always the prospect of moving from a consciousness of Christ to the Christ Consciousness.
28. For a complex of varied meanings inseparably related to my understanding of "Christ Consciousness," see the subsection, "The Christ," in Hanegraaff, *New Age Religion and Western Culture*, pp. 189-194, especially pp. 190-191. I have chosen here to emphasize the elements of love and compassion because, for me, there is no enduring enlightenment without them. I regard the two terms as interchangeable.
29. There are, of course, variations on the meaning of "cosmic consciousness," yet I simply do not accept any inseparable connection between experiencing a so-called "vast Ocean of Oneness" and an "Ocean of Living Love" (*ibid.*, p. 296). I do not believe that the testimony of religious history (confessional, but especially behavioral) confirms the practical unity of these two "Oceans," even though a multidimensional-universe perspective can acknowledge their coexistence. Divine Grace still remains the key to any "Ocean of Living Love."
30. I once read—but have forgotten where—a highly perceptive scholar who urged that what we would call "extraterrestrials" could be said to be *human*, if that term be understood in the sense of any being manifesting "intelligence," though probably in an obviously uncertain number of extraterrestrial cases, *extraordinary* intelligence.
31. Grace is as Augustine envisioned it; but, for me, in the matter of good and evil it still refers (1) to God's willingness to forgive us, though unworthy, for our sins (or violations of Cosmic Law), and (2) to His willingness to empower us to overcome sin (see I John 3:7, 9; 5:18-20). This view does not, as it might seem, deny that our ultimate choice is between spiritual knowledge and ignorance, but rather that there *is* sin (evil)—and there *are* victims, though it has its ultimate roots in spiritual ignorance. But though sin does

indeed exist, it cannot be overcome without God's "Cooperative Grace"; for contrary views (e.g., by Shirley MacLaine and Kevin Ryerson) and a rather complex general problem, see Hanegraaff, *op. cit.*, chapter 10, especially pp. 281, 295, and pp. 300-301. Cf. David Spangler's realistic attitude, p. 286. For the Holocaust, see pp. 284, 290.

32. See "Nice People or New Men, C.S. Lewis," in Streng, *et al.*, *Ways of Being Religious*, pp. 412-415. Lewis's description of "New Men" is truly remarkable.

33. In Christian terms, I regard *Brahman* as the Cosmic Field of the Creator's Glory (cf. John 17:21-24), which both engenders a knowledge of the unity of all things and is the universal essence of the mystical experience.

34. This element stands out among all others as actually the most controversial and goes to the heart of the gnostic vision of Jesus of Nazareth. I intend to enter fully into the controversy in my next volume.

35. Maurice Bucke, *Cosmic Consciousness: A Study in the Evolution of the Human Mind* (New York, N.Y.: E.P. Dutton and Company, Inc.), p. 79. Bucke deserves much credit for introducing many modern Westerners to the esoteric way of interpreting Scripture and the lives of outstanding personalities. He seems to have considered Walt Whitman as "par excellence," i.e., "the best, most perfect example the world has so far had of the Cosmic Sense"; see his chapter 13, especially p. 225.

36. *Ibid.*, p. 4 of a nonpaginated introduction entitled "The Man and His Book."

37. J. Christie Kumar, "An Indian Christian Appreciation of the Doctrine of the Holy Spirit: A Search into the Religious Heritage of the Indian Christian," *The Indian Journal of Theology*, Vol. 3:1 (January-March 1981); see pp. 29-35. Italics added.

38. See John 13:34-35.

39. Henry Nelson Wieman, "Transcendence and Cosmic Consciousness," in Richardson and Cutler, *Transcendence*, p. 158.

40. This does not, of course, mean that these attitudes have not been countered all throughout European-American religious history by authentic ethical-spiritual attitudes. For instance, the role of the Roman Catholic Church in having integrated schools during South Africa's time of "apartheid" is probably not widely known. One should also recall the role of religious souls in giving sanctuary and in the abolition of slavery.

41. See I Corinthians 12:1-13:1.

42. See John 10:22-39.

43. Cited in W.C. Beane, "The Nature and Meaning of Modern Religious Experience," in *World Faiths Insight*, New Series 6 (January 1983), p. 21. This insight and the emphasis on "purification" above have significant implications for certain early sectors of new age thought. For some, while repugnant to the idea of reincarnation, look insistently forward via further postmortem *purgatorial* experiences to "spiritual progress through higher worlds"; see Hanegraaf, *New Age Religion and Western Culture, op. cit.*, p. 473ff.

44. Matthew 5:44-45; 39; Luke 6:35; 27-28.

45. Isaiah 1:17.

46. I Corinthians 13:2, 13.

47. From Latin *quinta* ("fifth") and *essentia* (essence); defined by *The American Heritage Dictionary of the English Language* as "the pure, highly concentrated essence of something." Though in philosophy the term is

much more complex, my use of it refers to the possession and the goal of acquiring all the attributes of God that make for soul-perfection. Solomon had wisdom, but his potential for its becoming increasingly "highly concentrated" was largely arrested by his love of women (he "clung to these in love"), many with detracting religious customs; see I Kings 11:1-4.

48. I said earlier that every believer loves a miracle! But how many miracle-lovers remember John the Divine's words that we cannot be anything but liars if we say that we love God and hate our neighbors (I John 4:20); or remember that being in love with the miraculous or the supernatural—or even the metaphysical—does not automatically mean that we are spiritually developed (I Corinthians 13:2).

49. See, for example, chapter 14: "East-West Meditation," in Mark Thurston (and the editors of the A.R.E.), *More Great Teachings of Edgar Cayce* (Virginia Beach, Virginia: A.R.E. Press, 1997).

50. Latin *gratitudo*, but related to "grace" *(gratia)*, the word *gratitude* has been greatly underestimated in terms of its religious instructional potential. For those who cannot accept a blood-sacrificial view of atonement, it can indeed become an authentic and profound way of understanding the saving significance of the life of Jesus of Nazareth; see Abelard, in chapter 3, p. 48 in this book.

Epilogue

The End of Faith and the Beginning of Knowledge

W*e cannot say* with certainty, after all that has been said and done, why we have been called at this stage in our cosmic spiritual development to have faith, as such. Or why it is that so much has been made of faith in doctrinal terms by the very guardians of the treasuries of "saving knowledge," especially in the West. A dual alternative view says that we all once had potential (or actual) knowledge of the Truth and have since wandered either by way of an Original Fall into sin in an earthly Paradise, or that we descended from a Cosmic Realm of Light into soul entrapment along the Great Chain of Being. This, of course, refers, respectively, to the "terrestrial" Fall in the Garden of Eden for conventional Christians, or the "cosmic" Fall of various Gnostics of the ancient world. There is, then, in one case, the need to be "redeemed" or be "reconciled" to God through the Way; and in the other, to "return" by way of mystical attunement through a reincarnation process because we have somehow forgotten "who we really are." One must remember, however, that there is no inherent contradiction between a traditional doctrine of Original Sin and a gnostic cosmic Fall, since in either case the soul practically always enters the earth with karmic residues trailing after it. Thus, more than trying to remember previous lives for their own sake, we should be trying to recover and deepen the virtues that previous lives have engendered in us; but ultimately it is only through the Grace of our Eternal Divine Source that we can learn from them and thereby find final salvation.

At any rate, there are situations to be lived, lessons to be learned, and beings to be loved. Be that as it may, it is surely the Christ-conscious gnostic way to perceive that faith, as such, is neither intended to remain a pious psychological fixation on Jesus Christ, nor is it intended to be the ultimate end of religion. I perceive, through the insights in the Gospels themselves, especially the Gospel of John, that such is not the case; and that surpassing all the emphasis placed on the idea of justification by faith in Protestant circles, and on the idea of sacramental grace in Catholic circles, there remains the intended priority of "saving knowledge" (gnosis). The foregoing medium of doctrine and mode of liturgy can be truly beneficial, but their final aim should be twofold: (1) to communicate that "the righteous live by their faith" (Habakkuk 2:4) but that faith is not the end of righteousness (I John 3:7); and (2) that what all sacraments are intended to point to is the real and fulfillable promise of *sacramental existence* beyond (i.e., without) recurrent sacramental celebration, as if salvation depended on it. For the final and consummate aim of all religiosity is a form of spirituality which Jesus indicated in the most revolutionary terms in John 4:24.

Hence faith begins to end when one feels the cumulative effects of a continuity of faith in God swelling up in one's being to the extent that one has the power to grasp, to know what God is doing in one's life in practically every momentous situation (John 5:20), even without knowing everything that God is doing. It is in fact the Creator's invitation to the soul to participate, cumulatively, in the omnipresence, omniscience, and omnipotence of the Creator through a supersensory, mystical, intuitive knowledge of the omni-Providence of the Creator. Augustine was all too right when he thought that it is really through love (*caritas*) that we truly can know the Creator.

By now, it must be at least certain in your mind that the aim of this book has not been to diminish, certainly not to ridicule, the role of faith in the history of human religious experience. Rather it has been to say that the importance of faith in both Testaments—and in some Eastern traditions (e.g., Buddhism)—is not the end, but instead the beginning of a journey that is finally aimed at each one of us becoming knowledgeable in our practical, everyday understanding of the nature of reality, human nature, and human destiny.

John the Divine's portrait of Jesus is thus inseparable from the insight that we are destined "to *know* the truth, and [that] the truth will make [us] free" (8:32). Free from fear to believe new things about God, humankind, and the universe; free to live a life being true to oneself, knowing that if you can trust yourself, God can trust you; free to learn new ways of doing old things; free to do new things in old ways; free to love unselfishly whom you please; free from false and frustrating preventions of love across diverse boundaries; free even to lay down one's life for the sake of a larger freedom of the Spirit; free from preachers who may choose to frighten the soul into submission. For the prophet Jeremiah shared that vision in his foresight of a people who will, each, come to know the Lord without anyone having to bid one to do so (Jeremiah 31:31-34). While Paul of Tarsus in typical style could say through a paradox that "I *know* in whom I have *believed*," (II Timothy 1:12; italics added) he, too, knew that it was the ultimate intention of the Eternal God of the Fullness of Inner Light that we come to "*know fully*, even *as* . . . [we] have been *fully known*" (I Corinthians 13:12; italics added). But then, ask yourself this crucial question, asked of us by an authentic Christian seer (Edgar Cayce): "How sincere *is* the *desire* on the part of each *to* know The Lord Thy God Is One?" (262-42)

Be that as it may, it is still true that faith has proved to be indispensable to the beginnings of the odysseys of countless souls as they have sought to make their way through the maze of human madness toward what Hindus have tended to call *Brahmaloka* (the Realm of the Creator) or *Moksha* (Liberation); to many popular Buddhists of faith, the "Pure Land"; to many Jews and Muslims, "Paradise"; and to Christians, the "Kingdom of God" or just "Heaven."

This book has sought in part to encourage those who are becoming increasingly restless with traditional dogmatic assumptions that they were never intended from eternity to be free to explore the mysteries of the Kingdom of God with the Creator's blessing; that faith was never intended to evolve beyond faith into a form of spiritual, intuitive knowledge. But it is, in fact, that knowledge (gnosis) which ultimately places the human consciousness on a plane that is metaphysically attuned to the experience of being *in* the Realm of the Creator, while *in* this world. This dimension of spiritual experience is what again motivated the seer, Edgar Cayce, and which led his original Study Group to reaffirm, in spirit and in truth, that "Faith . . . is the inner spiritual knowledge of the Creative Forces of the universe." (*A Search for God, Book I,* 50th Anniversary Edition, p. 43)

About the Author

Dr. Wendell Charles Beane is professor of history of religions at the University of Wisconsin Oshkosh and does comparative research in his approach to the study of the major world religious traditions. He studied history, French, and pastoral theology at Howard University. He has been an elder in the United Methodist Church since 1961. A student of the world-renowned historian of religions, Mircea Eliade, and a graduate of the University of Chicago (Ph.D. 1971), he has been a fellow of the American Institute of Indian Studies and of Pilgrim Institute in West Yarmouth, Massachusetts. At present he teaches world religions, Hinduism, issues in contemporary world religions, perennial myths and modern mysteries; a seminar on comparative religious views of suffering; religion, faith, and healing; and comparative mysticism. He was awarded the Distinguished Teaching Award in 1990 and the University of Wisconsin Board of Regents Award for Teaching Excellence in 1992. He has written scholarly articles for international journals, such as *History of Religions* (Chicago), *Religious Studies* (Cambridge), and *World Faiths Insight* (London). He is the author of *Myth, Cult, and Symbols in Śākta Hinduism* (E.J. Brill), and editor (with W.G. Doty) of *Myths, Rites, Symbols: A Mircea Eliade Reader* (two volumes, Harper & Row). He has delivered papers before the American Academy of Religion, the Society for the Scientific Study of Religion, the University of Wisconsin Madison annual conference on south Asia, the National Medical Association, and the Association for Research and Enlightenment. He has traveled widely and has spoken on various subjects ranging from biblical mysteries and spirituality to meditation and mysticism. He is a former chair of the department of religious studies and anthropology at the University of Wisconsin Oshkosh and was a visiting scholar at Andover Newton Theological Seminary for the year 1992-1993. He is now undertaking the writing of a book on the application of the "Gnostic Spirit" to practical problems in the modern world.

A.R.E. Press

The A.R.E. Press publishes quality books, videos, and audiotapes meant to improve the quality of our readers' lives—personally, professionally, and spiritually. We hope our products support your endeavors to realize your career potential, to enhance your relationships, to improve your health, and to encourage you to make the changes necessary to live a loving, joyful, and fulfilling life.

For more information or to receive a free catalog, call

1-800-723-1112

Or write

A.R.E. Press
P.O. Box 656
Virginia Beach, VA 23451-0656

Discover How the Edgar Cayce Material Can Help You!

The Association for Research and Enlightenment, Inc. (A.R.E.®), was founded in 1931 by Edgar Cayce. Its international headquarters are in Virginia Beach, Virginia, where thousands of visitors come year round. Many more are helped and inspired by A.R.E.'s local activities in their own hometowns or by contact via mail (and now the Internet!) with A.R.E. headquarters.

People from all walks of life, all around the world, have discovered meaningful and life-transforming insights in the A.R.E. programs and materials, which focus on such areas as holistic health, dreams, family life, finding your best vocation, reincarnation, ESP, meditation, personal spirituality, and soul growth in small-group settings. Call us today on our toll-free number

1-800-333-4499

or

Explore our electronic visitor's center on the
INTERNET: **http://www.are-cayce.com**

We'll be happy to tell you more about how the work of the A.R.E. can help you!

A.R.E.
67th Street and Atlantic Avenue
P.O. Box 595
Virginia Beach, VA 23451-0595